AMERICAN ENGLISH READER

SAXON SERIES IN ENGLISH AS A SECOND LANGUAGE

GRANT TAYLOR, Consulting Editor

AMERICAN

ENGLISH

READER

STORIES FOR READING AND VOCABULARY
DEVELOPMENT

BY GRANT TAYLOR, Consulting Editor, McGraw-Hill Book Company;
Formerly: Associate Professor of English, Director of American
Language Institute, New York University; Senior English Language
Advisor, English Language Education Council, Tokyo; English Lan-
guage Consultant, U.S.I.A.; Chairman, English Language Section,
National Association for Foreign Student Affairs; Lecturer in English,
Columbia University; Associate Editor, *Thorndike-Barnhart Compre-
hensive Desk Dictionary*.

McGRAW-HILL BOOK COMPANY

NEW YORK   LONDON   MEXICO CITY   SYDNEY   TORONTO

The United States Library of Congress Catalog Card Number 60-12950.
ISBN 07-062944-7

21 22 23 24 25 EBEB 9 8 7 6

TAYLOR/AMERICAN ENGLISH READER

DERECHOS RESERVADOS © 1988, respecto a la primera edición por
McGRAW-HILL/INTERAMERICANA DE MEXICO, S.A. de C.V.
Atlacomulco 499-501, Fracc. Ind. San Andrés Atoto
53500 Naucalpan de Juárez, Edo. de México
Miembro de la Cámara Nacional de la Industria Editorial, Reg. Núm. 1890

ISBN 968-422-467-2

Reimpreso con permiso

Copyright © MCMLX by McGraw-Hill, Inc., U. S. A.

ISBN 0-07-062944-7

Impreso en México   Printed in Mexico

Esta obra se terminó de
imprimir en septiembre de 1990
en Multidiseño Gráfico
Oaxaca No. 1
01000 México, D.F.

Se tiraron 1 000 ejemplares

IN TODAY'S WORLD, the teaching and learning of foreign languages has taken on greater importance and dimension than ever before. Among the countless languages of the world, English has assumed a leading role in diplomatic, commercial, and all other types of international communication. To provide the many thousands of teachers of English in the United States and abroad with materials of unquestioned excellence, the editors of Saxon Press created almost a decade ago the English as a Second Language Series. The American English Reader is the seventh in this distinguished series of textbooks for teaching American English.

THE ILLUSTRATION on the left page by Leonard Everett Fisher* depicts Independence Hall in Philadelphia, Pennsylvania, where the signing of the Declaration of Independence was announced by the Continental Congress on July 4, 1776.

*Illustration from *America Is Born*
by Gerald W. Johnson, New York,
William Morrow and Company, Copyright 1959

PREFACE

★ ★ ★ ★ ★ ★ ★ ★ ★ ★ ★ ★ ★ ★

Achieving a high degree of proficiency in English as a foreign language is not a mysterious process without scientific basis. It is simply a result of study and practice—the more systematically and efficiently guided, the better the result. Systematic guidance presumes controls, and efficient guidance presumes maximum utilization of all stimuli. The purpose of the author in creating his *American English Reader* was, therefore, to provide the teacher of American English with a collection of interesting stories which would (a) allow maximum opportunity for useful vocabulary study within the framework of controlled and limited sentences and (b) emphasize the conversion of "passive" language ability (reading and listening) into its "active" counterpart (writing and speaking).

The *American English Reader* is designed then for "intensive" rather than "extensive" reading practice in American English. Intensive reading calls for close attention to vocabulary and the structure within which this vocabulary occurs; it also calls for thorough study and careful home preparation. Of course, it is essential to keep language practice stimulating for students, and arousing their curiosity about the information in a story is an excellent procedure. In intensive reading, however, knowledge of the plot or the ideas set forth in any story becomes secondary in importance. Extensive reading, on the other hand, is generally done outside of the class and there is little concentration on reproducing with any degree of exactness the vocabulary or structures from the text. The emphasis in this case is on increasing reading speed, gathering information, and the collection of ideas. Gaining active control of English vocabulary and structure first requires intensive study, to be followed later by extensive, uninterrupted reading to develop further familiarity with the lexicon and to develop speed and ease in silent reading for communication.

Teachers will find in using the *American English Reader* that each of the stories has been presented in the same format. This was done purposely to aid students in becoming familiar with the plan of the text in as brief a time as possible. More specifically, the arrangement of materials is the following: (a) *the story with footnoted word study lists,* (b) *questions for oral and written practice,* (c) *summary sentences for laboratory practice,* and (d) *exercise and study materials* comprising at least one each of the following types: (d1) the synonym exercise, (d2) the missing word exercise, (d3) the preposition exercise, (d4) the matching sentence parts exercise, (d5) the word form chart, (d6) the word form example list, (d7) the word form selection exercise, (d8) the correct sentence completion exercise.

From the plan in the foregoing paragraph, it will be apparent at once that the *American English Reader* was developed with the thought in mind that the student should not only see and hear but should also repeat and write new words or the alternate forms of known words in the course of going through each story. Further, the text was developed with consideration of the need for frequent repetition of vocabulary and making the student "word-and-structure conscious." The reading assignment is, of course, highly effective for vocabulary expansion. It was the author's aim to make his *American English Reader* particularly well suited for this task by developing special ways of clearly illustrating derivative forms and providing for practice with these forms. The teacher will also note that, throughout the text, great emphasis has been placed on oral and written questioning, one of the most valuable exercises which can be used in connection with the reading assignment. Finally, the audio-oral approach to language learning has been even further stressed in the *American English Reader* through the presentation of summary sentences for listening and repetition practice in the laboratory or the classroom.

Since it has been convincingly demonstrated that, in all language learning situations, the more frequently a word is encountered the more likelihood there is that it will be permanently retained, the author has placed great emphasis on the frequent recurrence of vocabulary items. This was done purposely to expedite the permanent addition of these items to the student's total active and passive vocabulary in accordance with the principle previously stated. How the repetition of vocabulary items was handled can be illustrated by several brief examples: In the first story ("He Saw Texas First"), the word *adventurous* occurs on page four, and the word *adventure* occurs in the same paragraph; thereafter, both words are noted in the word study list

SAXON SERIES IN ENGLISH AS A SECOND LANGUAGE

GRANT TAYLOR, Consulting Editor

ADVANCED ENGLISH EXERCISES

AMERICAN ENGLISH READER

AMERICAN READINGS

ENGLISH CONVERSATION PRACTICE

INDEX TO MODERN ENGLISH

LEARNING AMERICAN ENGLISH

MASTERING AMERICAN ENGLISH

MASTERING SPOKEN ENGLISH, Tapes 1

MASTERING SPOKEN ENGLISH, Records 1

MASTERING SPOKEN ENGLISH, Workbook 1

MODERN ENGLISH ESSAYS

MODERN ENGLISH WORKBOOK

MODERN SPOKEN ENGLISH

PRACTICING AMERICAN ENGLISH

READING AMERICAN HISTORY

culty. It is quite essential for this sort of questioning to proceed at a fairly rapid clip without delaying for the student who has to search for his answer. In this procedure, there is a conscious effort on the part of the student to memorize briefly and then recall. In order to get full benefit from this type of practice, the student should be required to answer in a complete sentence. It will be noted, in this connection, that the actual words and constructions from the stories in the *American English Reader* have been closely followed in forming the questions. This allows minimal variation from the text and forces students to note exactly the structure and vocabulary used in the reading. Both the linking of the oral English and the written English and the many brief periods of memorization and recall in this type of practice speed up language learning considerably. The entire questioning process, carried out in this manner, is not only simple and highly effective but it also becomes in a very short time an interesting procedure for students.

The summary sentences for laboratory practice following each story have been taken from the story but have been adapted to spoken English form and are especially suitable for language laboratory work. An effort was made in all cases to reduce sentences to a manageable length for oral reproduction; in addition, words, expressions, or sentence structures which would not normally occur in oral discourse were eliminated. Although excellent high fidelity recordings of the summary sentence sections are available from the publishers of the *American English Reader,* some teachers may prefer to use the summaries for classroom repetition or for pronunciation practice. The sentences in this section can also be used for combined reading comprehension, vocabulary review, and oral drill. In this type of practice, the teacher asks an isolated question about the story while the student has his text open to the summary sentences. The student is asked (a) to find the sentence which answers the question, (b) to give the number of the sentence, and (c) to give the complete sentence orally without looking at the lines in the book. In a variation of this exercise, the teacher gives the student five or six questions on the blackboard or a duplicated page, and the student writes the answers.

The problem of style is always a difficult one for the author of a reading text for non-native speakers, especially so if vocabulary is to be kept within an intermediate range and the types of sentence structures which can be used are to be limited. While the problem in original writing is difficult at best, the problem in adapting stories is even more tortuous. For example, however beautifully constructed, very complicated sentences have to be simplified; cultural or social references which students from other countries would not understand, no matter how well these references present a concise picture, have to be avoided; literary, poetic, regional, and technical language have likewise to be avoided. By the same token, frequent repetition of sentence patterns or vocabulary items, ordinarily a violation of good style, must be deemed valuable.

For all the reasons enumerated above, the author feels very obligated to express his special appreciation to those authors and publishers who were kind enough to permit the adaptation (or rewriting in many cases) of articles or stories which they had originally created or made available to the public. It should be kept firmly in mind that the articles and stories as they appear in the *American English Reader* are not representative or typical in any way of the individual professionally excellent writing styles of their creators. In this connection, the author wishes to express his gratitude to all those authors, illustrators, and publishers who have been kind enough to allow the use or adaptation of their materials in the *American English Reader.* In particular, the author extends his thanks to: The Humble Oil & Refining Company, Houston for "He Saw Texas First," by B. T. Fields, illustrations by E. M. Schiwetz from the *Texas Sketchbook;* Simon and Schuster, Publishers, and Bernard Jaffe, author of *Men of Science in America,* Copyright 1944, from which "Man in Flight" was adapted; The Association Press for the articles "Charles A. Lindbergh" by James V. Thompson and "Thomas Alva Edison" by Marshall C. Harrington, both from *Vocations and Professions,* edited by P. H. Lotz, Copyright 1940; the editors of *Pageant Magazine* and the author, Thomas Gallagher, for "The End of the Shenandoah" from *Pageant Magazine,* Copyright 1958; Random House and Jacob Landau for his illustrations from *The Wright Brothers, Pioneers of American Aviation* by Quentin Reynolds, Landmark Books, Random House, Copyright 1955; McGraw-Hill Book Co., Inc. and W. N. Wilson for his illustration from *Ships that Made American History* by Mitchell and Wilson, Whittlesey House, McGraw-Hill Book Co., Inc., Copyright 1950; Houghton Mifflin Company and William Barss for his illustrations from *Young Tom Edison* by Sterling North, Copyright 1958; William Morrow and Company and Leonard Everett Fisher for his illustrations

at the foot of the page and occur in Exercises 4, 5, 6, and 7. Taking another instance, the word *greedy* also occurs on page four; thereafter, it occurs in the footnoted word study list, in sentence 10 of the sentences for laboratory practice, and in Exercises 1, 2, 4, 6, 7, and 8. The student would, therefore, in doing all the work connected with the first story encounter the word *greedy* at least 10 times! In this connection, the words in the footnoted word study lists which accompany each story are those which have been proven to cause non-native speakers difficulty for one or more of the following reasons: the vocabulary range within which they fall, the spelling, or the attached usage problems. The words have been placed at the foot of the page on which they occur to call them to the attention of students, and some teachers may find it convenient to use these words as the basis for dictations or spelling exercises.

The study of alternate or derivative word forms is another highly important aspect of vocabulary expansion. In order to make his vocabulary serviceable for as many situations as possible, the student must not only learn to use words in one form but also to alter the forms of words to fit different contexts. As previously stated, it was the author's aim to make the *American English Reader* particularly well-suited for this type of vocabulary practice. To help achieve this aim, a special word form chart was developed for each story in the reader; further, a section providing extensive examples of all derivatives and important idiomatic usages was made up to accompany each chart. These items provide the student with the opportunity to enlarge his vocabulary considerably by encountering and being asked to use alterations or variations of known vocabulary. To assure that the student would be provided with an actual opportunity to practice with the alternate forms (rather than just to work with "meaning"), the author has also developed for each story a word form exercise based on the word form chart and example section. In using the word form charts, the teacher should be aware that often word forms *do exist* where the chart has X X X X X (indicating no form). In all cases, these forms have been omitted by virtue of rarity, shifts in meaning, or complicated usage problems, and the student should not be expected to deal with these omitted forms until a later stage in his language learning process. The teacher should also note in using the word form charts that present and past participles (the *-ing* and *-ed* forms of verbs) have not been given as distinctive adjectival forms; however, in cases where the use of either participle form as an adjective is very common, the author has included an example of the usage in the word form example section. It should be pointed out that the word form charts are very useful in demonstrating to students how derivatives are formed through the use of prefixes and suffixes. The charts can also be useful to the teacher who wishes to make up further exercises. By using the charts, for example, many excellent exercises can be developed on forming adjectives from nouns, nouns from verbs, etc. The word form examples associated with each chart were carefully planned to be useful in supplementary audio-oral drill. Wherever possible, the sentences were based directly on the story and the use of unknown words was avoided; further, the sentences were kept short and contractions were purposely used. The sentences in the word form example section can, therefore, be used for effective audio-oral drill in the laboratory or the classroom.

As the teacher will quickly notice upon examining the text, the "question-density" for each story is relatively high, i.e. there are covering questions for a large percentage of the sentences in each story. In line with the principles of intensive reading practice, high question-density gives the teacher the maximum opportunity to stress the observation of structural detail (tenses, plural forms, articles, etc.). Also it should be noted that high question-density simplifies the reading assignment for the student and facilitates the use of controls by the teacher; conversely, the lower the question-density, the more difficult the reading assignment becomes for the student and the less opportunity the teacher has for controls or reinforcement. The questions in the *American English Reader* may be used for either oral or written practice although care was taken to make them especially suitable for the following type of simple but highly effective oral practice: The student keeps his book open in front of him and is permitted to look at it as the teacher asks a question. The student to whom the question is directed (after a suitable pause, of course) is asked to look at the teacher, not the book, and give his reply. In answering, the student is told to look at the teacher during the entire time that he is answering, not just for a moment after which he glances back to the lines of the story. This can be done successfully, of course, only after the student is familiar with the story, the vocabulary, and the structure of the sentences. The questions in the text progress from sentence to sentence and ask about the people, actions, and other details mentioned in the story. Students are, therefore, able to follow along with little diffi-

from *America Is Born* by Gerald W. Johnson, Copyright 1959; Little, Brown and Company for the use of the map in "The Louisiana Purchase" from *The American Pageant* by T. A. Bailey, Copyright 1956. The original illustrations for "The Legend of Sleepy Hollow" and "Seeds for the Future" were the work of Mr. Arck D'Agostino. All of the portraits in the *American English Reader* as well as the illustrations for "The End of the Shenandoah" and "Wings Across the Atlantic" were the original work of Mr. Juan Carlos Barberis.

During the time the *American English Reader* was being developed, revised, and tested in the classroom, ideas and advice were freely given by most of the members of the faculty of the English Language Program, New York University as well as by a number of teachers of English from other parts of the world. I wish, therefore, to express my special gratitude to all these colleagues. In this respect, particular credit for the generous contribution of their time and effort is due Mr. Gordon Ericksen, the Assistant Director of the English Language Program, Mr. John B. Henry, Dr. Martha Salmon, and Miss Bibi Abril-Lamarque. I wish also to thank Mrs. Sara Quimby and Miss Roberta Schissel for their help in the typing and preparation of the final manuscript.

G. E. T.

Washington Square
New York City
1960

CONTENTS

★ ★

HE SAW TEXAS FIRST 2–17

Story 2
Questions 7
Summary Sentences 9
Exercises 1-8 10

THE FIRST THANKSGIVING 18–33

Story (Part One) 18
Questions (Part One) 21
Story (Part Two) 22
Questions (Part Two) 24
Summary Sentences 25
Exercises 9-16 26

THE LEGEND OF SLEEPY HOLLOW 34–57

Story (Part One) 34
Questions (Part One) 37
Story (Part Two) 38
Questions (Part Two) 44
Story (Part Three) 45
Questions (Part Three) 47
Summary Sentences 48
Exercises 17-24 50

THE LOUISIANA PURCHASE 58–77

Story 58
Questions 64
Summary Sentences 65
Exercises 25-32 69

★ ★

FIRST ACROSS THE CONTINENT **78–101**

    Story (Part One) 78

    Questions (Part One) 81

    Story (Part Two) 82

    Questions (Part Two) 85

    Story (Part Three) 88

    Questions (Part Three) 89

    Summary Sentences 90

    Exercises 33-44 91

SEEDS FOR THE FUTURE **102–117**

    Story (Part One) 102

    Questions (Part One) 104

    Story (Part Two) 105

    Questions (Part Two) 108

    Summary Sentences 108

    Exercises 45-52 110

BETTER KNOWN AS MARK TWAIN **118–133**

    Story 118

    Questions 123

    Summary Sentences 124

    Exercises 53-60 126

THE WIZARD OF MENLO PARK **134–153**

    Story (Part One) 134

    Questions (Part One) 138

    Story (Part Two) 139

    Questions (Part Two) 141

    Summary Sentences 142

    Exercises 61-68 144

★ ★

FROM SLAVE TO TEACHER **154–177**

   Story (Part One) 154
   Questions (Part One) 158
   Story (Part Two) 160
   Questions (Part Two) 164
   Summary Sentences 166
   Exercises 69-80 167

MAN IN FLIGHT **178–197**

   Story (Part One) 178
   Questions (Part One) 181
   Story (Part Two) 182
   Questions (Part Two) 185
   Summary Sentences 188
   Exercises 81-88 189

THE END OF THE SHENANDOAH **198–217**

   Story (Part One) 198
   Questions (Part One) 201
   Story (Part Two) 204
   Questions (Part Two) 206
   Summary Sentences 207
   Exercises 89-96 209

WINGS ACROSS THE ATLANTIC **218–235**

   Story 218
   Questions 224
   Summary Sentences 225
   Exercises 97-104 227

HE SAW TEXAS FIRST

By B. T. Fields

ONE WARM MORNING in June 1527, five Spanish ships left Spain for the West Indies. This was just 35 years after Columbus had discovered the New World. Panfilo Narvaez was in command of the expedition. The king had appointed him to conquer and colonize the

---

discover   in command   appoint   conquer   colonize

territory between the Rio Grande and Florida. The story of the fate of
Narvaez and the 600 soldiers on the boats is one of the most remarkable
in the history of American exploration.

After the expedition reached the West Indies, many of the men

---

territory   fate   remarkable   exploration   expedition   reach deserted. Many others died in hurricanes. Only four of the 300 men who finally reached Florida lived to tell the story of their incredible trip from Florida to the Pacific coast of Mexico! One of the four survivors was Alvar Nuñez Cabeza de Vaca who was the treasurer and second-in-command of the expedition. He was a proud, adventurous, and truthful man, and he wrote many stories about his adventures.

The expedition reached the west coast of Florida on April 15, 1528. From the beginning, the Indians were hostile. By the way they acted, they clearly told Narvaez to leave—the sooner the better. But the greedy Narvaez had already seen some gold jewelry worn by the Indians. He learned that it came from a place called "Apalachen," and he decided to find this golden kingdom and take away its treasure.

Narvaez decided to send the ships along the coast to the Rio Grande. He instructed the rest of the expedition to make the trip by land. Obviously, he did not know the great distance between Florida and the Rio Grande and the difficulty of getting supplies. Cabeza de Vaca was against the plan because the men and horses were in poor condition. Narvaez said that he could go with the ships if he was afraid. De Vaca was a proud man, and he replied that he would go with the expedition. He made the choice in pride and anger, and it almost cost him his life.

On May 1, 1528, Narvaez and his 300 men began the search for Apalachen. Nearly two months later, they found it. Apalachen was only a poor native village. The Spaniards were tired, hungry, and disappointed. Although they had dreamed about gold and jewels, they were now satisfied with corn, beans, and pumpkins.

The Spaniards continued to search for gold for another month. However, a third of the men got sick, and the unhappy Narvaez decided to travel by sea. There was only one problem. They didn't have any ships. They didn't even have the materials and tools to build a ship. In desperation, they tried to build a few flimsy rafts. They even melted their helmets and other metal objects to make nails, saws, and axes.

desert	hostile	difficulty	disappoint	desperation
hurricane	greedy	supplies	dream	flimsy
incredible	jewelry	condition	jewel	raft
coast	decide	afraid	satisfy	melt
survivor	golden	reply	corn	helmet
treasurer	kingdom	choice	beans	object
proud	treasure	pride	pumpkin	nail
adventurous	instruct	anger	unhappy	saw
truthful	obviously	search	material	axe
adventure	distance	native	tool	

4

They made ropes from the tails and manes of horses. By September 20, 1528, they had completed five crude rafts. Two days later, 242 desperate men climbed onto these rafts and started out.

The men stayed as close to the coast as possible. When they reached the area where the city of Mobile, Alabama, is located today, two men went for water and never returned. The rest started out again and soon found themselves in dangerous circumstances. Their water was useless, and they needed food. Men died of thirst, and the survivors were so weak that they could hardly use the oars. Somehow, they continued their voyage until they finally came to the entrance of the Mississippi River. Here they found fresh water to drink. However, they could not sail up the river because of the strong current.

After a few more days of sailing, the rafts became separated. De Vaca found himself and his men alone. Towards evening, he saw two of the other rafts. Narvaez was in one of them. De Vaca called to Narvaez and asked for help, but Narvaez refused. He selfishly replied that each man should try to save his own life. Then he sailed away. It was justice, perhaps, that Narvaez later lost his life in the Gulf of Mexico while Cabeza de Vaca survived.

Somehow, de Vaca found enough strength to stay awake and hold the steering oar weakly. Then, just before dawn, he heard a familiar sound. The sea was washing against a beach not far away! After 45 days, de Vaca's barge had reached an island on the coast of Texas.

That evening, the Spaniards found a large and curious group of Indians. They were friendly and promised food in the morning. After they had rested and eaten, the Spaniards felt strong enough to continue their voyage. Unfortunately, a big wave turned over the raft, and three men died in the sea. De Vaca did the only sensible thing. He asked the Indians for food and shelter in their village. The Indians carried the weak men to a hut. Later, men from another boat which had reached another part of the island arrived. There were now 80 Spaniards.

As food became more scarce, the Indians became unfriendly. This unfriendliness became hostility when an epidemic began to kill both

rope	useless	refuse	steer	sensible
tail	thirst	selfishly	oar	shelter
mane	hardly	justice	dawn	hut
crude	voyage	perhaps	familiar	scarce
desperate	entrance	gulf	curious	unfriendly
start out	sail	survive	promise	unfriendliness
dangerous	current	strength	unfortunately	hostility
circumstances	separate	stay awake	turn over	epidemic

CAST ASHORE IN TEXAS

Indians and Spaniards. By spring, only 15 white men were alive. The Spaniards named their island prison *Malhado (*Misfortune). When the epidemic was at its worst, the warriors wanted to kill the Spaniards. They blamed them for all the tribe's troubles. At the last moment, a wise chief saved them. He pointed out that the Spaniards were dying too. However, the warriors did succeed in one thing. They persuaded their chief that the Spaniards should try to cure the sick Indians. As de Vaca wrote, "They wished to make us physicians without any examination or without inquiring for diplomas."

Although he earned some respect as a physician, de Vaca was practically a slave. The Indians forced him to work. He even had to dig roots with his fingers. Finally, he decided to escape. He left the island and joined a tribe on the mainland. They treated him better, gave him more liberty, and encouraged him to become a traveling trader. They needed someone to exchange goods with unfriendly tribes. Because of

alive	succeed	diploma	force	liberty
misfortune	persuade	although	dig	encourage
blame	cure	earn	root	trader
tribe	physician	respect	escape	exchange
moment	examination	practically	join	goods
point out	inquire	slave	treat	

this new freedom, he began to explore the country more thoroughly. A short time later, he successfully escaped from these Indians and headed westward toward New Spain. On the way, he met some Indians who told him about three other Christians in a nearby village. There he met Dorantes, Castillo, and a Moorish slave, Estevanico. These three men were the only other survivors.

Although the tribe treated the four men well, they still wanted to escape. One day they started on a journey that would take them over a large part of Texas and northwestern Mexico before they finally reached civilization. They wandered from tribe to tribe. They helped many sick Indians as they moved along.

Eventually the four men reached the Rio Grande and crossed into Mexico. As they traveled from village to village, the four men began to see signs that other Spaniards had come that way. At last, they met a group of Spanish slave-hunters who helped and protected them. Soon after that, the four survivors of the unsuccessful Narvaez Expedition rejoined their countrymen on the western coast of Mexico. On May 18, 1536—eight years after they had landed on the coast of Texas—they arrived at Caluiacan. They were truly men who refused to die!

After Cabeza de Vaca returned to Spain, he asked the king for permission to conquer and colonize Florida. However, it was too late! The king had already given permission to Hernando de Soto. De Soto offered de Vaca the position of second-in-command of the expedition, but he refused. Instead, he became the Governor of Uruguay. After even more adventures, he became a judge in Seville, where he died about 1564. It was a quiet end for one who had lived such a wild and dangerous life.

QUESTIONS FOR ORAL AND WRITTEN PRACTICE

(1) How many Spanish ships left Spain for the West Indies? (2) When did the expedition leave? (3) How many years before had Columbus discovered the New World? (4) Who was in command of the expedition? (5) What had the king appointed him to do? (6) What did many men do after the expedition reached the West Indies? (7) How did other men die? (8) How many men finally

freedom	westward	civilization	unsuccessful	instead
explore	Christians	wander	rejoin	governor
thoroughly	nearby	eventually	truly	judge
successfully	survivor	sign	permission	wild
head toward	northwestern	protect	offer	dangerous

7

reached Florida? (9) When did the expedition reach Florida? (10) Why did Narvaez want to search for Apalachen? (11) What did Narvaez decide to do with the ships? (12) What did he instruct the rest of the expedition to do? (13) Why was Cabeza de Vaca against the plan? (14) What did Narvaez tell Cabeza de Vaca he could do? (15) What did de Vaca reply? (16) When did Narvaez and his men begin the search for Apalachen? (17) When did they find it? (18) What had the Spaniards dreamed about? (19) What were they now satisfied with? (20) What did the unhappy Narvaez decide to do? (21) What was the one problem? (22) What did they try to do in desperation? (23) What had the Spaniards completed by September 20, 1528? (24) How many men climbed onto the rafts? (25) What happened when they reached Mobile? (26) What did men die of? (27) What did the Spaniards finally come to? (28) What did they find there? (29) What happened to the rafts? (30) What did Cabeza de Vaca see towards evening? (31) What did he ask Narvaez for? (32) What did he reply? (33) What did Narvaez do then? (34) What happened just before dawn? (35) What had Cabeza de Vaca's raft reached after 45 days? (36) What did the Spaniards find that evening? (37) What did the Indians promise? (38) What happened after the Spaniards continued their voyage? (39) What did Cabeza de Vaca ask the Indians for? (40) Who arrived later? (41) How many Spaniards were there now on the island? (42) When did the Indians become hostile? (43) How many Spaniards were now alive? (44) What did the Spaniards name their island prison? (45) What did the warriors want to do? (46) Who saved the Spaniards? (47) What did the warriors succeed in? (48) What did the Indians force de Vaca to do? (49) What did he finally decide to do? (50) How did the tribe on the mainland treat him? (51) What did the tribe need? (52) Where did Cabeza de Vaca head after he escaped from the new tribe? (53) Whom did he finally meet? (54) What did the four men want to do? (55) Where did their journey take them? (56) What did they begin to see as they traveled from village to village? (57) Whom did they meet at last? (58) Where did they finally rejoin their countrymen? (59) How long was it after they had landed on the coast of Texas? (60) What did Cabeza de Vaca ask the king for after his return to Spain? (61) To whom had the king already given permission? (62) What position was Cabeza de Vaca offered? (63) What did he become instead? (64) What did de Vaca finally become?

SUMMARY SENTENCES FOR LABORATORY PRACTICE

(1) It was a warm morning in June 1527. (2) Five Spanish ships left Spain for the West Indies. (3) Columbus had discovered the New World 35 years before. (4) Panfilo Narvaez was in command of the expedition. (5) Cabeza de Vaca was the treasurer of the expedition. (6) He wrote many stories about his adventures. (7) The expedition reached the west coast of Florida in 1528. (8) The Indians were hostile from the beginning. (9) They clearly told the Spaniards to leave. (10) The greedy Narvaez had already seen some gold jewelry. (11) The jewelry was worn by the Indians. (12) He learned that it came from a place called Apalachen. (13) The Spaniards began the search for that place. (14) They found it nearly two months later. (15) It was only a poor native village. (16) The Spaniards were tired, hungry, and disappointed. (17) They had dreamed about gold and jewels. (18) They were now satisfied with corn, beans, and pumpkins. (19) A third of the men got sick. (20) The unhappy Narvaez decided to travel by sea. (21) They tried to build a few flimsy rafts. (22) They had completed five crude rafts by September. (23) The desperate men climbed onto these rafts. (24) De Vaca's raft reached an island on the coast of Texas. (25) The Spaniards found a curious group of Indians. (26) De Vaca asked the Indians for food and shelter. (27) The Indians carried the weak men to a hut. (28) The Indians became unfriendly as food became scarce. (29) An epidemic began to kill both Indians and Spaniards. (30) Only 15 white men were alive by spring. (31) The warriors wanted to kill the Spaniards. (32) They blamed them for all the tribe's troubles. (33) A wise chief saved them. (34) The Spaniards tried to cure the sick Indians. (35) De Vaca earned some respect as a physician. (36) He escaped and joined a tribe on the mainland. (37) They encouraged him to become a traveling trader. (38) He successfully escaped from these Indians also. (39) He met the only three other survivors. (40) The tribe treated the four men well. (41) They still wanted to escape. (42) They wandered from village to village, helping the sick. (43) They met a group of Spanish slave-hunters. (44) The slave-hunters helped and protected them. (45) They rejoined their countrymen on the western coast of Mexico. (46) De Vaca asked the king for permission to colonize Florida. (47) The king had already given permission to Hernando de Soto. (48) He became the Governor of Uruguay instead. (49) He became a judge later. (50) He had lived a dangerous life.

EXERCISE 1. From the column at the left, select the best synonym for the italicized word in each sentence. Rewrite the sentences using the synonyms.

greedy
extraordinary
contented
completely
feebly
declined
guide
inquisitive
intelligent
achieved
liberty
roamed
conditions
well-known
decision
unbelievable

1 He made his *choice* in pride and anger.
2 The warriors *succeeded in* one thing.
3 He did the only *sensible* thing.
4 The men *wandered* from tribe to tribe.
5 They were now *satisfied* with corn and beans.
6 De Vaca held the steering oar *weakly.*
7 Their story is a most *remarkable* one.
8 He could explore because of his *freedom.*
9 He tried to explore the region *thoroughly.*
10 He heard a *familiar* sound just before dawn.
11 They found a group of *curious* Indians.
12 De Vaca used an oar to *steer* the raft.
13 He *refused* the position of second-in-command.
14 They made an *incredible* trip to Mexico.
15 They were often in dangerous *circumstances.*

EXERCISE 2. From the column at the left, select the correct word for each blank space in the sentences at the right. Use each word only once. Do not change the forms of the words.

justice
obviously
pride
greedy
selfishly
appointed
current
epidemic
survivors
blamed
separated
tools
succeeded
oars
persuaded
cure

1 The Indians _____ them for their troubles.
2 The _____ began to kill all of the people.
3 He decided to go because of his _____.
4 _____ he didn't realize the great difficulty.
5 There was a strong _____ in the river.
6 He answered the request for help _____.
7 The _____ of the trip were very weak.
8 After several days, the rafts became _____.
9 He was _____ to colonize the territory.
10 The men needed _____ to build a ship.
11 The Spaniards tried to _____ the sick Indians.
12 They couldn't move the boat with the _____.
13 Their _____ leader wanted to get the treasure.
14 He _____ them not to kill the Spaniards.
15 They _____ in reaching the coast of Texas.

EXERCISE 3. Supply the correct preposition for each blank space.

1 Five Spanish ships left Spain _____ June 1527.
2 Panfilo Narvaez was _____ command _____ the expedition.
3 Many men died _____ hurricanes; others died _____ thirst.
4 They reached the coast _____ Florida _____ April 15, 1528.
5 The Indians were hostile _____ the beginning.
6 Part of the expedition made the trip _____ land.
7 The horses and men were _____ poor condition.
8 They continued to search _____ gold _____ another month.
9 They made ropes _____ the tails and manes _____ horses.
10 They finally reached an island _____ the coast _____ Texas.
11 There were 80 Spaniards _____ the island.
12 _____ spring, only 15 white men were alive.
13 De Vaca had to dig roots _____ his fingers.
14 De Vaca had to exchange goods _____ unfriendly tribes.
15 The four men wandered _____ village _____ village.

EXERCISE 4. From the column at the right, select the correct line to complete each of the numbered lines at the left. Write each sentence in its correct form.

1 De Vaca wrote many stories
2 Many men were killed
3 Narvaez was greedy
4 De Vaca's pride and anger
5 The Spaniards were often
6 Because the water was useless
7 Just before dawn, he
8 He asked the Indians
9 An epidemic began to kill
10 De Vaca had to dig roots
11 He earned some respect
12 They blamed the Spaniards
13 De Vaca requested permission
14 The four men wandered
15 They were truly men

(A) almost cost him his life
(B) men died of thirst
(C) for the tribe's troubles
(D) with his fingers
(E) as a physician
(F) about his adventures
(G) from village to village
(H) who refused to die
(I) to colonize Florida
(J) heard a familiar sound
(K) in hurricanes
(L) both Spaniards and Indians
(M) for food and shelter
(N) without food and water
(O) for gold and jewels

EXERCISE 5. Study the following word form chart carefully.

	ADJECTIVE	NOUN	VERB	ADVERB
1	x x x x x	commander command	*command*	x x x x x
2	x x x x x	appointment	*appoint*	x x x x x
3	colonial	colonist colony	*colonize*	x x x x x
4	*adventurous*	adventurer *adventure*	x x x x x	*adventurously*
5	true *truthful*	*truth* truthfulness	x x x x x	truly truthfully
6	*hostile*	*hostility*	x x x x x	x x x x x
7	*greedy*	greediness	x x x x x	greedily
8	obvious	obviousness	x x x x x	*obviously*
9	x x x x x	reply	*reply*	x x x x x
10	angry	*anger*	anger	angrily
11	x x x x x	*search*	search	x x x x x
12	*hungry*	hunger	x x x x x	hungrily
13	x x x x x	disappointment	*disappoint*	x x x x x
14	*desperate*	*desperation*	x x x x x	desperately
15	thirsty	*thirst*	x x x x x	thirstily
16	x x x x x	refusal	*refuse*	x x x x x
17	selfish	selfishness	x x x x x	*selfishly*
18	*weak*	weakness	x x x x x	*weakly*
19	*flimsy*	flimsiness	x x x x x	flimsily
20	x x x x x	*permission*	permit	x x x x x
21	*curious*	curiosity	x x x x x	curiously
22	x x x x x	promise	*promise*	x x x x x
23	*scarce*	scarcity	x x x x x	x x x x x
24	x x x x x	blame	*blame*	x x x x x
25	persuasive	persuasion	*persuade*	persuasively
26	*sick*	sickness	x x x x x	x x x x x
27	x x x x x	treatment	*treat*	x x x x x
28	x x x x x	encouragement	*encourage*	x x x x x
29	*quiet*	quietness	x x x x x	quietly
30	*sensible*	sensibility	x x x x x	sensibly
31	respectful	*respect*	respect	respectfully
32	thorough	thoroughness	x x x x x	*thoroughly*

12

EXERCISE 6. Use the correct form of each italicized word in the sentence which follows. Notice the first two examples. Refer to the word form chart and examples whenever necessary.

1. *selfishly* — The leader acted in a *selfish* way.
2. *command* — The king appointed him *commander* of the expedition.
3. *truthful* — He always spoke to the men _____.
4. *curious* — The explorers had a lot of _____ about the gold.
5. *colonize* — He wanted to establish _____ in the New World.
6. *persuade* — Their leader was a very _____ speaker.
7. *quiet* — All of the men left _____ during the night.
8. *flimsy* — They were afraid of the _____ of the rafts.
9. *weakly* — They could not walk because of their _____.
10. *hostile* — Their unfriendliness soon became great _____.
11. *appoint* — He was proud of his _____ to lead the expedition.
12. *permission* — The king did not _____ him to lead the expedition.
13. *scarce* — There was a great _____ of food at that time.
14. *desperation* — The men tried _____ to reach the island.
15. *anger* — He _____ the men when he refused to help them.
16. *refuse* — His _____ to help surprised everyone greatly.
17. *blame* — The Indians _____ them for all of the trouble.
18. *sick* — At first, his _____ was not very serious.
19. *adventure* — His life as an explorer was always _____.
20. *greedy* — The hungry men ate their food _____.
21. *respect* — The men _____ the courage of their leader.
22. *hungry* — The explorers looked at the fresh food _____.
23. *disappoint* — Of course, the men's _____ was very great.
24. *thirst* — The men got _____ after days without water.
25. *sensible* — He acted _____ when he asked for assistance.
26. *reply* — When he _____, he gave the leader his opinion.
27. *thoroughly* — The commander planned the trip with great _____.
28. *treat* — The explorer appreciated the Indian's kind _____.
29. *encourage* — He received a great deal of _____ from them.
30. *promise* — The Indians kept their _____ to the Spaniards.
31. *obvious* — The leader _____ did not realize the problems.
32. *search* — The group _____ for gold for almost two months.

EXERCISE 7. Study the following examples for the preceding word form chart. The numbers correspond to those on the word form chart.

1 **commander, command.** He was the *commander* of the ships. The *command* of the ships was his responsibility. The men *followed his commands.* He was *in command of* the entire expedition. He *commanded* the expedition. He *commanded* the soldiers to follow him.

2 **appointment, appoint.** The king *appointed* him to lead the expedition. He received the *appointment* to lead the expedition.

3 **colonial, colonist, colony, colonize.** The king wanted to *colonize* the territory. He sent *colonists* to the territory. They established *colonies.* He appointed a *colonial* governor.

4 **adventurous, adventurer, adventure, adventurously.** He wrote about his *adventures* in the New World. He was truly an *adventurer.* He was an *adventurous* man. He lived *adventurously.*

5 **true, truthful, truth, truthfulness, truly, truthfully.** The facts were *true.* He was a *truthful* man. He was *truly* an adventurer. He told his story *truthfully.* He *told the truth.* The *truth* was hard to believe. People respected his *truthfulness.*

6 **hostile, hostility.** The Indians showed *hostility* toward the men. Their *hostility* was very apparent. They acted in a *hostile* way.

7 **greedy, greediness, greedily.** The explorer was a *greedy* man. He looked at the jewelry *greedily.* He showed his *greediness* in many ways.

8 **obvious, obviousness, obviously.** His greediness was *obvious* to the men. He made *obvious* plans to get the gold. *Obviously,* he wanted to get the gold. His *obviousness* made the men angry.

9 **reply.** He *replied* to the leader's question. His *reply* to the question made the other man angry.

10 **angry, anger, angrily.** He was *angry.* The man's reply *made him angry.* The *angry* man spoke loudly. He spoke to the other man *angrily.* His *anger* showed in his voice. The leader *angered* the men.

11 **search.** They began their *search* for gold in May. They *searched* for the village.

12 **hungry, hunger, hungrily.** The men were *hungry.* They were dying of *hunger.* They thought about food *hungrily.*

13 **disappointment, disappoint.** Their *disappointment* was very obvious. They *suffered disappointment* several times. The results *disappointed* them. They were *disappointed* by the results. The *disappointed* men returned. It was *disappointing* news.

14 **desperate, desperation, desperately.** The *desperation* of the men was understandable. They acted *in desperation*. The *desperate* men tried to save their lives. They were *in desperate circumstances*. They were *desperately* trying to save their lives.

15 **thirsty, thirst, thirstily.** The men were *thirsty*. They drank the water *thirstily*. Some of the men died of *thirst*.

16 **refusal, refuse.** He *refused* to help the other soldiers. His *refusal* made them angry.

17 **selfish, selfishness, selfishly.** He was a *selfish* man. He frequently acted *selfishly*. The men knew about his *selfishness*.

18 **weak, weakness, weakly.** They couldn't row because of their *weakness*. They were *weak* from hunger. The *weak* men were unable to row. They held the oars *weakly*.

19 **flimsy, flimsiness, flimsily.** Their *flimsy* raft wasn't safe. The raft was *flimsily* made. They weren't safe because of the *flimsiness* of the raft.

20 **permission, permit.** He received *permission* from the king. The king *granted permission*. The king *permitted* him to leave.

21 **curious, curiosity, curiously.** The Indians were *curious* about the men. The *curious* Indians looked at them. They showed their *curiosity* in many ways. They looked at the white men *curiously*.

22 **promise.** The Indians *promised* to help them. They *promised* assistance. Their *promise* encouraged the men. They *kept their promise* to the men. They didn't *break their promise*.

23 **scarce, scarcity.** Food was *scarce*. There was a *scarcity* of food.

24 **blame.** The Indians *blamed* the men for their troubles. The men *were to blame* for everything. They *placed the blame on* the men.

25 **persuasive, persuasion, persuade, persuasively.** He *persuaded* them not to kill the Spaniards. He used *persuasion* instead of force. He argued *persuasively*. His arguments were *persuasive*. He was a *persuasive* person.

26 **sick, sickness.** There were many *sick* men. They were *sick* from lack of food. They *looked sick*. Some of them died of *sickness*.

27 **treatment, treat.** The Indians *treated* them well. They *received good treatment* from the Indians. Their *treatment* was good.

28 **encouragement, encourage.** The Indians *encouraged* him to become a trader. He was *encouraged* by their treatment. He obtained *encouraging* information. Their *encouragement* helped him very much. They *gave him encouragement*.

29 **quiet, quietness, quietly.** It was a *quiet* night. The men sat there *quietly*. The *quietness* of the night worried them.

30 **sensible, sensibility, sensibly.** His *sensibility* was respected by the other men. They trusted him because he acted *sensibly*. He usually did the *sensible* thing.

31 **respectful, respect, respectfully.** The men *respected* their leader. Their *respect* for him was obvious. They *showed respect* for him. He *earned respect* in many ways. They were *respectful* men. They were *respectful* of their leader. They treated their leader *respectfully*.

32 **thorough, thoroughness, thoroughly.** Their leader planned everything *thoroughly*. He was a *thorough* man. Their success depended on his *thoroughness*.

EXERCISE 8. Select the correct way to complete each of the following sentences. Write each sentence in its correct form.

1 The Indians in Florida (*a*) wanted Narvaez and his men to stay. (*b*) promised to show Narvaez their golden kingdom. (*c*) were hostile. (*d*) were greedy.

2 De Vaca did not want to make the trip by land because (*a*) the men and horses were in poor condition. (*b*) he was afraid. (*c*) of his pride. (*d*) he did not like Narvaez.

3 Narvaez finally decided to travel by sea because (*a*) the gold was too heavy to carry by land. (*b*) many of his men were sick. (*c*) the Indians were always fighting with them. (*d*) he found some rafts.

4 When de Vaca asked him for help, Narvaez (*a*) gave him some food and water. (*b*) took the sick men on his raft. (*c*) ordered his men to pull de Vaca's raft. (*d*) refused and sailed away.

5 Just before dawn, de Vaca (*a*) heard the voices of Indians. (*b*) went to sleep. (*c*) saw the rest of the rafts. (*d*) heard the sea washing against a beach.

6 When they landed on the island, the Spaniards found (*a*) a number of other rafts. (*b*) a group of curious Indians. (*c*) an epidemic. (*d*) their ships.

7 The Indians became hostile (*a*) when too many other Spaniards arrived. (*b*) because the Spaniards treated them badly. (*c*) because the Spaniards refused to work. (*d*) when an epidemic killed many of them.

8   The chief ordered the Spaniards (*a*) to leave the village immediately.   (*b*) to cure the sick Indians.   (*c*) to stay in their huts.   (*d*) to build new rafts.

9   The tribe on the mainland (*a*) encouraged de Vaca to become a traveling trader.   (*b*) ordered de Vaca to return to the island prison.   (*c*) wanted de Vaca to explore the country more thoroughly.   (*d*) sent de Vaca westward toward New Spain.

10 After his escape, de Vaca (*a*) decided to travel alone.   (*b*) met three of his countrymen.   (*c*) searched for Narvaez.   (*d*) discovered Apalachen.

11 As the four men roamed from tribe to tribe, they (*a*) stole food from the Indians.   (*b*) made slaves of the Indians.   (*c*) became sick.   (*d*) helped the sick Indians.

12 A group of Spanish slave-hunters (*a*) tried to kill them.   (*b*) showed them the way to the Rio Grande.   (*c*) helped and protected them.   (*d*) refused to die.

13 De Vaca now wanted to (*a*) become the Governor of Uruguay.   (*b*) conquer and colonize Florida.   (*c*) be second-in-command of de Soto's expedition.   (*d*) stay in Spain.

14 De Vaca finally (*a*) died quietly in Seville.   (*b*) was killed by unfriendly Indians in Uruguay.   (*c*) died in a hurricane.   (*d*) received permission to colonize Florida.

15 This story is remarkable because (*a*) almost all of the men survived.   (*b*) the Spaniards made the trip from Florida to the Rio Grande so quickly.   (*c*) the four men survived great dangers and difficulties.   (*d*) of the great success of the expedition.

The story "He Saw Texas First" by B. T. Fields and the accompanying illustrations by E. M. Schiwetz originally appeared in *The Texas Sketchbook* published by the Humble Oil & Refining Company, Houston, Texas. Permission to use and rewrite these materials was kindly approved by the Supervisor of Publications, Humble Oil & Refining Company.

17

The First Thanksgiving

PART ONE

In 1620, a small sailboat named the *Mayflower* left England for the New World. The *Mayflower* headed for the Jamestown colony on the warm shore of Virginia. Its one hundred passengers were the Pilgrims. They were looking for a place where they could worship God in their own way.

Because of strong winds and severe storms, the *Mayflower* lost its course. The brave group of colonists finally had to land at Plymouth on the rocky coast of Massachusetts in December 1620. It was the

sailboat	shore	severe	colonist	rocky
head for	passenger	course	land	coast
colony	worship			

middle of the stern northern winter. Terrible months of starvation, disease, and death were ahead of them. Only the strongest of the Pilgrims survived that winter. Many women gave their own pitiful rations to their children and died for lack of food for themselves. The Governor of the Plymouth Colony, John Carver, died in April 1621. In his place, the Pilgrims elected William Bradford.

Conditions began to improve in the spring of 1621. There were wild vegetables. There were berries and fruit. Fish and game were

stern	disease	survive	for lack of	berry
terrible	death	pitiful	elect	game
starvation	ahead of	rations	condition	

plentiful. Therefore, they were able to get enough fresh meat despite their lack of skill or experience in hunting and fishing. The colonists' health improved with the warm weather and their better diet.

In the fall, they looked back over the past year. They were both regretful and thankful. Only fifty of the original one hundred passengers remained. The price in human lives and tragedy had been great. On the other hand, they saw new hope for the future. A splendid harvest was behind them. They were ready for the second winter with confidence. They had eleven crude houses for protection against the severe winter. Seven were for families, and four were for communal use. Best of all, they had established a treaty of friendship with their Indian neighbors under Chief Massasoit in the summer. The woods and forests became safe. When the *Mayflower* returned to England that summer, there were no colonists aboard.

At the end of their first year in their new home, the Pilgrims wanted to celebrate with a real holiday. Governor Bradford decided on December 13, 1621 as the day for giving thanks to God.

The colonists fired a cannon as a salute at dawn on that first Thanksgiving Day. Afterwards they moved to the meeting house in a procession. This house took the place of a church for them. There they offered humble thanks to God. After the religious ceremony, a great feast and three days of celebration began. Massasoit and his Indian warriors were guests.

The hunters came back with wild turkeys, geese, and ducks. The Indians brought deer meat. In addition, there were fish, clams, and oysters. The Pilgrim housewives probably cooked some of their dried strawberries or cherries. However, there was no sugar. Therefore, they were unable to prepare English jam or jelly. The Indians contributed many kinds of vegetables, especially pumpkins. Today pumpkins are both food and decoration for almost every Thanksgiving table.

plentiful	harvest	celebrate	celebration	housewife
therefore	confidence	fire	guest	probably
despite	crude	cannon	hunter	strawberry
skill	protection	salute	turkey	cherry
experience	communal	dawn	goose	unable
diet	best of all	procession	duck	jam
regretful	establish	offer	deer	jelly
thankful	treaty	humble	in addition	contribute
original	friendship	religious	clam	pumpkin
remain	chief	ceremony	oyster	decoration
tragedy	aboard	feast		

During the three days of celebration, the small group of women worked very hard. There were only a few young girls and a small number of children to help them. This little group provided food for the three-day feast for one hundred and forty people, including the Indian guests.

In the meantime, the men took part in various contests and games. The Indians competed with their bows and arrows. Both red men and white men competed in sports. The Pilgrim leaders usually considered games and sports a waste of time. Of course, on this holiday their discipline was not so strict. However, there were constant prayers during the three days. Miles Standish and his soldiers marched for their guests. Every man except Governor Bradford and Elder Brewster joined the parade. Everyone was very excited when the soldiers shot their rifles and blew their bugles.

On the whole, it was a wonderful holiday for the Pilgrims after their winter of starvation and tragedy. However, they paid for this luxury during the following winter. There was very little food for anyone. They did not have a Thanksgiving feast the next fall. The harvest was too small for that. In spite of everything, they never had any regrets about their first holiday.

QUESTIONS FOR ORAL AND WRITTEN PRACTICE

(1) When did the *Mayflower* leave England for the New World? (2) Where did the *Mayflower* head for? (3) How many passengers were there? (4) Who were the passengers? (5) What were they looking for? (6) Why did the *Mayflower* lose its course? (7) Where did the colonists finally have to land? (8) When did they land there? (9) What was ahead of them? (10) Who survived the winter? (11) To whom did many women give their rations? (12) What happened to these women? (13) When did their first Governor die? (14) Whom did the Pilgrims elect in his place? (15) What things could they eat in the spring of 1621? (16) Why did their health improve? (17) How did they feel about the past year in the fall of 1621? (18) How many of the original passengers remained? (19) How did they feel about the second winter?

provide	compete	waste	prayer	bugle
including	bow	of course	march	on the whole
in the meantime	arrow	discipline	join	luxury
take part in	sports	strict	parade	in spite of
various	leader	constant	excite	regret
contest	consider			

(20) How many houses did they have?   (21) What had they established with their Indian neighbors?   (22) How many colonists returned to England on the *Mayflower* that summer?   (23) What did the Pilgrims want to do at the end of their first year in their new home?   (24) What day did Governor Bradford decide on?   (25) What happened at dawn on that first Thanksgiving Day?   (26) Where did the colonists go after that?   (27) When did the great feast and celebration begin?   (28) What did the hunters come back with?   (29) What did the Indians bring?   (30) What other kinds of food did they have?   (31) What did the small group of women do during the three days?   (32) What did the men do during the three days?   (33) How did the Pilgrim leaders usually feel about games and sports?   (34) What did Miles Standish and his soldiers do for their guests?   (35) Who joined the parade?   (36) How did the Pilgrims pay for this luxury during the following winter?   (37) Did they have a Thanksgiving feast the next fall? Why not?   (38) How did they feel about their first holiday when it was over?

PART TWO

IN THE FOLLOWING DECADES, Thanksgiving Days were frequently held, sometimes twice a year, sometimes every other year, depending on the circumstances. Thanksgiving lost some of its New England character during the Revolutionary War. The Continental Congress recommended eight days of Thanksgiving in April, May, July, and December. Congress interrupted its regular business on those days. General George Washington issued a proclamation for a general Thanksgiving for the Continental Army on Thursday, December 18, 1777 and again at Valley Forge on May 7, 1778. Washington became the first President of the United States in April 1789. Just before the adjournment of Congress in September of that year, President Washington issued a proclamation for a Thanksgiving Day on November 26. He announced a second Thanksgiving Day six years later. After that, there were no Thanksgiving Days until 1812. President James Madison announced a Thanksgiving Day at the end of the War of 1812.

decade	character	interrupt	largely	constant
frequently	revolutionary	issue	responsibility	suggestion
twice	continental	proclamation	realize	national
every other	congress	adjournment	for the first time	bitter
depending on	recommend	announce	in agreement with	civil war
circumstance				

The history of Thanksgiving as a national holiday is largely the responsibility of Mrs. Sarah J. Hale. Mrs. Hale moved from Boston to Philadelphia in 1830. Then she realized for the first time that Thanksgiving was not celebrated at all in many states. In agreement with Mrs. Hale's constant suggestions, President Abraham Lincoln announced the first national Thanksgiving Day Proclamation on October 3, 1863. At that time, the country was in the middle of a bitter civil war. Lincoln

appoint	nation	hardly	manner	generosity
proclaim	as a whole	intention	denomination	

23

appointed the last Thursday in November as Thanksgiving Day. Each president since Lincoln has proclaimed a Thanksgiving Day for the nation as a whole.

Thanksgiving has hardly changed at all since 1621 in its intention and manner of celebration. Churches of all denominations are open on this day to give thanks for God's generosity. Thanksgiving is a family holiday. All over the country, husbands and wives, grandchildren, and great-grandchildren travel from city to town, from town to village, or from village to farm to spend the day at their old home. Many speak to their parents or grandparents by long-distance telephone.

Thanksgiving dinner is practically the same all over the country. The table is always loaded with delicious food of many different kinds. Naturally, the main course is the turkey. Pumpkin pie is often served in remembrance of the Indians' gift to the first settlers. In most homes, there are traditional games after dinner.

Thanksgiving is a happy celebration. It is a family day and a chance to renew friendships. Above all, Thanksgiving Day is a time for remembrance and for giving thanks.

QUESTIONS FOR ORAL AND WRITTEN PRACTICE

(39) How often were Thanksgiving Days held in the following decades? (40) How did the character of the holiday change? (41) What did the Continental Congress recommend? (42) Who was George Washington? (43) What kind of proclamation did he issue about Thanksgiving Day? (44) When did he announce the second Thanksgiving Day? (45) What happened in 1812? (46) Who worked to make Thanksgiving Day a national holiday? (47) Where did she move to in 1830? (48) What did she then realize for the first time? (49) What was the country in the middle of at that time? (50) What day did President Lincoln proclaim as Thanksgiving Day in 1863? (51) What has each president since Lincoln done in connection with Thanksgiving Day? (52) How much has Thanksgiving changed since 1621 in its intention? In its manner of celebration? (53) In what way is Thanksgiving a family holiday? (54) In what way is Thanksgiving a religious holiday? (55) Where do many people celebrate this holiday? (56) How do many people celebrate this holiday? (57) Why do many people celebrate this holiday? (58) Since what year have people celebrated this

| load | naturally | serve | traditional | renew |
| delicious | main course | remembrance | | |

holiday? (59) What is the traditional food for Thanksgiving Day?
(60) Why are pumpkins associated with this holiday?

SUMMARY SENTENCES FOR LABORATORY PRACTICE

(1) A small sailboat left England for the New World in 1620. (2)
The boat headed for a colony on the shores of Virginia. (3) The ship
had one hundred passengers. (4) There were strong winds and severe
storms. (5) The ship lost its course. (6) The colonists had to land on
the rocky coast of Massachusetts. (7) They landed in December 1620.
(8) It was the middle of the winter. (9) Only the strongest of the
colonists survived the winter. (10) Starvation and disease caused death.
(11) The governor of the colony died in the spring. (12) A new governor was elected. (13) Conditions began to improve in the spring.
(14) There were wild vegetables. (15) There were berries and fruit.
(16) Fish and game were plentiful. (17) The colonists lacked skill and
experience. (18) But they were able to get fresh meat despite this.
(19) Their health improved with the warm weather. (20) Only fifty
of the original passengers survived. (21) In the fall, they looked back
over the year. (22) They were regretful. (23) But they were also
thankful. (24) The price had been great. (25) But they saw hope for
the future. (26) They were confident because of their harvest. (27)
They had houses for protection against the winter. (28) They established a treaty with the Indians. (29) The woods and forests became
safe. (30) None of the colonists returned to England. (31) At the end
of the year, they wanted to celebrate. (32) They decided on December
13 as a holiday. (33) Three days of celebration began on December 13.
(34) After a religious ceremony, there was a feast. (35) Their Indian
neighbors were guests. (36) The hunters came back with wild turkeys
and ducks. (37) The Indians contributed meat and vegetables. (38)
The small group of women worked very hard. (39) There were only a
few young girls to help them. (40) The group provided food for the
feast. (41) There were one hundred and forty people including the
guests. (42) The men took part in contests and games. (43) Everyone
competed in sports. (44) On the holiday, their discipline wasn't strict.
(45) There was a parade for the guests. (46) Everyone was excited when
they shot their rifles. (47) It was a wonderful holiday for the Pilgrims.
(48) But they paid for it during the following winter. (49) There was
very little food for anyone. (50) But they never had any regrets about
their first holiday.

EXERCISE 9. From the column at the left, select the best synonym for the italicized word in each sentence. Rewrite the sentences using the synonyms.

appoint
scarcely
principal
got better
almost
searching
parade
stayed
completely filled
primarily
violent
remained alive
shot
memory
roughly finished
furnished

1 The Pilgrims were *looking* for a new home.
2 The *severe* storms damaged the little ship.
3 Their health *improved* in the spring.
4 Only the strongest Pilgrims *survived*.
5 They built *crude* houses for protection.
6 On that day, there was a *procession*.
7 The colonists *fired* a cannon as a salute.
8 The group *provided* the food for the feast.
9 All the colonists *remained* in New England.
10 The celebration has *hardly* changed.
11 It is *practically* the same everywhere.
12 It was *largely* the responsibility of Mrs. Hale.
13 The table is always *loaded* with food.
14 The *main* course usually consists of turkey.
15 It is served in *remembrance* of their gifts.

EXERCISE 10. From the column at the left, select the correct word for each blank space in the sentences at the right. Use each word only once. Do not change the forms of the words.

tragedy
aboard
recommended
skill
issued
feast
stern
unable
communal
dried
crude
discipline
humble
served
salute
interrupted

1 The price in lives and _____ had been great.
2 The first winter in Massachusetts was _____.
3 The colonists lacked _____ in hunting for food.
4 They built eleven _____ houses for protection.
5 Four of the houses were for _____ use.
6 The ship returned with no colonists _____.
7 At dawn, they fired a cannon as a _____.
8 They offered _____ thanks for the harvest.
9 They provided food for the three-day _____.
10 They were _____ to prepare jam or jelly.
11 The housewives probably cooked _____ berries.
12 Much delicious food was _____ by the women.
13 Their _____ wasn't strict during the celebration.
14 Congress _____ its regular business for Thanksgiving.
15 Congress _____ eight days of Thanksgiving.

EXERCISE 11. Supply the correct preposition for each blank space.

1 The *Mayflower* left England _____ the New World _____ 1620.
2 Many women died _____ lack _____ food _____ themselves.
3 They had to land _____ the rocky coast _____ Massachusetts.
4 The Governor _____ the colony died _____ April 1621.
5 _____ his place, the colonists elected William Bradford.
6 Conditions began to improve _____ the spring _____ 1621.
7 The price _____ lives and tragedy had been great.
8 _____ the other hand, they saw new hope _____ the future.
9 They were ready _____ the future _____ great confidence.
10 They moved _____ the meeting house _____ a procession.
11 They wanted to celebrate _____ the end _____ their first year.
12 The governor decided _____ December 13 _____ the best day.
13 They provided food _____ the three-day feast _____ 140 people.
14 _____ the meantime, the men took part _____ various games.
15 _____ the whole, it was a wonderful holiday _____ the colonists.

EXERCISE 12. From the column at the right, select the correct line to complete each of the numbered lines at the left. Write each sentence in its correct form.

1 The Pilgrims were looking for
2 The ship lost its course
3 Their health improved
4 When the ship returned
5 No one had regrets
6 The men took part in
7 It was a wonderful holiday
8 They usually considered sports
9 In spite of everything, they
10 The holiday has hardly changed
11 The dinner table is always
12 The country was in the middle
13 Many people died
14 Terrible months of starvation
15 The colonists finally had

(A) various contests and games
(B) after their tragic winter
(C) loaded with delicious food
(D) of a bitter civil war
(E) were ahead of them
(F) about their holiday
(G) no colonists were aboard
(H) with a better diet
(I) because of severe storms
(J) for lack of food
(K) never had any regrets
(L) a place to worship God
(M) to land at Plymouth
(N) at all since 1621
(O) a waste of time

EXERCISE 13. Study the following word form chart carefully. The word forms which occurred in the preceding story are italicized.

ADJECTIVE	NOUN	VERB	ADVERB
1 *severe*	severity	x x x x x	severely
2 stormy	*storm*	x x x x x	stormily
3 x x x x x	starvation	starve	x x x x x
4 x x x x x	survivor / survival	*survive*	x x x x x
5 x x x x x	election	*elect*	x x x x x
6 x x x x x	improvement	*improve*	x x x x x
7 *plentiful*	plenty	x x x x x	plentifully
8 skillful	*skill*	x x x x x	skillfully
9 regrettable / *regretful*	*regret*	regret	regrettably / regretfully
10 *thankful*	thanks (always pl.)	thank	thankfully
11 x x x x x	remainder	*remain*	x x x x x
12 hopeless / hopeful	*hope*	hope	hopelessly / hopefully
13 confident	confidence	x x x x x	confidently
14 protective	*protection*	protect	protectively
15 *safe*	safety	save	safely
16 x x x x x	*celebration*	celebrate	x x x x x
17 *religious*	religion	x x x x x	religiously
18 preparatory	preparation	*prepare*	x x x x x
19 x x x x x	contribution	*contribute*	x x x x x
20 decorative	*decoration*	decorate	decoratively
21 competitive	competition	*compete*	competitively
22 wasteful	*waste*	waste	wastefully
23 x x x x x	excitement	*excite*	x x x x x
24 luxurious	*luxury*	x x x x x	luxuriously
25 characteristic	*character*	characterize	characteristically
26 x x x x x	recommendation	*recommend*	x x x x x
27 x x x x x	interruption	*interrupt*	x x x x x
28 x x x x x	announcement	*announce*	x x x x x
29 responsible	*responsibility*	x x x x x	responsibly
30 x x x x x	appointment	*appoint*	x x x x x
31 intentional	*intention*	intend	intentionally
32 generous	*generosity*	x x x x x	generously

EXERCISE 14. Use the correct form of each italicized word in the sentence which follows. Notice the first two examples. Refer to the word form chart and examples whenever necessary.

1	*improve*	There was an *improvement* in their conditions.
2	*celebrate*	They decided on December 13 for the *celebration*.
3	*plentiful*	There were _____ of strawberries and cherries.
4	*regretful*	They had many _____ about their decisions.
5	*thankful*	They were very _____ for the good harvest.
6	*confidence*	They were _____ that the future would be better.
7	*protection*	Their houses gave them _____ against the weather.
8	*prepare*	Much _____ was necessary for the celebration.
9	*remain*	The _____ of the people decided not to return.
10	*safe*	They could go into the forests with _____.
11	*compete*	There was _____ in sports and games.
12	*character*	Certain things are _____ of New England.
13	*announce*	The governor read the _____ to the people.
14	*appoint*	The president _____ a specific day for Thanksgiving.
15	*severe*	The _____ of the storms caused great trouble.
16	*starvation*	Many people _____ during the terrible winter.
17	*skill*	At first, the men were not _____ hunters.
18	*storm*	They had a _____ trip across the Atlantic.
19	*hope*	The colonists were _____ that it would change
20	*religious*	The colonists felt that _____ was important.
21	*contribute*	The Indians made _____ to the celebration.
22	*responsibility*	The president was _____ for the change.
23	*waste*	They tried not to be _____ with food.
24	*decoration*	The children _____ the table for the feast.
25	*interrupt*	There was an _____ during that time.
26	*generosity*	Everyone appreciated the _____ assistance.
27	*recommend*	People thought it was a good _____.
28	*luxury*	They never regretted this great _____.
29	*intention*	They _____ to celebrate for three days.
30	*survive*	The colonists were thankful for their _____.
31	*excite*	There was much _____ before the celebration.
32	*elect*	The _____ took place in the month of April.

EXERCISE 15. Study the following examples for the preceding word form chart. The numbers correspond to those on the word form chart.

1 **severe, severity, severely.** There were *severe* storms. The storms damaged the boat *severely*. No one had expected such *severity*.

2 **stormy, storm.** There were many *storms*. The weather was *stormy* for many days. They lost their course in the *stormy* weather.

3 **starvation, starve.** There was much *starvation* during the winter. Many people *starved*. Some of them *starved to death*. The *starving* people searched for food.

4 **survival, survivor, survive.** About half of them *survived* that winter. Their *survival* depended on their strength. The *survivors* elected a governor. The *surviving* colonists elected a governor.

5 **election, elect.** A new governor was *elected* in the spring. The *election* was held in April 1621.

6 **improvement, improve.** Their health *improved* in the spring. They could work harder because of their *improved* health. They were happy about the *improving* conditions. Their better diet caused the *improvement*.

7 **plentiful, plenty, plentifully.** There was *plenty* of food during the summer. There were *plenty* of vegetables to eat. Fish and game were *plentiful*. Berries grew in the woods *plentifully*.

8 **skillful, skill, skillfully.** They didn't have much *skill* in hunting. They weren't *skillful* workers. They weren't *skilled* workers. They didn't hunt for food *skillfully*.

9 **regretful, regrettable, regret, regretfully, regrettably.** They were *regretful* that many had died. They thought about the past winter *regretfully*. There had been many *regrettable* events. *Regrettably*, about half of them had died. However, they didn't *regret* their decision. They *had no regrets* about it. They didn't mention any *regrets*.

10 **thankful, thanks** (pl. noun), **thank, thankfully.** They were *thankful* for their good harvest. They spoke about their good harvest *thankfully*. They *gave thanks to* God in their church. They expressed their *thanks*. They *thanked* God in their prayers.

11 **remainder, remain.** Only fifty colonists *remained* in the spring. The *remainder* of the colonists had died.

12 **hopeful, hopeless, hope, hopefully, hopelessly.** They had much *hope* for the future. They *hoped* for better conditions. They *hoped* to establish a treaty with the Indians. They were *hopeful* for the

future. They were *hopeful* that the future would be better. They prepared for the winter *hopefully*. The situation wasn't *hopeless*. They didn't wait aboard the ship *hopelessly*.

13 **confident, confidence, confidently.** They were ready for the winter with *confidence*. They *had confidence in* their ability to survive. They were *confident* in their ability. They prepared for the winter *confidently*.

14 **protective, protection, protect, protectively.** They had houses for *protection* against the weather. The houses *protected* them against the weather. They built *protective* frames around the doors. Trees were located *protectively* around the houses.

15 **safe, safety, safely.** Because of the treaty, they were *safe* in the woods. They could walk through the woods *safely*. They could walk through the woods with *safety*.

16 **celebration, celebrate.** The *celebration* began on December 13. They *celebrated* with a real holiday. They *celebrated* their first year in the New World.

17 **religious, religion, religiously.** They were *religious* people. They tried to live *religiously*. *Religion* was very important in their lives.

18 **preparatory, preparation, prepare.** The women *prepared* food for the celebration. The *preparation* of the food took much time. The men took care of the *preparatory* work.

19 **contribution, contribute.** The Indians *contributed* food for the celebration. They brought their *contribution* on the day of the feast.

20 **decorative, decoration, decorate, decoratively.** Families *decorate* their tables with pumpkins. Pumpkins are used in the *decoration* of the table. Pumpkins are *decorative* because of their color. Pumpkins are used *decoratively*.

21 **competitive, competition, compete, competitively.** The colonists and Indians *competed* in sports. The colonists *competed* against the Indians. The *competition* was friendly. There were *competitive* games. They shot their bows and arrows *competitively*.

22 **wasteful, waste, wastefully.** They felt it was *a waste of time*. They tried to avoid *waste* of any kind. They didn't want to *waste time*. They didn't *waste* any food. They weren't *wasteful* with food. They didn't do things *wastefully*.

23 **excitement, excite.** Everyone was *excited* about the holiday. The plans *excited* everyone. The *exciting* plans were finally completed. The *excited* children shouted loudly. There was much *excitement*.

24 luxurious, luxury, luxuriously. The feast was their first *luxury* of the year. They had very few *luxuries*. They had very few *luxurious* things. They couldn't live *luxuriously*.

25 characteristic, character, characterize, characteristically. The celebration originally had a New England *character*. It was *characteristic* of New England customs. The people celebrated the holiday *characteristically*. Certain customs *characterized* their manner of celebration.

26 recommendation, recommend. They *recommended* eight days of celebration. The *recommended* period of celebration was eight days. Their *recommendation* wasn't followed very long.

27 interruption, interrupt. They *interrupted* their regular meetings. During the *interruption,* no business took place.

28 announcement, announce. He *announced* his decision to the public. His *announcement* concerned the official holiday. He *made an announcement* to the public.

29 responsible, responsibility, responsibly. It became a national holiday through her *responsibility*. She was largely *responsible* for Lincoln's announcement. She acted *responsibly* to establish this holiday.

30 appointment, appoint. He *appointed* a specific day for the celebration. Thanksgiving was held on the *appointed* day. He *appointed* General Grant commander-in-chief. He announced the *appointment* publically.

31 intention, intend. They *intended* the holiday to be a day for giving thanks. They *intended* to celebrate their plentiful harvest. They explained their *intention* to everyone.

32 generous, generosity, generously. They appreciated his *generosity*. They appreciated his *generous* assistance. He gave his assistance *generously*.

EXERCISE 16. Select the correct way to complete each of the following sentences. Write each sentence in its correct form.

1 The *Mayflower's* passengers were (*a*) looking for gold and wealth. (*b*) trying to increase interest in the New World. (*c*) hoping to establish new holidays. (*d*) looking for religious liberty.

2 During the first winter, many women died for lack of food because (*a*) they had no skill or experience. (*b*) they gave their own pitiful rations to their children. (*c*) there were severe storms. (*d*) the ship lost its course.

3 Conditions began to improve in the spring of 1621 because (a) the *Mayflower* headed back for England. (b) they elected William Bradford as their governor. (c) they were able to get fresh meat and other food. (d) they were ready for a celebration.

4 The colonists' health improved (a) with the warm weather and better food. (b) with medicine which was contributed by the Indians. (c) with the establishment of a treaty. (d) with the increase in their confidence.

5 Of the original one hundred passengers, (a) only eleven remained. (b) most of them returned to England. (c) only the children survived. (d) there were fifty survivors.

6 At the end of the Pilgrims' first year in their new home, (a) discipline became very strict. (b) an important election was held. (c) they decided to interrupt their regular meetings. (d) they wanted to celebrate with a real holiday.

7 The colonists were confident about the future because (a) the Indians made a contribution for the feast. (b) religion was very important in their lives. (c) the harvest had been good and they had crude houses. (d) the small group of women provided food for the three-day feast.

8 At dawn on the first Thanksgiving Day, (a) the men took part in various contests and games. (b) the colonists fired a cannon as a salute. (c) the governor appointed a specific day for the celebration. (d) some of the New England character was lost.

9 At the first Thanksgiving dinner, the Indians (a) came without invitations. (b) set the houses on fire. (c) shot off rifles. (d) brought vegetables and meat.

10 The colonists did not usually compete against each other in sports because (a) a plentiful harvest was behind them. (b) they were not very skillful hunters. (c) they considered it a waste of time. (d) they were regretful about their decision.

The illustration by W. N. Wilson on pages 18 and 19 originally appeared in Mitchell and Wilson, *Ships that Made United States History*, New York, Whittlesey House, McGraw-Hill Book Co., Inc., Copyright 1950. The illustration has been reproduced with the permission of the publisher.

The illustration by Leonard Everett Fisher on page 23 originally appeared in *America Is Born* by Gerald W. Johnson, New York, William Morrow and Company, Copyright 1959. The illustration has been reproduced with the permission of the publisher.

The Legend of Sleepy Hollow

From *The Sketch Book of Geoffry Crayon* by Washington Irving

NOT FAR FROM TARRYTOWN along the Hudson River, there is a little valley among the high hills. It is one of the quietest places in the whole world. Because it is so peaceful and quiet, this lovely valley is called Sleepy Hollow.

The people of Sleepy Hollow believe all kinds of strange things. They often see strange sights and hear music and voices in the air. According to many people, the valley is visited regularly by a ghost. The ghost always rides a horse and has no head. Some people say it is the spirit of a soldier who lost his head in a nameless battle during the Revolutionary War. They say the body of the soldier lies under the earth of the churchyard. As the story goes, the ghost rides away every night to hunt for its head and then rushes back like the wind to get to

legend	lovely	spirit	revolutionary	churchyard
sleepy	sight	nameless	lie (*irreg.*)	rush
hollow	regularly	battle	earth	wind
peaceful	ghost			

the churchyard before dawn. The ghost is known in all the country homes by the name of the Headless Horseman of Sleepy Hollow.

Once in the early history of this region, a man named Ichabod Crane came to Sleepy Hollow as a teacher. The name Crane suited him. He was tall and thin with narrow shoulders, long arms and legs, and big feet. His hands hung a mile out of his sleeves. His head was flat at the top, and he had a long pointed nose. On a windy day, he looked exactly like a scarecrow, some people said. His school stood alone in a rather pleasant place at the foot of a hill. It was a log cabin with one large room and a low roof. The broken windows were covered with pieces of old paper.

Ichabod was not a cruel teacher. On the contrary, he punished his students as fairly as possible. After school hours, he was friendly with the children. Indeed, it was tactful of him to be their friend. The pay for teaching was small, and even though he was thin, Ichabod liked to eat. In that part of the country, the teacher lived in the homes of the children's parents. He went to all their farms in turn for a week at a time. He carried all his belongings from house to house in a handkerchief.

Because he went from one farmhouse to another, Ichabod became a kind of traveling newspaper. People were glad to see him because he carried the news from house to house. The mothers thought well of Ichabod because he was gentle and kind with their children. He often sat with a little child on his knee for hours at a time. The women also thought well of him because of his great knowledge. He had read several books completely. He had also studied a whole book about witches.

Of course, Ichabod firmly believed in witches. He also believed all the stories about the various ghosts of Sleepy Hollow. He loved to sit in front of a fire with the old Dutch wives on long winter evenings and talk about ghosts, haunted houses, and the Headless Horseman of Sleepy Hollow. There was pleasure in all this while he was in a warm lighted room among the company. No ghost dared to show its face there! How-

dawn	flat	on the contrary	handkerchief	believe
headless	point	punish	think well of	various
horseman	windy	fairly	gentle	in front of
region	exactly	indeed	knee	Dutch
crane	scarecrow	tactful	knowledge	haunt
suit	pleasant	even though	whole	pleasure
narrow	at the foot of	in turn	witch	dare
shoulder	log cabin	at a time	of course	show one's face
hang	roof	belongings	firmly	however
sleeve	cruel			

ever, that pleasure was always followed by the fears of his walk home. He sometimes jumped in fear at the sight of a bush covered with snow. He often stopped at the sound of his own steps and was afraid to look over his shoulder. All of these, however, were just fears of the night.

Many young people came to Ichabod's singing class one evening each week. Among them, there was a pretty girl of eighteen named Katrina Van Tassel. She was the daughter and only child of a rich farmer. She was known far and wide not only for her beauty but also for the money which she would have some day. Katrina knew that she was pretty, and she liked to catch the boys' eyes. Her short skirt showed the prettiest feet in the whole valley. Old Belthus Van Tassel, her father, was a perfect picture of a happy, kind-hearted farmer. He enjoyed his wealth, but he made no great show of it. The Van Tassel farm was almost like a nest in a quiet green place along the Hudson River. The large barn near the house was as big as a church. Men were busy in the barn from morning until night. There were birds on the roof, fat pigs in the pens, turkeys in the farmyard, geese and ducks in the fresh water of their stream. The farmhouse had plenty of room for everything. There were bags of wool in the corners, and the shelves were filled with Indian corn and apples.

Ichabod Crane had a soft and foolish heart toward girls. Naturally, Katrina's youthful beauty pleased him very much, especially after he had visited her father's farm. He rolled his large green eyes over the rich fields of wheat and the trees which were heavy with fruit, and his heart longed for the girl. When he entered the house, he wanted to become a member of the family more than ever. From then on, his peace of mind was at an end. How could he win Van Tassel's beautiful daughter?

QUESTIONS FOR ORAL AND WRITTEN PRACTICE

(1) Where is Sleepy Hollow? (2) What kind of place is Sleepy Hollow? (3) Why is this lovely valley called Sleepy Hollow? (4) What do the people of Sleepy Hollow believe? (5) What do they

fear	catch one's eye	pen	shelf	wheat
jump	skirt	turkey	corn	long for
bush	kind-hearted	goose	foolish	member
snow	wealth	duck	naturally	from then on
sound	make a show of	fresh	youthful	peace of mind
step	nest	stream	beauty	at an end
afraid	barn	bag	especially	win
far and wide	pig	wool	roll	

often see and hear?   (6) By whom is the valley regularly visited according to many people?   (7) How does the ghost travel?   (8) What does the ghost look like?   (9) What do some people say about the ghost?   (10) Why does the ghost ride away every night according to the story?   (11) Why does the ghost rush back to the churchyard?   (12) By what name is the ghost known in all the country homes?   (13) When did Ichabod Crane come to Sleepy Hollow?   (14) What was Ichabod's profession?   (15) What did Ichabod look like?   (16) Why did the name Crane suit him?   (17) What did he look like on a windy day?   (18) Where was his school located?   (19) What kind of building was the school?   (20) What kind of teacher was Ichabod?   (21) In what manner did he punish his students?   (22) How did Ichabod treat the children after school hours?   (23) Why was it tactful of him to be the children's friend?   (24) How long did Ichabod stay at each family's farm?   (25) How did he carry his possessions from one farmhouse to another?   (26) Why were people glad to see Ichabod?   (27) Why did the mothers think well of Ichabod?   (28) For what other reason did the women think well of him?   (29) How had Ichabod educated himself?   (30) What did Ichabod believe in firmly?   (31) What else did he believe in?   (32) What did he love to do?   (33) Why was there pleasure in talking about ghosts while he was in a warm lighted room among company?   (34) What was that pleasure always followed by?   (35) What did Ichabod often do along his way home?   (36) What kind of fears were these?   (37) How often did young people come to his singing class?   (38) Who was among those young people?   (39) Who was Katrina?   (40) For what was Katrina known far and wide?   (41) What did Katrina know?   (42) What did Katrina like to do?   (43) What did her short skirt show?   (44) What was Katrina's father a perfect picture of?   (45) What was the Van Tassel farm like?   (46) How big was the barn?   (47) What animals were there at the farm?   (48) What was in the house?   (49) What kind of heart did Ichabod have toward girls?   (50) Why did Ichabod long for Katrina?   (51) What was the big question in Ichabod's mind?

PART TWO

At the time Ichabod became interested in Katrina, many young men were trying to win Katrina. They watched each other carefully, and they were ready to fight together against any new fellow. Among

38

these, the most dangerous was a big, loud fellow named Brom Van Brunt. The countryside was full of stories of his strength. He had broad shoulders and curly black hair. His face was bold but pleasant. He was famous as a brave horseback rider. He was first at all races. He was always ready for a fight, but he liked fun even more than a fight. Whenever any wild trick was played, everyone knew Brom was at the bottom

dangerous	fellow	curly	horseback	wild
loud	countryside	bold	race	trick
broad	strength	brave	whenever	at the bottom of

of it. For some time, Brom had wanted to win Katrina. Whenever Brom's horse was outside Van Tassel's farmhouse, everyone else kept away.

Naturally, no one dared to go against Brom openly. Therefore, Ichabod went on in a quiet and gentle manner. As the singing teacher, he often visited the Van Tassel farmhouse. In this way, Ichabod often had a chance to sit with Katrina or walk with her in the evening. Of course, bad feelings developed between Brom and the teacher of Sleepy Hollow, but Ichabod was too wise to quarrel openly with Brom.

Matters went on this way for some time. Then, on a fine fall afternoon, Ichabod was sitting on the tall chair where he usually watched over his school. All the boys and girls were busy with their books or were whispering behind them with one eye on the schoolmaster. Suddenly, a boy rode up on the back of a wild little horse. He ran into the schoolhouse loudly and asked Ichabod to attend a party at the Van Tassel farm that evening. Then the boy left in a hurry. In a moment, everything became alive in the schoolroom. The children raced through their lessons. The whole school was let out an hour before the proper time.

Ichabod took at least a half hour to get ready for the party. He brushed up his best and only suit and combed his hair in front of a piece of mirror on the schoolhouse wall. Of course, he wanted to appear before his lady in a fine manner. Therefore, he borrowed a horse from a cross old Dutchman named Hans Van Ripper. When he started, the afternoon sky was clear, and nature was dressed in rich gold colors. Wild ducks flew high in the air. The sound of squirrels echoed among the trees.

The schoolmaster arrived at Balthus Van Tassel's home toward evening. People from all over the country were there. Naturally, Brom Van Brunt was there too. He had come to the gathering on a big horse named Daredevil. The old farmers wore homemade suits, blue stockings, big shoes with shining buckles. Their wives wore tight caps and

for some time	wise	alive	appear	all over
keep away	quarrel	race through	borrow	gathering
therefore	matters	let out	cross	daredevil
manner	go on	proper	Dutchman	homemade
in this way	whisper	get ready	nature	shine
have a chance	suddenly	brush up	fly	buckle
feeling	ride up	comb	squirrel	tight
develop	attend	mirror	echo	cap
between	in a hurry			

long dresses. The young girls were dressed like their mothers. Plenty of food waited for the Van Tassels' company. There were cakes of all kinds. There were peach and pumpkin pies, ham, roast beef, and chicken together with bowls of milk and cream.

Ichabod was not in a hurry. He took time to eat all that he could hold. His heart warmed with thanks as he filled himself with food. He smiled at the thought of owning all this some day. Old Balthus Van Tassel moved about among the company. His face was spread with joy and was as round as the full moon. Then the musicians began to play. Ichabod was almost as proud of his dancing as of his singing. The lady of his heart danced with him and smiled in reply to all his smiles. Brom sat by himself in one corner jealously.

When the dance was at an end, Ichabod joined some of the older people. They told stories about ghosts and the strange things people had seen and heard. Many people had heard terrible cries near the tree by the church where Major Andre had been captured. Most of the stories were about the Headless Horseman of Sleepy Hollow. Several people had seen this ghost lately. Old Brouwer, who did not believe in ghosts, said he had met the Horseman on his ride into Sleepy Hollow. Then Brom said that he had met the Horseman one night. Brom had offered to race with the Horseman. Brom had almost won the race too. But the Horseman had rushed on at the bridge by the church and had disappeared in a flash of fire. These stories were told in front of the fire in a low voice. Ichabod listened to everything. Then he told about parts of his book about witches.

At last the party began to break up. The old farmers gathered their families in their wagons. Some of the girls sat on horses behind their young men. The sound of their laughter soon died away in the distance. At last, everything was quiet at the Van Tassel farm. Ichabod stayed behind for a moment to speak to Katrina. He was sure that he was going to win her. But apparently something went wrong. After a while, he walked away with a sad expression on his face. Without looking to the right or left to notice Van Tassel's rich lands, he went straight to his horse.

company	spread	join	disappear	die away
peach	joy	terrible	flash	stay behind
pumpkin	full moon	cry	at last	apparently
ham	proud	major	break up	go wrong
roast beef	reply	capture	gather	after a while
bowl	jealously	lately	wagon	expression
take time	at an end	offer	laughter	straight

(52) What were many young men trying to do at the time Ichabod became interested in Katrina? (53) What were these young men ready to do? (54) Who was the most dangerous among these young men? (55) What kind of stories was the countryside full of? (56) What did Brom look like? (57) As what was he famous? (58) What did Brom like even more than a fight? (59) What did everyone know whenever any wild trick was played? (60) What had Brom wanted to do for some time? (61) Why didn't anyone dare to go against Brom openly? (62) In what way did Ichabod go on? (63) For what reason did Ichabod often visit the Van Tassel farmhouse? (64) In this way, what did he have a chance to do? (65) What kind of feelings developed between Brom and Ichabod? (66) Who rode up to the school on a horse on one fine afternoon? (67) What did the boy ask Ichabod to do? (68) What did the children do then? (69) When was the school let out? (70) How long did Ichabod take to get ready for the party? (71) How did Ichabod get ready? (72) Why did Ichabod borrow a horse from Hans Van Ripper? (73) Who was at the party? (74) When did Ichabod arrive at the Van Tassel home? (75) How had Brom come to the party? (76) What did the old farmers wear? (77) What did their wives wear? (78) How were the young girls dressed? (79) What kind of food was there for the Van Tassels' company? (80) How much did Ichabod eat? (81) Why did Ichabod smile? (82) What did Balthus Van Tassel's face look like? (83) How did Ichabod feel about his dancing? (84) Who danced with Ichabod? (85) Where did Brom sit? (86) What did Ichabod do at the end of the dance? (87) What did the older people tell stories about? (88) What had many people heard near the tree by the church? (89) What were most of the stories about? (90) Whom had Old Brouwer met on his ride into Sleepy Hollow? (91) What did Brom say then? (92) What had Brom offered to do? (93) Why didn't Brom win the race? (94) Where were these stories told? (95) How were they told? (96) What did Ichabod tell about then? (97) What did the old farmers do when the party began to break up? (98) Where did some of the girls sit? (99) Why did Ichabod stay behind for a moment? (100) What was Ichabod sure of? (101) What kind of expression was on his face when he walked away? (102) Why didn't he look to the right or left to notice Van Tassel's rich lands?

44

PART THREE

When Ichabod left the Van Tassel farm, it was the exact time of night for witches. As he rode along the sides of the hills above Tarrytown, he could hear the sound of a dog from the other side of the river. There was no sign of life near him except from some little animal in the woods. All the stories of ghosts and strange things came back to Ichabod's mind. As he came near Major Andre's tree, he began to whistle. He thought his whistle was answered, but it was the wind in the dry leaves. Suddenly he heard a groan. He began to shake, and his knees hit against the saddle. But it was only one large branch which was rubbing against another in the wind.

About two hundred yards from the tree, a small stream crossed the road and entered the woods. A few logs side by side formed a crude bridge over the stream. Passing this bridge was the hardest part of Ichabod's journey. His heart began to jump, but he tried to be brave. He gave his old horse a few kicks and tried to rush across the bridge. But it was no use. His horse took a step forward and then jumped into the bushes along the side of the road.

Just at this moment, Ichabod heard a step by the side of the bridge. In the darkness beside the stream, he saw a peculiar black shape. The poor schoolmaster's hair rose on his head in fear. What could he do? It was too late to turn around and go back.

"Who are you?" Ichabod called. Then he asked the question again in a shaking voice. There was still no answer.

Once more, he beat the sides of the old horse. At the same time, he started to sing a church song. Just then, the black object moved to the side of the road. Ichabod could see its form. It was a large horseman on a black horse with a big body. The horseman kept off to one side of the road and moved at the same speed as Ichabod. The schoolmaster remembered Brom's meeting with the Headless Horseman. Although Ichabod's horse moved a little faster, the other came on just as fast.

---

exact	hit	form	peculiar	form
sign	saddle	crude	shape	keep off
whistle	branch	journey	rise	to one side of
leaf	rub	kick	turn around	speed
groan	cross	no use	beat	although
shake	side by side	darkness	object	

Ichabod's heart stood still. He tried to sing again, but his tongue was dry. Finally, Ichabod could see the horseman clearly against the open sky. He was headless! Then the teacher's horror was increased. The horseman carried his head in front of him on the saddle!

Ichabod suddenly kicked his heels, and his old horse began to run. The horseman started right behind him. The two horses galloped down the road madly. Stones flew, and sparks flashed at every step. Ichabod's loose clothes flew in the wind. They reached the road to Sleepy Hollow, but Ichabod's horse made the wrong turn down the hill to the left. This road crossed a bridge close beside the white church. By the bridge, Ichabod's saddle started to slip off. Ichabod threw his arms around the neck of his horse to save himself, and the saddle fell to the ground.

Then the schoolmaster saw the walls of the church under the trees. This gave him hope. The ghost usually disappeared by the church bridge. "I am safe if I can reach the bridge," Ichabod thought.

At that moment, he heard the black horse behind him. Ichabod's horse rushed over the boards of the bridge. Then Ichabod looked behind himself. The Headless Horseman rose in his stirrups and threw his head at Ichabod! The poor schoolmaster tried to dodge, but the awful thing hit him with a great noise. Ichabod fell into the dust, and the two horses and the ghost passed by like the wind.

The next morning, the old horse was found without his saddle at his master's gate. Ichabod did not appear at breakfast. The boys came to school and walked along the banks of the stream, but there was no schoolmaster. The neighbors started to hunt for Ichabod. After a while, they came upon the marks of his horse's shoes. The saddle was found alongside of the road by the church. Ichabod's hat was found by the broad part of the stream. Beside the hat, there was a broken pumpkin. The neighbors hunted in the stream, but the schoolmaster's body was not discovered.

Hans Van Ripper looked after Ichabod's things. There were a few clothes and a book of church songs. Van Ripper also found his book about witches and a paper with several lines in honor of Katrina Van

stand still	gallop	slip	dodge	alongside of
tongue	madly	throw	awful	broad
horror	spark	fall	dust	pumpkin
increase	flash	board	pass by	discover
heel	loose	stirrup	come upon	in honor

Tassel. Hans Van Ripper burned these books and decided not to send his children to school any more. He said that nothing good ever came from reading and writing.

The event was talked of at church on the following Sunday. People gathered in the churchyard at the bridge. They began to shake their heads. They decided that the Headless Horseman had taken Ichabod away. No one worried about Ichabod any more. The school was moved to a different place, and another schoolmaster came to teach.

Soon after Ichabod disappeared, Brom Van Brunt married the beautiful Katrina. He always laughed loudly when people spoke of Ichabod and the pumpkin. Some people even thought that Brom knew a great deal about the matter. However, the old country wives are the best judges of these things. To this day, they say that Ichabod was taken away by some strange means. The story is often told by neighbors in front of a fire on cold winter evenings.

QUESTIONS FOR ORAL AND WRITTEN PRACTICE

(103) What time was it when Ichabod left the Van Tassel farm? (104) Where did the teacher ride? (105) What could he hear? (106) What was the only sign of life near him? (107) What came back to his mind? (108) What did he do as he came near Major Andre's tree? (109) What did he think then? (110) What did he suddenly hear? (111) What did the teacher begin to do? (112) Where did the groan come from? (113) What formed a crude bridge over the stream? (114) What was the hardest part of Ichabod's journey? (115) How did he try to get across the bridge? (116) What did his horse do? (117) What did Ichabod see in the darkness beside the stream? (118) What happened to Ichabod's hair? (119) What did Ichabod call? (120) What was the answer to his question? (121) What did Ichabod begin to sing? (122) Where did the black object move just then? (123) What was the black object? (124) How fast did the horseman move? (125) What did Ichabod's heart do? (126) Why was Ichabod's horror suddenly increased? (127) Where did the horseman carry his

burn	event	marry	judge	means
decide	worry	laugh	to this day	

head? (128) What did Ichabod's horse begin to do when Ichabod kicked his heels? (129) What did the horseman do? (130) In what manner did the two horses go down the road? (131) What happened to Ichabod's clothes? (132) What did Ichabod's horse do at the road to Sleepy Hollow? (133) Where did this road go? (134) What happened to Ichabod's saddle by the bridge? (135) How did Ichabod save himself? (136) What did Ichabod see then? (137) Why did this give him hope? (138) What did Ichabod think? (139) What did the horseman do as Ichabod rushed over the bridge? (140) What happened to Ichabod? (141) When was the old horse found? (142) Why did the neighbors start to hunt for Ichabod? (143) What did they come upon after a while? (144) Where was the saddle found? By whom? (145) Where was Ichabod's hat found? (146) What was there beside the hat? (147) Where did the neighbors hunt then? (148) What did Van Riper find among Ichabod's things? (149) What did Van Riper do with the books? (150) What did Van Riper decide? (151) What did the people decide the following Sunday? (152) What did Brom Van Brunt do soon after Ichabod disappeared? (153) What did Brom always do when people spoke about Ichabod? (154) What did some people think? (155) What do the old country wives say about the matter to this day?

SUMMARY SENTENCES FOR LABORATORY PRACTICE

(1) There's a little valley not far from Tarrytown. (2) It's a very quiet place. (3) The valley is called Sleepy Hollow. (4) Many people there believe in ghosts. (5) They believe a ghost visits the valley regularly. (6) The ghost rides a horse and has no head. (7) Ichabod Crane came to Sleepy Hollow as a teacher. (8) He was tall and thin. (9) He had narrow shoulders. (10) He had a long, pointed nose. (11) He looked exactly like a scarecrow. (12) His school was a log cabin with one large room. (13) The broken windows were covered with pieces of paper. (14) He wasn't a cruel teacher. (15) After school hours, he was friendly with the children. (16) He lived at different farms for a week at a time. (17) He carried all his belongings in a handkerchief. (18) He became a kind of traveling newspaper.

(19) He'd studied a book about witches. (20) He liked to sit in front of a fire at night. (21) Then he liked to talk about haunted houses. (22) But he was afraid of darkness. (23) Katrina was the daughter of a rich farmer. (24) She was the farmer's only child. (25) Her youthful beauty pleased the tall teacher very much. (26) He longed for the girl very much. (27) He also longed for her father's farm. (28) Many young men were trying to win the beautiful farmer's daughter. (29) They all watched each other carefully. (30) Brom had a bold but pleasant face. (31) He was famous as a brave horseback rider. (32) He liked fun even more than a fight. (33) He'd wanted to win the beautiful girl for some time. (34) No one dared to go against him openly. (35) But the teacher went on in a quiet manner. (36) Matters went on this way for some time. (37) Then one day, a little boy rode up to the school. (38) He asked the teacher to attend a party. (39) The school was let out an hour before the proper time. (40) The teacher brushed his best suit and combed his hair. (41) He wanted to make a good appearance. (42) The old farmers wore homemade suits. (43) People from all over the country were there. (44) There was plenty of food for the company. (45) There were chickens and roast beef. (46) There were also pies and cake. (47) Then the musicians played for dancing. (48) Stories were told about ghosts and witches. (49) At last, the party began to break up. (50) The teacher stayed behind for a moment. (51) Then he walked away with a sad expression. (52) He whistled as he rode through the forest. (53) He tried to be brave. (54) His horse jumped into the bushes. (55) He saw a large horseman on a black horse. (56) The horseman carried his head in front of him. (57) The teacher kicked his horse with his heels. (58) The two horses galloped down the road. (59) Stones flew, and sparks flashed at every step. (60) The road crossed a bridge beside a white church. (61) The horseman threw his head at the frightened teacher. (62) It hit the teacher with a loud noise. (63) The next morning, the teacher didn't appear at breakfast. (64) His hat was found by the stream. (65) There was a broken pumpkin beside the hat. (66) The neighbors hunted around the stream. (67) But the teacher's body wasn't discovered. (68) People decided that the horseman had taken the teacher away. (69) A new schoolmaster came to teach in the valley. (70) Brom always laughed loudly when people spoke of Ichabod Crane.

EXERCISE 17. From the column at the left, select the best synonym for the italicized word in each sentence. Rewrite the sentences using the synonyms.

strongly
possessions
correct
shape
entire
courageous
recently
guests
search
opportunity
continued
method
strangely
rubbed
directly
display

1 He was famous in the *whole* region.
2 The ghost rode away to *hunt* for its head.
3 Several people had seen the ghost *lately*.
4 He believed in witches very *firmly*.
5 The horseman was dressed *peculiarly*.
6 They left school at the *proper* time.
7 Things *went on* this way for some time.
8 He was taken away by some strange *means*.
9 He could see the *form* of the black object.
10 He wasn't famous as a *brave* man.
11 There was plenty of food for the *company*.
12 He carried his *belongings* in a handkerchief.
13 He made no great *show* of his wealth.
14 He had a *chance* to sit with Katrina.
15 Ichabod walked *straight* to his horse.

EXERCISE 18. From the column at the left, select the correct word for each blank space in the sentences at the right. Use each word only once. Do not change the forms of the words.

quarrel
dared
broad
loudly
bushes
slip
rose
curly
suited
joined
crude
spread
kicks
gathered
horror
boards
whistle

1 His family name _____ him very well.
2 He was too wise to _____ with his rival.
3 No one _____ to go against Brom openly.
4 He had _____ shoulders and _____ black hair.
5 Ichabod _____ the older people by the fire.
6 Her father's face was _____ with joy.
7 A few logs formed a _____ bridge.
8 The horse jumped into the ____ beside the road.
9 The sight of the horseman increased his _____.
10 His hair _____ because of his great terror.
11 He gave the old horse a few hard _____.
12 His horse rushed over the _____ of the bridge.
13 The saddle began to _____ off the old horse.
14 People _____ in the churchyard to discuss it.
15 He laughed _____ when people said it.

EXERCISE 19. Supply the correct preposition for each blank space.

1 He loved to sit _____ front _____ a warm fire.
2 He was often afraid to look _____ his shoulder _____ night.
3 She was known far and wide _____ her beauty.
4 Men were busy _____ the barn _____ morning _____ night.
5 The farmhouse had plenty _____ room _____ everything.
6 His peace _____ mind was _____ an end _____ then on.
7 Brom had wanted to win Katrina _____ some time.
8 Katrina smiled _____ reply _____ all his own smiles.
9 Brom sat _____ himself _____ one corner jealously.
10 Some people didn't believe _____ ghosts _____ all.
11 He walked away _____ a sad expression _____ his face.
12 One branch was rubbing _____ another _____ the wind.
13 The awful thing hit Ichabod _____ a loud noise.
14 He had written several lines _____ honor _____ Katrina.
15 They thought he knew a great deal _____ the matter.

EXERCISE 20. From the column at the right, select the correct line to complete each of the numbered lines at the left. Write each sentence in its correct form.

1 The broken windows were   (A) because of his knowledge
2 The shelves were filled   (B) over the rich fields
3 He punished them as   (C) covered with old paper
4 He rolled his eyes   (D) with plenty of food
5 Of course, he firmly   (E) a member of the family
6 His peace of mind   (F) fairly as possible
7 He became a kind   (G) of night for witches
8 The most dangerous was   (H) pleased him very much
9 They thought well of him   (I) of his ability to dance
10 Her youthful beauty   (J) believed in witches
11 He wanted to become   (K) but his tongue was dry
12 He had a chance   (L) a big, loud fellow
13 He was very proud   (M) was at an end
14 It was the exact time   (N) to sit with Katrina
15 He tried to sing   (O) of traveling newspaper

EXERCISE 21. Study the following word form chart carefully. The word forms which occurred in the preceding story are italicized.

	ADJECTIVE	NOUN	VERB	ADVERB
1	*peaceful*	peace	x x x x x	peacefully
2	regular	regularity	x x x x x	*regularly*
3	*cruel*	cruelty	x x x x x	cruelly
4	x x x x x	punishment	*punish*	x x x x x
5	fair	fairness	x x x x x	*fairly*
6	*kind*	kindness	x x x x x	kindly
7	firm	firmness	x x x x x	*firmly*
8	*pleasant*	*pleasure*	please	pleasantly
9	fearless	*fear*	fear	fearlessly
	fearful			fearfully
10	x x x x x	interest	*interest*	x x x x x
11	strong	*strength*	strengthen	strongly
12	famous	fame	x x x x x	x x x x x
13	brave	bravery	x x x x x	bravely
14	x x x x x	quarrel	quarrel	x x x x x
15	x x x x x	whisper	whisper	x x x x x
16	apparent	appearance	*appear*	*apparently*
17	joyful	enjoyment	enjoy	joyfully
		joy		
18	jealous	jealousy	x x x x x	*jealously*
19	*terrible*	terror	terrify	terribly
20	x x x x x	offer	*offer*	x x x x x
21	x x x x x	disappearance	*disappear*	x x x x x
22	x x x x x	*laughter*	laugh	x x x x x
23	sad	sadness	x x x x x	sadly
24	x x x x x	*whistle*	*whistle*	x x x x x
25	*dry*	dryness	dry	x x x x x
26	x x x x x	*kick*	*kick*	x x x x x
27	x x x x x	*step*	step	x x x x x
28	*peculiar*	peculiarity	x x x x x	peculiarly
29	horrible	*horror*	horrify	horribly
30	mad	madness	x x x x x	*madly*
31	*loose*	looseness	loosen	loosely
32	x x x x x	discovery	*discover*	x x x x x

EXERCISE 22. Use the correct form of each italicized word in the sentence which follows. Notice the first two examples. Refer to the word form chart and examples whenever necessary.

1	*cruel*	He never treated the children with *cruelty*.
2	*famous*	His *fame* as a rider spread throughout the region.
3	*appear*	He wanted to make a good _____ at the party.
4	*brave*	The schoolmaster was not famous for his _____.
5	*jealously*	His rival suffered from a great deal of _____.
6	*sad*	There was _____ in the expression on his face.
7	*kick*	Ichabod _____ the horse with his heels.
8	*loose*	All of his clothes hung from his body _____.
9	*whistle*	He thought he heard an answer to his _____.
10	*peaceful*	The people lived together _____ in the valley.
11	*firmly*	The schoolmaster had _____ opinions about ghosts.
12	*fear*	He always walked home _____ at night.
13	*regularly*	People said the ghost visited the valley _____.
14	*interest*	He told the company _____ stories about witches.
15	*quarrel*	He was too wise to _____ openly with Brom.
16	*disappear*	Everyone thought his _____ was very strange.
17	*discover*	The _____ of his hat caused much discussion.
18	*dry*	The _____ of the leaves caused strange sounds.
19	*strength*	People heard stories about his great _____.
20	*pleasant*	It was a _____ for him to be with the beautiful girl.
21	*fair*	The schoolmaster always treated them _____.
22	*whisper*	Ichabod _____ something to the farmer's daughter.
23	*joy*	Everyone _____ the music and the dancing.
24	*offer*	His _____ for a race was not accepted.
25	*madly*	The two horses galloped down the road _____.
26	*step*	Ichabod thought he heard _____ in the darkness.
27	*horror*	He was _____ by the sight of the horseman.
28	*punish*	It was sometimes necessary to use _____.
29	*kind*	Ichabod always tried to treat the children with _____.
30	*terrible*	His hands were shaking because of his _____.
31	*peculiar*	The horseman was dressed very _____.
32	*laugh*	There was much _____ at the Van Tassels' party.

EXERCISE 23. Study the following examples for the preceding word form chart. The numbers correspond to those on the word form chart.

1 **peaceful, peace, peacefully.** There was a great deal of *peace* in the valley. The valley was very *peaceful*. The people lived in the valley *peacefully*.

2 **regular, regularity, regularly.** The ghost visited the valley *regularly*. The ghost was a *regular* visitor. The ghost visited the valley with great *regularity*.

3 **cruel, cruelty, cruelly.** He wasn't a *cruel* teacher. He didn't treat the children *cruelly*. He didn't show any *cruelty*.

4 **punishment, punish.** He *punished* the children. His *punishment* was fair.

5 **fair, fairness, fairly.** He was a *fair* teacher. He treated the children *fairly*. The children noticed his *fairness*.

6 **kind, kindness, kindly.** He was *kind* to the children. He treated the children *kindly*. He showed a great deal of *kindness*.

7 **firm, firmness, firmly.** He had a *firm* belief about it. He believed it *firmly*. The *firmness* of his belief was apparent.

8 **pleasant, pleasure, please, pleasantly.** The girl's beauty *pleased* everyone. She had a *pleased* expression on her face. She had a *pleasing* personality. She had a *pleasant* face. She smiled at everyone *pleasantly*. It was a *pleasure* to be with her.

9 **fearful, fearless, fear, fearfully, fearlessly.** He *feared* the walk home in the darkness. His *fear* was very apparent. He was *fearful* of the darkness outside. He was *fearless* inside the house. He walked along the road *fearfully*. He didn't walk *fearlessly*.

10 **interest.** Stories about ghosts *interested* him. He was *interested* in stories about ghosts. His stories were always *interesting*. He told *interesting* stories. He was always an *interested* listener too. His *interest* was apparent to everyone.

11 **strong, strength, strengthen, strongly.** He was a *strong* person. He had great *strength*. He *strengthened* his grip on the saddle. He had *strong* opinions. He believed certain things *strongly*.

12 **famous, fame.** He was *famous* as a rider. Everyone talked about his *fame*.

13 **brave, bravery, bravely.** He was a *brave* rider. He rode *bravely* in races. He was famous for his *bravery*.

14 **quarrel.** The men *quarreled* with each other. People heard about the *quarrel*.

54

15 **whisper.** He heard a *whisper* in the room. One of the students *whispered* to his friend. The student *whispered* a message.

16 **apparent, appearance, appear, apparently.** He *appeared* to be sad. His *appearance* was peculiar. His sadness was *apparent. Apparently,* he had received bad news. He had *apparently* received bad news.

17 **joyful, joy, enjoyment, enjoy, joyfully.** He smiled with great *joy.* He was *joyful* about everything. He smiled *joyfully.* He *enjoyed* the music. His *enjoyment* was apparent.

18 **jealous, jealousy, jealously.** He was *jealous* of his rival. He sat in the corner *jealously.* His *jealousy* was apparent.

19 **terrible, terror, terrify, terribly.** He heard a *terrible* sound in the darkness. The voice cried *terribly* in the darkness. The sound *terrified* him. He had great *terror* of ghosts.

20 **offer.** He *offered* to race to the bridge. His *offer* wasn't accepted.

21 **disappearance, disappear.** The teacher *disappeared* completely. Everyone talked about his strange *disappearance.*

22 **laughter, laugh.** The young people *laughed* loudly. He heard the sound of their *laughter.*

23 **sad, sadness, sadly.** He had a *sad* expression on his face. He looked down *sadly.* His *sadness* was apparent.

24 **whistle.** He heard a *whistle.* Someone *whistled* quietly.

25 **dry** (adjective and verb), **dryness.** The leaves were very *dry.* The sun had *dried* the leaves. The leaves made little sounds because of their *dryness.*

26 **kick.** He *kicked* the horse with his heels. The horse responded to his *kick.*

27 **step.** Each *step* made noise. He *stepped* on the leaves carefully. He *took careful steps* in the darkness.

28 **peculiar, peculiarity, peculiarly.** The person wore *peculiar* clothes. The person was dressed *peculiarly.* He noticed the *peculiarity* of the person's clothes.

29 **horrible, horror, horrify, horribly.** The sight increased his *horror.* The sight *horrified* him. He saw a *horrible* thing. He cried out *horribly.*

30 **mad, madness, madly.** They moved down the road at a *mad* speed. They moved down the road *madly.* They moved down the road with *madness.*

31 **loose, looseness, loosen, loosely.** His clothes hung on his body *loosely.* His *loose* clothes flew in the wind. The *looseness* of his clothes made him look thin. He *loosened* his tie in order to breathe better.

32 **discovery, discover.** They *discovered* his hat by the stream. A young boy *made the discovery.* The *discovery* caused much discussion.

EXERCISE 24. Select the correct way to complete each of the following sentences. Write each sentence in its correct form.

1 It was tactful of Ichabod to be friendly with the children because (*a*) he firmly believed in witches. (*b*) his rival was a dangerous fellow. (*c*) the whole school was let out an hour before the proper time. (*d*) he lived in the homes of the children's parents.

2 There was pleasure for the school teacher in talking about ghosts (*a*) in the bushes near the bridge. (*b*) while he was with company in a lighted room. (*c*) at night under a full moon. (*d*) when he was walking home through the woods.

3 Katrina's father was a perfect picture of (*a*) a scarecrow on a windy day. (*b*) a brave horseback rider with curly hair. (*c*) a happy, kind-hearted farmer. (*d*) a major in the Revolutionary Army.

4 Katrina was known far and wide not only for her beauty but also (*a*) for her tight caps and long dresses. (*b*) for the parties at which she served plenty of food. (*c*) for her dancing and singing. (*d*) for the money which she would have some day.

5 Whenever Brom's horse was outside Van Tassel's farmhouse, (*a*) the countryside was full of stories of his strength. (*b*) they all watched each other carefully. (*c*) the event was talked of at church the following Sunday. (*d*) everyone else kept away.

6 Because no one dared to go against Brom openly, Ichabod (*a*) joined the older people in front of the fire. (*b*) took time to eat all that he could hold. (*c*) borrowed a horse from a cross old Dutchman. (*d*) went on in a quiet and gentle manner.

7 After the party, Ichabod stayed behind for a moment (*a*) to race with Brom. (*b*) to speak to Katrina. (*c*) to eat more ham and roast beef. (*d*) to look at the rich wheat fields.

8 Ichabod thought he heard a groan, (*a*) and he began to whistle a church song.   (*b*) but he knew it was the sound of a dog from the other side of the river.   (*c*) so he disappeared in a flash of fire. (*d*) but it was only a large branch which was rubbing against another.

9 The teacher's horror was increased (*a*) by the sight of the horseman with his head on the saddle.   (*b*) because he heard the terrible cries of Major Andre.   (*c*) because stones flew and sparks flashed. (*d*) by the echo of squirrels among the trees.

10 To this day, the old country wives say that (*a*) nothing good ever came from reading and writing.   (*b*) Ichabod was taken away by some strange means.   (*c*) Brom knew a great deal about the matter. (*d*) Ichabod almost won the race with the horseman.

The Louisiana Purchase

In 1803, the United States paid France $15,000,000 for the Louisiana Territory, an area more than four times the size of France. The land which was bought included everything between the Rocky Mountains and the Mississippi River except Texas. The principal port for the second longest river system in the world was located within this territory. Although few realized it at that time, the purchase included the vast forests of Arkansas and Minnesota, the oil deposits of Oklahoma, the cornfields of Iowa, the wheatlands of the Dakotas, the copper, silver,

---

purchase	rocky	system	vast	cornfield
territory	principal	locate	deposit	wheatland
include	port	realize		

— Barberis —

THOMAS JEFFERSON

59

and gold of Colorado and Montana, the rice and sugar of Louisiana. Without doubt, the Louisiana Purchase was one of the greatest events in the history of the United States. In a single action, a third-class nation doubled its size, united its states and population, and became a great power in the world.

Shortly before 1800, half a million Americans were living west of the Allegheny Mountains. The settlers in the towns and villages there needed trade. In order to get trade, they had to send their flour, tobacco, and whisky by water. There were no usable roads to the eastern cities and ports. The Ohio River and the Mississippi served as direct highways. The entire Mississippi, except its mouth at New Orleans, was open to the settlers. Spain owned New Orleans and the great Louisiana Territory to the west of the river. The western settlers solved their problem by obtaining the "right of deposit" from Spain. This gave the settlers the right to unload their freight at New Orleans and put it in warehouses before shipping it to the east.

On paper, Don Carlos IV ruled the great Spanish Empire. However, Don Carlos was a weak ruler, and Europe was controlled by Napoleon Bonaparte's armies. England was the only nation not under French control. The Spanish ruler was forced to turn over Louisiana to Napoleon through a secret treaty in 1800. This was part of Napoleon's plan. At that time, Napoleon boasted that he would soon be the master of the world. He planned to rebuild the French Empire in the New World. Napoleon called off the war against England. He could not continue his war against England and win the New World at the same time. Napoleon needed a naval base in order to defend his new lands in America. In 1801, Napoleon attacked the West Indian island of Santo Domingo. This island was a French colony, but the Negro slave Toussaint L'Ouverture had weakened French power on this island through revolt.

President Jefferson was greatly concerned over these developments. In a letter to Robert R. Livingston, the American minister to France, he

without doubt	flour	right	force	attack
event	tobacco	unload	turn over	colony
single	whisky	freight	treaty	slave
third-class	usable	warehouse	boast	weaken
unite	serve	on paper	master	revolt
population	direct	rule	rebuild	concern
power	highway	empire	call off	development
settler	solve	ruler	naval base	minister
trade	obtain	control		

pointed out that three eighths of the nation's annual product had to pass through New Orleans. Jefferson saw one possible solution. He asked Congress to grant the great amount of $2,000,000. Then he instructed Livingston to try to buy New Orleans and West Florida from Napoleon. In Paris, Livingston presented the offer to the clever Talleyrand, Napoleon's Foreign Minister. Livingston tried to talk down the value of the port, but Talleyrand showed no interest.

In 1803, Jefferson's worst fears came true. Spain took the "right of deposit" at New Orleans away from American citizens. The news began to travel through the Kentucky and Ohio region. Many of the settlers prepared to go to New Orleans to fight. Alexander Hamilton wanted to take New Orleans by force. The Westerners, who were Jefferson's principal supporters, turned to him for help. President Jefferson was in a difficult position. He wanted to keep peace, but he knew the importance of New Orleans to the Westerners and to the entire national economy.

Jefferson decided to send James Monroe to help Livingston in Paris. In the meantime, Livingston had another talk with Talleyrand. After a short conversation, Talleyrand asked an amazing question. "What will you give us for the whole Louisiana Territory?" Of course, Livingston was shocked. He had the authority to buy only a little city and the coastline of Florida. Nevertheless, he decided to offer $4,000,-000. This was not enough for Louisiana, Talleyrand said, but Livingston had made the decision to buy Louisiana. Shortly after that, Monroe arrived in Paris with the authority to offer as much as $10,000,000 for New Orleans and West Florida. Monroe immediately agreed that Livingston had made the correct decision regarding the larger territory. They sent a message to President Jefferson, but they knew that they could not receive a reply in less than a month and a half. Although they had no authority from Congress or the Constitution, Livingston and Monroe had to act quickly.

For many days, the two Americans discussed details concerning the price with Barbe-Marbois, Napoleon's Minister of the Treasury. The

point out	offer	supporter	whole	agree
annual	clever	keep peace	shock	regard
product	talk down	importance	authority	message
solution	value	national	coastline	Congress
grant	take away	economy	nevertheless	Constitution
amount	region	in the meantime	decide	detail
instruct	prepare	conversation	decision	treasury
present	Westerner	amaze	immediately	

last days of April 1803 were the critical period. At last, Livingston and Monroe could bring the price no lower. Napoleon wanted $15,000,000 for the Louisiana Territory. This sum was more than the total annual income of the United States! Livingston and Monroe courageously decided to trust their government to support them. They signed an agreement with Barbe-Marbois on May 2, 1803. On May 18, war broke out between England and France. Four days later, Napoleon signed the agreement.

President Jefferson and Congress were enthusiastic about the purchase. A great celebration was held when the news reached Washington. Crowds of happy people came to the White House to congratulate Jefferson. On the Fourth of July, a salute was fired by 21 cannons to announce the bloodless victory. Before the purchase, Jefferson had always followed the Constitution strictly. However, he knew this was the greatest bargain in history even though the Constitution did not give the government the power to acquire more territory. He finally accepted the agreement and asked Congress to support him. Of course, some people objected loudly, but the vast majority of the population supported Jefferson. The Senate ratified the agreement and the Louisiana Territory became part of the United States.

Why did Napoleon decide to sell the Louisiana Territory? Probably no one will ever know all of the facts. However, it is possible to guess certain things. His plan of conquering the New World had not gone well. His French soldiers had won an important battle and had captured Toussaint, the Negro leader. However, the Haitians continued to attack the French, and then yellow fever destroyed Napoleon's army. In January of 1803, Napoleon received the news that General Leclerc was dead in Santo Domingo. Napoleon also received the news that there were 20 British warships in the Gulf of Mexico. These British ships were ready to capture New Orleans. Napoleon knew that he could not defend Louisiana without strong support from Santo Domingo. He was on the verge of war with England anyway, and the French treasury was

critical	support	cannon	object	capture
period	agreement	announce	loudly	leader
at last	break out	bloodless	majority	fever
sum	enthusiastic	victory	ratify	destroy
income	celebration	strictly	probably	warship
courageously	congratulate	bargain	guess	gulf
trust	salute	acquire	conquer	defend
government	fire	accept	go well	on the verge

NAPOLEON BONAPARTE

not in good condition. It was better, he probably decided, to sell this wasteland immediately and use the money for gunpowder and ships.

A few days after the news of the purchase reached Washington, Jefferson sent Lewis and Clark on an expedition to the Pacific Ocean in the Northwest. Today this epic journey is called the Lewis and Clark Expedition. Because of their reports, the United States began to realize the true value of this great territory. The reports of these two men also prepared the way for a great westward movement of settlers from Ohio, Kentucky, and every other part of the United States.

QUESTIONS FOR ORAL AND WRITTEN PRACTICE

(1) When did the U.S. buy the Louisiana Territory? (2) How much did the U.S. pay for the Louisiana Territory? (3) How large was the Louisiana Territory in comparison with France? (4) How large was the Mississippi River system? (5) What land was included in the purchase? (6) Which present-day states are located within the limits of the original Louisiana Territory? (7) What natural resources did the purchase include? (8) How does the purchase of Louisiana compare with other events in the history of the United States? (9) How did the United States compare with the other nations of the world in 1803? (10) What were some of the effects of the purchase? (11) Before 1800, how many Americans were living west of the Alleghenies? (12) What did the western settlers need? (13) What did they have to do to get trade? (14) What kind of roads were there over the mountains? (15) What highway did the settlers use? (16) Who owned New Orleans? (17) How did the western settlers solve their freight problem? (18) What was "the right of deposit"? (19) Who was ruler of the Spanish Empire at that time? (20) Who controlled Europe? (21) When and how did Napoleon obtain Louisiana? (22) What did Napoleon boast at that time? (23) What did he plan to do in the New World? (24) Why did Napoleon call off the war against England? (25) What did he need in order to defend his new lands in America? (26) What did Napoleon do in 1801? (27) Why was it necessary for Napoleon to attack Santo Domingo? (28) What was President Jefferson's attitude over those developments? (29) What was Robert Livingston's official position? (30) What economic fact did Jefferson point out to Livingston? (31) What did Jefferson fear

| wasteland | expedition | journey | westward | movement |
| gunpowder | epic | | | |

most of all? (32) What did Jefferson ask Congress to do? (33) What did Jefferson then instruct Livingston to do? (34) To whom did Livingston present his offer? (35) What technique did Livingston use with Talleyrand? (36) What was Talleyrand's response? (37) What action did Napoleon take in Louisiana in 1803? (38) What was the effect of this action on the western settlers? (39) What did Alexander Hamilton want to do? (40) Who were Jefferson's principal supporters? (41) Why was Jefferson in a difficult position? (42) What did Jefferson decide to do? (43) What kind of authority did Jefferson give Monroe? (44) What did Livingston do in the meantime? (45) With what question did Talleyrand shock Livingston? (46) How much authority did Livingston have? (47) What decision did Livingston make? (48) What was Talleyrand's answer to Livingston's offer? (49) How did Monroe feel about Livingston's decision? (50) In 1803, how long did it take for a message to get from Europe to the U. S. and back again? (51) What did Monroe and Livingston have to do because of the time required for communication with Washington? (52) With whom did they discuss details concerning the price? (53) What was the critical period? (54) What was Napoleon's lowest price? (55) What did this amount mean in terms of the economy of the United States at that time? (56) What did Monroe and Livingston decide to do? (57) When did Napoleon sign the agreement? (58) What was the political event that had pushed Napoleon to conclude the sale? (59) What was the reaction of Jefferson and Congress to the purchase? (60) What happened when the news of the purchase reached Washington? (61) When and how was the purchase officially announced? (62) Why did Jefferson hesitate to accept the agreement? (63) What formal action did the Senate take? (64) What had happened to Napoleon's army in Haiti? (65) What were British warships in the Gulf of Mexico ready to do? (66) What did Napoleon need in order to defend New Orleans? (67) What kind of condition was the French treasury in? (68) What did Napoleon plan to do with the money from the Louisiana Purchase? (69) What action did Jefferson take to determine the value of the new land? (70) What was one of the results of the reports from the expedition?

SUMMARY SENTENCES FOR LABORATORY PRACTICE

(1) The United States bought the Louisiana Territory in 1803.
(2) The government paid fifteen million dollars for all the land.

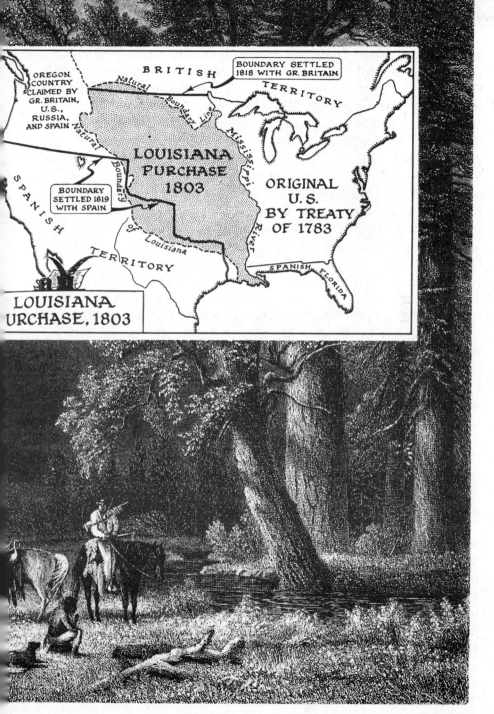

LOUISIANA
PURCHASE, 1803

BRITISH TERRITORY

BOUNDARY SETTLED
1818 WITH GR. BRITAIN

OREGON
COUNTRY
CLAIMED BY
GR. BRITAIN,
U.S.,
RUSSIA,
AND SPAIN

Natural Boundary Line

LOUISIANA
PURCHASE
1803

Mississippi River

ORIGINAL
U.S.
BY TREATY
OF 1783

SPANISH

Natural Boundary

BOUNDARY
SETTLED 1819
WITH SPAIN

TERRITORY

of Louisiana

SPANISH FLORIDA

(3) The area is more than four times the size of France. (4) It was one of the greatest events in American history. (5) The nation doubled its size with this purchase. (6) Many Americans were living west of the Allegheny Mountains. (7) These western settlers needed trade. (8) They used the Mississippi River as a direct highway. (9) The entire river was open to the settlers. (10) But Spain owned the port at the mouth of the river. (11) The settlers obtained the right to unload their freight in this port. (12) Europe was controlled by the armies of France. (13) The Spanish ruler was forced to turn over Louisiana to Napoleon. (14) Napoleon planned to create an empire there. (15) But he needed a naval base to defend his new lands. (16) He attacked the West Indian island of Santo Domingo. (17) Jefferson was greatly concerned about these developments. (18) New Orleans was important for the nation's economy. (19) He saw one possible solution to the problem. (20) He asked Congress to grant two million dollars. (21) He wanted to buy New Orleans and West Florida from Napoleon. (22) The American minister to France presented the offer. (23) But the Foreign Minister of France showed no interest. (24) Then Spain closed New Orleans to Americans. (25) Many of the settlers prepared to fight. (26) Some people wanted to take the port by force. (27) The President was in a difficult position. (28) He wanted to keep peace. (29) But he knew the importance of the port. (30) He decided to send James Monroe to Paris. (31) He wanted to buy the port for ten million dollars. (32) Monroe had the authority to offer as much as ten million dollars. (33) In the meantime, Napoleon decided to sell the land. (34) Livingston decided to offer four million dollars. (35) Monroe agreed that the decision to buy the territory was correct. (36) The two Americans discussed the price. (37) At last, they could bring the price no lower. (38) Napoleon wanted fifteen million dollars for the land. (39) This was more than the annual income of the United States. (40) They decided to trust their government to support them. (41) They signed an agreement. (42) Napoleon signed the agreement four days later. (43) Everyone in Washington was enthusiastic. (44) This was the greatest bargain in history. (45) The President finally accepted the agreement. (46) He asked Congress to support him. (47) Some people objected loudly. (48) But the vast majority of the people supported the President. (49) The Senate ratified the agreement. (50) The Louisiana Territory became part of the United States.

EXERCISE 25. From the column at the left, select the best synonym for the italicized word in each sentence. Rewrite the sentences using the synonyms.

guessed
legal power
physical power
contained
displayed
chief
protested
storage places
main road
ingenious
precisely
emphasized
crucial
astonishing
brave
comprehend

1 The land *included* a large area.
2 The Mississippi served as a *highway*.
3 They put it in *warehouses*.
4 He had *authority* to buy a city.
5 April 1803 was a *critical* period.
6 Livingston made a *courageous* decision.
7 The minister asked an *amazing* question.
8 Of course, some people *objected* loudly.
9 He wanted to take the port by *force*.
10 He presented the offer to the *clever* minister.
11 He had followed the Constitution *strictly*.
12 Jefferson *pointed out* some economic facts.
13 New Orleans was the *principal* port.
14 He *showed* no interest in the offer.
15 They began to *realize* its true value.

EXERCISE 26. From the column at the left, select the correct word for each blank space in the sentences at the right. Use each word only once. Do not change the forms of the words.

unloaded
solved
acquired
boasted
shocked
turned over
served
granted
weakened
forced
agreed
objected
supported
reached
included
realized

1 The Mississippi _____ as a direct highway.
2 The settlers _____ freight at New Orleans.
3 Don Carlos IV _____ the territory to Napoleon.
4 Congress _____ $2,000,000 for the purchase.
5 Napoleon _____ he would conquer the world.
6 Napoleon was _____ to call off the war.
7 The revolt _____ French power very much.
8 The minister was _____ by the unusual question.
9 The men finally _____ to pay $15,000,000.
10 The news _____ Washington 45 days later.
11 A majority of the people _____ the President.
12 Some people _____ to the agreement loudly.
13 The United States finally _____ the entire area.
14 Few people _____ that the land had great value.
15 The purchase _____ oil deposits and rich soil.

EXERCISE 27. Supply the correct preposition for each blank space.

1 The United States paid France $15,000,000 _____ Louisiana.
2 It included everything _____ the Rockies and the Mississippi.
3 _____ that time, few realized the value _____ the land.
4 The settlers _____ the West were _____ need _____ trade.
5 There were few roads _____ the cities _____ the Atlantic coast.
6 They solved their problem _____ obtaining rights _____ Spain.
7 Later Spain took these rights away _____ American citizens.
8 _____ the exception _____ England, Napoleon controlled Europe.
9 Monroe arrived _____ authority to offer more money.
10 The Negroes weakened his power _____ the island _____ revolt.
11 Jefferson was concerned _____ these developments.
12 _____ a letter _____ Livingston, he pointed out the danger.
13 He negotiated _____ Talleyrand _____ the help _____ Monroe.
14 They could not receive a reply _____ less than 45 days.
15 The ministers agreed _____ $15,000,000 as the final price.

EXERCISE 28. From the column at the right, select the correct line to complete each of the numbered lines at the left. Write each sentence in its correct form.

1 Napoleon obtained Louisiana		
2 There were no usable roads	(A)	in less than 45 days
3 The western settlers obtained	(B)	to gain a naval base
4 The settlers prepared to go	(C)	to the eastern coast
5 Jefferson asked Congress	(D)	about the purchase
6 New Orleans was in danger	(E)	were the critical period
7 He had already made	(F)	the decision to buy it
8 He tried to talk down	(G)	of capture by the British
9 They couldn't receive a reply	(H)	the general was dead
10 The last days of April	(I)	the value of the port
11 Napoleon attacked Santo Domingo	(J)	by yellow fever
	(K)	through a secret treaty
12 Napoleon's army was destroyed	(L)	to grant $2,000,000
13 He received the news that	(M)	reached the Pacific Ocean
14 Everyone was enthusiastic	(N)	rights to unload freight
15 The Lewis and Clark Expedition	(O)	to New Orleans to fight

EXERCISE 29. Study the following word form chart carefully. The word forms which occurred in the preceding story are italicized.

	ADJECTIVE	NOUN	VERB	ADVERB
1	doubtful	*doubt*	doubt	doubtfully
2	eventful	*event*	x x x x x	x x x x x
3	x x x x x	unity	*unite*	x x x x x
4	powerful	*power*	x x x x x	powerfully
5	serviceable	service	*serve*	serviceably
6	x x x x x	shipment	*ship*	x x x x x
7	controllable	*control*	control	x x x x x
8	*secret*	secrecy secret	x x x x x	secretly
9	forceful	*force*	force	forcefully
10	boastful	boast	*boast*	boastfully
11	x x x x x	defense	*defend*	x x x x x
12	x x x x x	concern	*concern*	x x x x x
13	x x x x x	*development*	develop	x x x x x
14	*possible*	possibility	x x x x x	possibly
15	x x x x x	offer	offer	x x x x x
16	*clever*	cleverness	x x x x x	cleverly
17	truthful true	truth	x x x x x	truthfully
18	x x x x x	*supporter* support	*support*	x x x x x
19	economic	*economy*	x x x x x	economically
20	x x x x x	amazement	*amaze*	x x x x x
21	x x x x x	shock	*shock*	x x x x x
22	x x x x x	*authority*	authorize	x x x x x
23	*correct*	correction	correct	correctly
24	courageous	courage	encourage	*courageously*
25	trustful	trust	*trust*	trustfully
26	*enthusiastic*	enthusiasm	x x x x x	enthusiastically
27	victorious	*victory*	x x x x x	victoriously
28	acceptable	acceptance	*accept*	x x x x x
29	objectionable	objection	*object*	objectionably
30	continuous	continuity	*continue*	continuously
	continual	continuation		continually
31	destructive	destruction	*destroy*	destructively
32	valuable	*value*	value	x x x x x

EXERCISE 30. Study the following examples for the preceding word form chart. The numbers correspond to those on the word form chart.

1 **doubtful, doubt, doubtfully, undoubtedly.** His *doubt* showed clearly. He *had doubt* about the offer. He *doubted* that they would consider it. He was *doubtful* about it. He spoke about it *doubtfully*. *Undoubtedly,* he expected the question. *Without doubt,* he expected it.

2 **eventful, event.** There were many important *events* during that period. It was an *eventful* period.

3 **unity, unite.** The purchase *united* the states and the population. An election was held in the *united* parts of the country. The *unity* made the country stronger.

4 **powerful, power, powerfully.** The nation's *power* was increased. The nation *gained power* through the purchase. The United States became *a world power*. The United States became a more *powerful* nation. Napoleon tried to move *powerfully*.

5 **serviceable, service, serve, serviceably.** The river *served* as a highway. The river gave good *service* as a highway. It was very *serviceable* as a highway. They could use it *serviceably*.

6 **shipment, ship.** They *shipped* their merchandise down the river. Each *shipment* was unloaded in New Orleans.

7 **controllable, controller, control.** Napoleon *controlled* all of Europe except England. He was the *controller* of the nation's future. His *control* of the island was weakened. He *lost control* of the island. The slaves were not *controllable*. The *controlled* nations couldn't help. France was the *controlling* nation.

8 **secret, secrecy, secretly.** *Secrecy* was necessary. It was an important *secret*. They tried to *keep it a secret*. It's hard to *keep secrets*. He had a *secret* agreement with them. They signed the agreement *secretly*.

9 **forceful, force, forcefully.** He felt that *force* was necessary. He wanted to take the port by using *force*. He wanted to *take it by force*. He wanted to use *forceful* methods. He wanted to act *forcefully*. He wanted to *force* France out of the port. Napoleon was *forced* to stop the war. His *forces* on the island were destroyed.

10 **boastful, boastfulness, boast, boastfully.** He *boasted* about his power. He *made a boast* that he would win. His *boast* was repeated by other people. They spoke about his *boastfulness*. They said that he was a *boastful* person. He made the statement *boastfully*.

11   **defense, defend.** His army *defended* the port. *Defense* was necessary.

12   **concern.** He was *concerned* about the situation. The situation *concerned* him. Congress understood his *concern*.

13   **development, develop.** Several unusual situations *developed* at that time. Everyone was concerned about these *developments*.

14   **possible, possibility, possibly.** He saw one *possible* solution. *Possibly,* he could solve the problem that way. It was a good *possibility*. There wasn't any other *possibility* for them.

15   **offer.** He *offered* them two million dollars. He *made an offer* of two million dollars. His *offer* wasn't accepted.

16   **clever, cleverness, cleverly.** He was a *clever* man. He handled situations *cleverly*. He was famous for his *cleverness*.

17   **true, truthful, truth, truthfully.** His information was *true*. It was a *truthful* report. His report was *truthful*. His report was *true to the facts*. It gave a *true* picture of the situation. He reported the facts *truthfully*. It was important to know the *truth* about everything. He *told the truth* about everything.

18   **supporter, support.** The western settlers *supported* the president. Their *support* was necessary. They were his principal *supporters*.

19   **economic, economy, economically.** The national *economy* depended on using the port. The *economic* situation was dangerous. It was important to the nation *economically*.

20   **amazement, amaze.** The minister's question *amazed* him. He was *amazed* when he heard the question. The minister asked an *amazing* question. The *amazed* minister tried to speak cautiously. His *amazement* was apparent.

21   **shock.** The question *shocked* him. He was *shocked* by the question. It was a *shocking* question. His *shock* was quite apparent. He *received a shock* when he heard this.

22   **authority, authorize.** The president *authorized* him to buy the land. He was *authorized* to buy the land. He was the *authorized* representative of the president. The president gave him the *authority* to buy it. He *had the authority* to offer two million dollars.

23   **correct, correction.** He *corrected* certain points. He *made the corrections* carefully. After that, no more *corrections* were necessary. He gave the *corrected* report to the president. The report was *correct*. It contained the *correct* information. The facts were reported *correctly*.

24 **courageous, courage, encourage, courageously.** He needed *courage* to make the decision. The president's reply gave him *courage*. The president's reply *encouraged* him. It was a *courageous* decision. He went ahead with the discussions *courageously*.

25 **trustful, trust, trustfully.** They *trusted* their government to support them. The president *trusted* his ministers. He was a *trusting* person. He was *trustful* of the men. They were *trustful* of their government. They had always done their work *trustfully*. They showed their *trust* by signing the agreement. The president had great *trust* in them.

26 **enthusiastic, enthusiasm, enthusiastically.** Everyone was *enthusiastic* about the purchase. The *enthusiastic* people celebrated the purchase. They received the news *enthusiastically*. Their *enthusiasm* was apparent. They *expressed enthusiasm* about it.

27 **victorious, victory, victoriously.** It was a *victory* for the small nation. The nation was *victorious*. The nation settled the situation *victoriously*.

28 **acceptable, acceptance, accept.** He *accepted* the offer. The offer was *acceptable* to him. His *acceptance* amazed everyone.

29 **objectionable, objection, object, objectionably.** Some people *objected* to the agreement. Some people *raised objections* to the agreement. The president considered their *objections*. The agreement was *objectionable* to them. They felt it was an *objectionable* arrangement. They felt matters had been handled *objectionably*.

30 **continual, continuous, continuation, continue, continually, continuously.** The soldiers *continued* to attack the cities. *Continuation* of the attack became impossible. They made *continual* attacks. They attacked the cities *continually*. The soldiers faced a *continuous* struggle against yellow fever. The insects bothered the soldiers *continuously*.

31 **destructive, destruction, destroy, destructively.** Disease *destroyed* the army. The army was almost completely *destroyed*. The *destruction* was almost complete. The *destructive* disease ruined Napoleon's plans. The disease passed among the soldiers *destructively*.

32 **valuable, value.** No one realized the *value* of the land. Before that time, no one had greatly *valued* the land. There were *valuable* forests in many parts of the territory.

EXERCISE 31. Use the correct form of each italicized word in the sentence which follows. Notice the first two examples. Refer to the word form chart and examples whenever necessary.

1	*accept*	The president's *acceptance* was necessary.
2	*value*	No one thought that the land was *valuable*.
3	*doubt*	He expressed his _____ to the president.
4	*serve*	There were no _____ roads to the east.
5	*possible*	He said that there were other _____.
6	*secret*	The minister felt that _____ was important.
7	*offer*	The minister _____ $2,000,000 for the land.
8	*support*	His principal _____ were the western settlers.
9	*amaze*	He tried not to show his _____.
10	*correct*	He made several _____ in the report.
11	*continue*	He decided against a _____ of the war.
12	*courageously*	He showed his _____ by making an offer.
13	*enthusiastic*	Everyone spoke about the purchase _____.
14	*development*	A dangerous situation _____ in New Orleans.
15	*economy*	The country was in a bad _____ situation.
16	*authority*	Congress _____ a payment of $2,000,000.
17	*clever*	The minister managed the arrangements _____.
18	*event*	It was an _____ period in history.
19	*unite*	Everyone agreed that _____ was important.
20	*power*	France was a _____ nation at that time.
21	*ship*	All _____ were unloaded and put in warehouses.
22	*force*	He wanted to act _____ in this matter.
23	*destroy*	The war caused the _____ of many cities.
24	*object*	Their principal _____ concerned land values.
25	*victory*	Napoleon was _____ in many battles.
26	*control*	His _____ of the island was weakened.
27	*boast*	He made several _____ remarks publicly.
28	*defend*	He needed a base for the _____ of his land.
29	*concern*	Everyone was _____ about his statements.
30	*true*	They told their leader the _____ about it.
31	*shock*	Everyone was _____ by the announcement.
32	*trust*	Jefferson _____ them to make the decision.

EXERCISE 32. Select the correct way to complete each of the following sentences. Write each sentence in its correct form.

1   The Louisiana Purchase included (*a*) everything west of the Mississippi River. (*b*) everything west of the Rocky Mountains. (*c*) New Orleans, the Florida Coastline and Texas. (*d*) everything between the Rocky Mountains and the Mississippi except Texas.

2   The western settlers usually transported their products to the east (*a*) over the usable roads to the east. (*b*) along the rivers of Santo Domingo. (*c*) along the western coastline of Florida. (*d*) down the Mississippi River.

3   Napoleon attacked the island of Santo Domingo because (*a*) England was the only country not under French control. (*b*) the settlers along the Mississippi needed trade. (*c*) he needed a base in order to defend his new lands. (*d*) he wanted to call off the war against England.

4   Napoleon called off the war against England because (*a*) he could not fight England and win the New World at the same time. (*b*) President Jefferson was greatly concerned about these developments. (*c*) there were 20 warships in the Gulf of Mexico. (*d*) Don Carlos of Spain was a weak ruler.

5   Jefferson knew the importance of New Orleans to the Westerners because (*a*) Hamilton wanted to take New Orleans by force. (*b*) the Westerners turned to Jefferson for help. (*c*) three-eighths of the national annual product had to pass through New Orleans. (*d*) Talleyrand showed no interest in an offer of two million dollars.

6   Livingston offered four million dollars to Talleyrand for Louisiana because (*a*) he expected Monroe to come to help him. (*b*) he had authority to buy New Orleans and Florida. (*c*) he had no authority from Congress. (*d*) he had made the decision to buy Louisiana.

7   Napoleon decided to sell Louisiana for fifteen million dollars because (*a*) he knew it was more than the total annual income of the United States. (*b*) he knew Congress would support Livingston and Monroe. (*c*) He needed the money for war with England. (*d*) Barbe-Marbois was his Minister of the Treasury.

8   Jefferson was enthusiastic over the purchase because (*a*) he knew this was the greatest bargain in history.   (*b*) the Constitution did not give the government the power to acquire more territory. (*c*) the vast majority of the population supported him.   (*d*) he expected Congress to ratify the agreement.

9   Napoleon decided to sign the sale agreement because (*a*) the French had won an important battle in Haiti.   (*b*) General Leclerc had died.   (*c*) There were 20 British warships in the Gulf of Mexico.   (*d*) a combination of economic, military and political considerations probably caused the decision.

10   The Lewis and Clark Expedition was of importance because (*a*) it informed the people of the beauty of Florida.   (*b*) the expedition reached the Pacific Ocean.   (*c*) it found Pike's Peak.   (*d*) it prepared the way for a westward movement of settlers.

The map on pages 66 and 67 originally appeared in *The American Pageant* by T. A. Bailey, published by Little, Brown and Company, Copyright 1956. The map has been reproduced with the permission of the publishers.

FIRST

ACROSS

THE

CONTINENT

PART ONE

In 1803, the United States doubled its size with the purchase of the Louisiana Territory for $15,000,000. But what kind of territory had the United States bought from Napoleon? The Westerners knew the land along the Mississippi River well. The city of New Orleans was familiar to almost everyone. On the other hand, President Jefferson had bought a very large farm west of the Mississippi, and he knew very little about it. No one else knew much about it either. There were vast areas which no white explorer had ever seen. Parts of the Louisiana Territory were not familiar even to the Indians.

President Jefferson decided to send out an expedition to explore the vast region. He chose two Virginians to lead the expedition. One of the Virginians was his young secretary, Meriwether Lewis. Lewis had been a fearless hunter and explorer since childhood, and he was deeply

double	familiar	explorer	explore	hunter
size	on the other hand	Indian	region	childhood
purchase	vast	decide	fearless	deeply
territory	area	send out		

interested in natural science. The other was William Clark, a captain in the army and a friend of Lewis'. William Clark was the brother of General George Rogers Clark, the hero of the battle of Vincennes in 1778. Like his brother George, William was very familiar with the customs and habits of the Indians. He was able to make use of this knowledge constantly on his western journey.

Lewis and Clark were accompanied on the expedition by 26 men. Nine of the men were from the Kentucky border where Clark lived. The other men were all soldiers or scouts. The leaders had complete instructions from President Jefferson. He wanted to know about many things. For example, he wanted to know about the location of the mouths of rivers, islands, and falls, the speech and customs of the Indian tribes, the plants and animals of the region. President Jefferson wanted complete notes and drawings of all these things.

In the fall of 1803, the expedition moved to a place opposite the mouth of the Missouri River. A small French village named St. Louis was located there. Ice began to form on the rivers, and the explorers decided to spend the winter there. During the winter, they collected information about the river from the French traders. They also gathered supplies and equipment for their trip. A great deal of their money was spent on bright cloth and jewelry for the Indians, but they also needed horses, food, clothes, guns, and ammunition. The men finally loaded their three long rowboats and 55-foot flatboat the following May and began to travel into the unknown territory.

The expedition moved up the Missouri slowly. They had to avoid shallow spots in the river and floating logs. They did not take along much food. They lived mainly on fish, buffalo, deer, and bear meat, but they occasionally ate wild fruit and made hard cornbread. They were constantly bothered by mosquitoes, flies, and other insects. They stopped to visit many Indian villages along the way. In the flat prairie region, they often built fires with dry grass. When the Indians saw these

natural science	border	collect	rowboat	bear
hero	scout	information	flatboat	occasionally
battle	location	trader	unknown	wild
custom	falls	gather	avoid	cornbread
habit	speech	supplies	shallow	bother
make use of	tribe	equipment	spot	mosquito
knowledge	plant	bright	float	fly
constantly	notes	cloth	log	insect
western	drawing	jewelry	mainly	flat
journey	opposite	ammunition	buffalo	prairie
accompany	form	load	deer	grass

smoke signals, they came to meet the explorers. Lewis and Clark collected much information about the geography of the region from the Indians. They also tried to explain that Spain was no longer the ruler of the territory, but this had little meaning to the Indian chiefs.

The expedition moved 1600 miles during the summer and fall. Along the way, Lewis and Clark picked up a lazy French-Canadian guide named Charbonneau to be their interpreter. Charbonneau's wife was a brave and intelligent 19-year-old Indian girl named Sacajawea. She had been stolen from her own tribe, the Shoshones, by an enemy tribe six years before. Lewis and Clark were hesitant to take a woman along, but they needed Charbonneau's help very much. Both Charbonneau and his wife accompanied the expedition. In November 1804, they reached a tiny Indian village named Mandan in North Dakota. Their trip had been hard and dangerous, and one of the members of the expedition had died along the way. They built a small camp and began to make plans for the next year. During the long, cold winter Sacajawea gave birth to a baby boy.

QUESTIONS FOR ORAL AND WRITTEN PRACTICE

(1) How did the purchase of the Louisiana Territory affect the size of the United States? (2) How much did the U.S. purchase the territory for? (3) How well did the Westerners know the land along the Mississippi River? (4) To whom was the city of New Orleans familiar? (5) How much did people know about the land west of the Mississippi? (6) How much did the Indians know about it? (7) What did President Jefferson decide to do? Why? (8) Whom did he choose to lead the expedition? (9) What had Lewis been since childhood? (10) What was Lewis interested in? (11) Who was William Clark? (12) Who was General George Rogers Clark? (13) What was William Clark familiar with? (14) How often was he able to make use of this knowledge? (15) How many men were Lewis and Clark accompanied by? (16) What was the occupation of many of these men? (17) From whom did they have instructions? (18) What specific things did President Jefferson want to know? (19) What kind

signal	meaning	interpreter	hesitant	dangerous
geography	chief	brave	reach	make plans
explain	pick up	intelligent	tiny	give birth to
no longer	guide			

of record of these things did he want? (20) Where was the French village named St. Louis located? (21) When did the expedition move there? (22) Why did the men decide to spend the winter there? (23) What did the men do during the winter? (24) What was a great deal of their money spent on? (25) What other things did they need for the trip? (26) When did the men leave St. Louis? (27) How did the men travel when they left St. Louis? (28) How fast did they travel up the Missouri River? (29) What did they have to avoid? (30) What kind of food did they live on? (31) Why didn't they take along much food? (32) What were they constantly bothered by? (33) Why did they stop along the way? (34) What did they often do in the flat prairie region? Why? (35) What did Lewis and Clark collect from the Indians? (36) What did they try to explain to the Indians? (37) How far did the expedition move during the summer and fall? (38) Why did they pick up a guide along the way? (39) Who was the guide's wife? (40) When had she last seen her own tribe? (41) Why did Lewis and Clark decide to take her along? (42) What place did they reach in November 1804? (43) What did they do at Mandan?

PART TWO

Early in the spring of 1805, the ice began to break up. The men were ready to continue their journey. Fourteen of the men were sent back toward St. Louis with complete reports, letters, drawings, and samples of plants, insects, and animals. The rest of the group started up the river again and traveled across North Dakota and Montana. The land became wilder, and food became scarce. The frontiersmen often met wild and ferocious grizzly bears. Sacajawea accompanied the expedition with her baby on her back. She was always loyal and helpful. She was valuable as an interpreter and helped to win the friendship of the Indians.

On June 13, Captain Lewis saw a cloud over the prairie ahead. It came from a great falls in the river. After a few hours, they reached the falls and discovered great rocky canyons and rapids which their boats

break up	frontiersman	helpful	cloud	rocky
report	ferocious	valuable	ahead	canyon
sample	grizzly bear	friendship	discover	rapids
scarce	loyal			

could not travel through. They spent several weeks there because they had to carry their boats and supplies thirteen miles to get past the dangerous spots in the river.

On July 4, 1805, the expedition led by Lewis and Clark was at the foot of the Rocky Mountains not far from the source of the Missouri River. Their supplies were very low, and everyone was discouraged by the sight of the huge mountains ahead. Sacajawea and her baby led the way. She was the only one who knew the way. She knew that her tribe lived near the mountains.

The weary group moved ahead. The men pulled their boats up the fast and narrow river with long ropes. They could not walk along the

| at the foot of | discourage | huge | weary | rope |
| source | sight | lead the way | narrow | |

steep banks, and the sharp stones in the river cut their feet. Near the top of the Bitter Root Mountains, the scouts could not find a way to go any farther.

Lewis realized that they had to find the Shoshone Indians or give up and return. The highest mountains were still ahead, and his men were exhausted. They needed horses. Their supplies were very low, and winter was near. Although they had seen no Indians for a month, Sacajawea insisted that she had seen the smoke signals of her tribe twice.

On August 9, 1805, Captain Lewis chose three men and went ahead. They climbed up the steep slopes until they found a narrow Indian road. On the morning of the fourth day, the four men ate their last piece of meat. By the afternoon, they had reached the high ridge which is called the "Great Continental Divide" today. From there, they could see the Pacific side of the Rocky Mountains. Shortly after that, they found Chief Cameahwait and 60 Shoshone Indians on horses. Lewis staggered toward the Indians with a flag above his head in friendship. The chief embraced Lewis and his men and called them "friends." Lewis offered to buy horses from the Indians. However, he had to go back to get the other members of the expedition. Although they were suspicious, the chief and the six other Indians rode back with Lewis. After much trouble, they finally found the main group. The Indian chief Cameahwait greeted Sacajawea very affectionately. They were brother and sister! However, Sacajawea chose to stay with her husband when the expedition moved to the west with 38 horses.

An old Indian accompanied the expedition across the Bitter Root Mountains as a guide. However, the old Indian led them in the wrong direction several times, and snow began to fill all the passes in the mountains. The members of the expedition were starving, and at one point, they had to kill some of their horses for food.

The group reached the Clearwater River. The men hardly had enough strength to make crude rafts and log boats. Even their leader was unable to move for several days. The expedition floated to the west on the Clearwater until they reached the junction of the Clearwater and the Snake River. Then they continued westward on the main river.

steep	although	divide	suspicious	hardly
bank	insist	shortly	main	strength
sharp	twice	stagger	greet	crude
farther	climb	flag	affectionately	raft
realize	slope	embrace	pass	unable
give up	ridge	offer	starve	junction
exhaust	continental	member	at one point	snake

In October, they reached the junction of the Snake River and a large river from the north. At this point, the two rivers formed the great Columbia River. For twenty or thirty years, stories of this great waterway had passed from trader to trader. They had always seemed to be legends, but Lewis and Clark had proved that the stories had been true.

While the men rested at the river junction, they were joined by large groups of Indians. They distributed many gifts to the Indians and received food in exchange. After resting for several days, the men and their leaders continued westward. The Indian villages along the river became more and more numerous. For the most part, these Indians lived on fish from the river, and they found many nets along the way.

After three more weeks of traveling, the men noticed that there were seagulls in the air and large salmon in the river. At noon on November 7, 1805, the expedition saw the large waves of the Pacific Ocean. Captain Clark wrote in his diary: "Oh the joy! We are in view of that great ocean which we have been anxious to see for so long!" The expedition had traveled 4000 miles in a year and a half.

QUESTIONS FOR ORAL AND WRITTEN PRACTICE

(44) When did the ice begin to break up? (45) How many men were sent back toward St. Louis? (46) What did those men take back with them? (47) What did the rest of the group do? (48) How many people continued with the expedition? (49) How did the land become? (50) What dangerous animals did they often meet? (51) How did Sacajawea travel? (52) How was she valuable to Lewis and Clark? (53) What did Captain Lewis see on June 13? (54) What did it come from? (55) How long did it take them to reach the falls? (56) What did they discover when they reached the falls? (57) How long did they stay there? Why? (58) Where was the expedition on July 4, 1805? (59) How were their supplies? (60) What was everyone discouraged by? (61) Who led the way? Why? (62) What did she know about her tribe? (63) How did the men move their boats up the fast and narrow river? (64) Why couldn't they walk along the banks? (65) What happened to their feet? (66) What did Lewis finally realize? (67) Why did they have to find the Shoshone Indians? (68) What did Sacajawea insist? (69) What did Captain Lewis do on

waterway	distribute	numerous	salmon	joy
legend	gift	for the most part	wave	view
prove	in exchange	net	ocean	anxious
join	westward	seagull	diary	

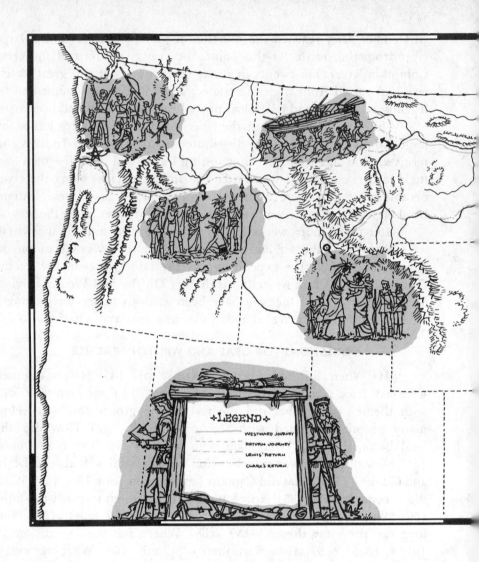

WESTWARD JOURNEY
RETURN JOURNEY
LEWIS' RETURN
CLARK'S RETURN

August 9, 1805? (70) How far did they climb up the steep slopes? (71) How far did they get by the afternoon of the fourth day? (72) What could they see from there? (73) What happened shortly after that? (74) How did Lewis meet them? (75) How did the chief respond? (76) What did Lewis offer to do? (77) Why did he have to go back? (78) Who rode back with Lewis? (79) How did the chief greet Sacajawea? Why? (80) What did Sacajawea choose to do then? (81) How many horses did Lewis and Clark have when they moved west? (82) Who accompanied the expedition across the Bitter Root

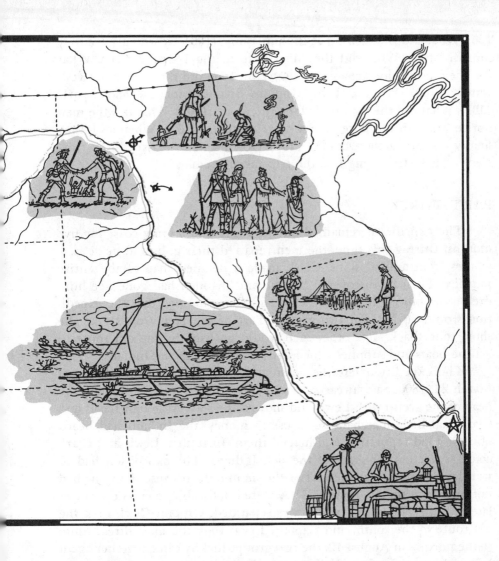

Mountains? (83) Why wasn't the old Indian a very good guide? (84) What did the snow begin to do? (85) What did they finally have to do for food? (86) What river did they reach next? (87) How much strength did they have? (88) How did they move along the Clearwater River? (89) What junction did they reach? (90) What other junction did they reach in October? (91) What great river did the two rivers form? (92) For how long had stories about this great river passed among traders? (93) What kind of stories had they always seemed to be? (94) What did Lewis and Clark prove?

(95) What did the men do at the junction? (96) By whom were they joined? (97) What did they distribute to the Indians? (98) What did they receive in exchange? (99) How soon did the men move westward? (100) What did the Indians live on for the most part? (101) What did the men find along the way? (102) What did the men notice after three more weeks of traveling? (103) When did they finally see the Pacific Ocean? (104) How far had the expedition traveled? (105) How long had the trip taken them?

PART THREE

The expedition remained on the foggy and stormy coast for five months. During this time, the men repaired their guns and made new clothes from animal skins. Clark made a detailed map of the entire journey. Then he discovered that he and his men had gone five hundred miles out of their way. Lewis and Clark decided that the expedition would go back in two groups. Part of the men would take the short route back. The other men would go back by the old route to get the boats and supplies which had been left with the Indians.

The expedition left the coast and started the journey back on March 23, 1806. Sacajawea was a valuable guide again. She rode at the head of the group with Lewis and showed the way. Although Lewis and Clark had little merchandise to use as money, the Indians had heard of their good reputation and helped them. In return, Lewis and Clark acted as doctors for some of the sick Indians. The expedition had to wait for one month at the foot of the mountains because the snow had not melted in the mountains. They were finally able to cross the ridges late in June. Then the two groups separated. Captain Clark took the old route to the south, and Captain Lewis took the most direct route to the north. On August 12, the two groups luckily came together again below the mouth of the Yellowstone River. They were all anxious to reach their homes again and traveled quickly. They reached St. Louis on September 23, 1806. The return trip from the Pacific had taken them six months.

No one had expected them to return. Everyone was sure that they had been killed. The people of St. Louis led the men through the

foggy	skin	reputation	cross	luckily
stormy	detail	in return	separate	return trip
coast	route	melt	direct	expect
repair	merchandise			

streets in joy. President Jefferson wrote the two leaders a warm letter of congratulation. Then President Jefferson announced the success of the expedition to Congress. The following year, Congress gave double pay and 300 acres of land to each of the men in the expedition. Lewis became the Governor of Louisiana, and Clark was promoted to the rank of general.

Today the Lewis and Clark Expedition is still considered the most important exploration in American history. It established the American claim of ownership of the Louisiana territory. Later, it was the basis of American claims of ownership of the Oregon territory.

QUESTIONS FOR ORAL AND WRITTEN PRACTICE

(106) What was the coast like? (107) How long did the expedition remain on the coast? (108) What did the men do during this time? (109) What did Clark do? (110) What did Clark discover then? (111) What did Lewis then decide? (112) How would the two groups go back? (113) Why did some of the men have to go back by the old route? (114) When did the expedition start the journey back? (115) Why was Sacajawea valuable to them again? (116) How much merchandise did Lewis and Clark have to use as money? (117) Why did the Indians help them despite the lack of merchandise? (118) What did Lewis and Clark do in return for the Indians' help? (119) Why did the expedition have to wait at the foot of the mountains? (120) When were they finally able to cross the ridges? (121) Which route did each of the men take when they separated? (122) When did the two groups come together again? (123) Where did they meet? (124) Why did they travel quickly? (125) When did they reach St. Louis? (126) How long had the return trip from the Pacific taken them? (127) Why hadn't anyone expected them to return? (128) What kind of letter did President Jefferson write? (129) What did President Jefferson announce to Congress? (130) What did Congress do for the members of the expedition? (131) What did Lewis become? (132) What rank was Clark promoted to? (133) How is the Lewis and Clark expedition considered today? (134) What did the expedition establish? (135) What was the expedition the basis of later?

congratulation	Congress	promote	consider	claim
announce	acre	rank	exploration	ownership
success	governor	general	establish	basis

SUMMARY SENTENCES FOR LABORATORY PRACTICE

(1) The United States doubled its size in 1803. (2) The United States bought the territory for $15,000,000. (3) What kind of territory had the United States bought? (4) No one knew much about it. (5) Parts were not familiar even to the Indians. (6) The president sent out an expedition to explore it. (7) He chose Lewis and Clark to lead the expedition. (8) Lewis was a fearless hunter and explorer. (9) He was deeply interested in natural science. (10) Clark was a captain in the army. (11) He was familiar with the customs of the Indians. (12) He was able to use this knowledge on his journey. (13) The two leaders were accompanied by 26 men. (14) Most of the men were soldiers or scouts. (15) The president wanted to know about many things. (16) He wanted complete notes and drawings. (17) The explorers decided to spend the winter in St. Louis. (18) They collected information about the Missouri River. (19) They gathered supplies and equipment for their trip. (20) They spent money on cloth and jewelry for the Indians. (21) The expedition moved up the river slowly. (22) They did not take along much food. (23) They lived mainly on fish and wild fruit. (24) They stopped to visit villages along the way. (25) They got information about the geography of the region. (26) They picked up a lazy guide. (27) His wife was a brave and intelligent Indian girl. (28) She was valuable as an interpreter. (29) She helped to win the friendship of the Indians. (30) The men reached the foot of the Rocky Mountains. (31) The girl was the only one who knew the way. (32) She knew that her tribe lived near the mountains. (33) They couldn't walk along the steep slopes. (34) The sharp stones in the river cut their feet. (35) They were joined by large groups of Indians. (36) They distributed many gifts to the Indians. (37) They received food in exchange. (38) The men and their leaders continued westward. (39) The men noticed that there were seagulls in the air. (40) The men finally saw the waves of the ocean. (41) They had traveled 4,000 miles in a year and a half. (42) They remained on the stormy coast for five months. (43) Then the expedition started the journey back. (44) They were all anxious to reach their homes again. (45) The return trip took them six months. (46) No one had expected them to return. (47) Everyone was sure that they had been killed. (48) The president announced their success to Congress. (49) He wrote the two leaders a letter of congratulation.

EXERCISE 33 (Part One). From the column at the left, select the best synonym for the italicized word in each sentence. Rewrite the sentences using the synonyms.

brave
signal
very small
extensive
filled
known
reluctant
gathered
existed
annoyed
purchased
regularly
miss
seriously
assistance
significance

1 The United States *bought* the territory in 1803.
2 There were *vast* areas no one had seen.
3 That land was *familiar* to everyone.
4 Captain Lewis was a *fearless* hunter.
5 He was *deeply* interested in that science.
6 He used his knowledge *constantly*.
7 In May, they *loaded* their four boats.
8 They often had to *avoid* shallow places.
9 The explorers were *bothered* by insects.
10 The men *lived* on fish and meat.
11 They needed the guide's *help* very much.
12 They were *hesitant* to take a woman along.
13 They *collected* information from the traders.
14 This had little *meaning* to the Indians.
15 They finally reached a *tiny* village.

EXERCISE 34 (Part One). From the column at the left, select the correct word for each blank space in the sentences at the right. Use each word only once. Do not change the forms of the words.

drawings
hero
lazy
habits
bright
border
childhood
form
supplies
floating
scouts
signals
opposite
size
natural
location

1 He was the _____ of an important battle.
2 The country doubled its _____ with the purchase.
3 He was familiar with the _____ of the Indians.
4 He had been an explorer since _____.
5 Clark's home was near the Kentucky _____.
6 They spent much money on _____ cloth.
7 The president wanted _____ of all these things.
8 In the prairies, they built fires as _____.
9 They had to avoid _____ logs in the river.
10 They picked up a _____ guide along the way.
11 Ice began to _____ on the rivers.
12 The men loaded their _____ in the boats.
13 Lewis was interested in _____ science.
14 They reported the _____ of the mouths of rivers.
15 The other men were soldiers or _____.

EXERCISE 35 (Part One).   Supply the correct preposition for each blank space.

1 The United States doubled its size _____ the purchase.
2 No one knew very much _____ the vast territory.
3 The territory was not familiar _____ the Indian guides.
4 Captain Clark was familiar _____ the Indians' customs.
5 Their leader was interested _____ natural science.
6 Lewis made good use _____ his knowledge _____ the journey.
7 Lewis and Clark were accompanied _____ twenty-six men.
8 _____ the fall _____ 1803, they moved _____ a French village.
9 They gathered equipment _____ their trip _____ St. Louis.
10 They got information _____ the river _____ the French traders.
11 They spent money _____ cloth and jewelry _____ the Indians.
12 The group visited many Indian villages _____ the way.
13 The men traveled 1600 miles _____ the summer and fall.
14 Their leaders often built signal fires _____ dry grass.
15 Their explanation had no meaning _____ the Indian chiefs.

EXERCISE 36 (Part One).   From the column at the right, select the correct line to complete each of the numbered lines at the left. Write each sentence in its correct form.

1 There were vast areas
2 Since childhood, Lewis had been
3 The men were sent out
4 Clark was familiar with
5 They were accompanied
6 The leaders had instructions
7 The men spent the winter
8 A village named St. Louis
9 In March, the ice
10 The men finally loaded
11 The expedition moved
12 They were bothered by
13 The men constantly had
14 The two leaders collected
15 The interpreter's wife

(A) from President Jefferson
(B) a hunter and explorer
(C) was located along the river
(D) to avoid shallow spots
(E) mosquitoes and flies
(F) to explore the vast region
(G) in a small French village
(H) which no one knew about
(I) their four long boats
(J) gave birth to a baby boy
(K) the habits of the Indians
(L) by scouts and soldiers
(M) information about the region
(N) up the river slowly
(O) began to break up

EXERCISE 37 (Part Two). From the column at the left, select the best synonym for the italicized word in each sentence. Rewrite the sentences using the synonyms.

distributed
origin
perilous
tremendous
remained
faithful
go on
admit failure
insisted
distrustful
savage
walk unsteadily
primitive
tired
hard to get
sight

1 The Indian girl was always *loyal*.
2 The slopes by the river were *dangerous*.
3 The expedition *stayed* for three weeks.
4 Most of the bears were *ferocious*.
5 In that region, food became *scarce*.
6 They were near the *source* of the river.
7 The *huge* mountains discouraged the men.
8 The *weary* men pulled their boats along.
9 They did not want to *give up* and return.
10 Why did he *stagger* toward the Indians?
11 The Indian chief was *suspicious*.
12 The men made *crude* rafts and boats.
13 They wanted to *continue* westward.
14 Finally, they were in *view* of the ocean.
15 They *passed out* gifts to the Indians.

EXERCISE 38 (Part Two). From the column at the left, select the correct word for each blank space in the sentences at the right. Use each word only once. Do not change the forms of the words.

trader
canyons
anxious
samples
ahead
junction
steep
joy
numerous
main
diary
members
ropes
waves
exchange
legends
sight

1 They sent _____ of plants and insects.
2 The men pulled the boats along with _____.
3 The men found rocky _____ by the falls.
4 Lewis saw a cloud over the prairie _____.
5 They couldn't walk along the _____ banks.
6 The other _____ of the expedition waited.
7 The two men finally found the _____ group.
8 The men reached the _____ of the two rivers.
9 The stories had always seemed to be _____.
10 The Indian villages became more _____.
11 They received food in _____ for their gifts.
12 All the men were _____ to see the Pacific Ocean.
13 They saw the _____ of the Pacific on November 7.
14 Captain Clark reported the event in his _____.
15 The men looked at the ocean with great _____.

EXERCISE 39 (Part Two). Supply the correct preposition for each blank space.

1. Fourteen men went back _____ St. Louis _____ complete reports.
2. Sacajawea accompanied them _____ her baby _____ her back.
3. Lewis saw a cloud _____ the prairie ahead.
4. The cloud came _____ a great falls _____ the river.
5. Their boat could not travel _____ the canyons and rapids.
6. They reached the Rocky Mountains _____ July 4, 1805.
7. They were discouraged _____ the sight _____ the mountains.
8. The men pulled their boats _____ long ropes.
9. The men had seen no Indians _____ an entire month.
10. _____ the afternoon, they had reached the high ridge.
11. Lewis held a flag _____ his head _____ friendship.
12. Sacajawea decided to stay _____ her husband.
13. The Indian led them _____ the wrong direction several times.
14. _____ one point, they had to kill horses _____ food.
15. They continued westward _____ resting _____ several days.

EXERCISE 40 (Part Two). From the column at the right, select the correct line to complete each of the numbered lines at the left. Write each sentence in its correct form.

1 The rest of the group	(A) their boats thirteen miles
2 As the land became wilder	(B) from the high ridge
3 She helped to win	(C) to move for several days
4 She was the only one	(D) food became scarce
5 At the falls, they discovered	(E) more and more numerous
	(F) her very affectionately
6 They had to carry	(G) started up the river
7 Sacajawea insisted that	(H) of the Pacific Ocean
8 They saw the Pacific side	(I) horses from the Indians
9 Lewis offered to buy	(J) great rocky canyons
10 The Indian chief greeted	(K) who knew the way
11 Their leader was unable	(L) by groups of Indians
12 At this point, the rivers	(M) she had seen signals
13 The men were joined	(N) the friendship of the Indians
14 The Indian villages became	dians
15 They saw the waves	(O) formed the great Columbia

EXERCISE 41. Study the following word form chart carefully. The word forms which occurred in the preceding story are italicized.

ADJECTIVE	NOUN	VERB	ADVERB
1 *familiar*	familiarity	familiarize	familiarly
2 exploratory	*exploration* explorer	*explore*	x x x x x
3 friendly	*friendship* *friend*	x x x x x	x x x x x
4 x x x x x	*location*	*locate*	x x x x x
5 informative	*information*	inform	informatively
6 *dry*	dryness	dry	dryly
7 explanatory	explanation	*explain*	explanatorily
8 meaningful	*meaning*	mean (irreg.)	meaningfully
9 *lazy*	laziness	x x x x x	lazily
10 *hesitant*	hesitation	hesitate	hesitantly
11 x x x x x	*plan*	plan	x x x x x
12 x x x x x	*birth*	be born	x x x x x
13 *ready*	readiness	ready	x x x x x
14 *loyal*	loyalty	x x x x x	loyally
15 *helpful*	help	help	helpfully
16 *valuable*	value	value	x x x x x
17 x x x x x	discoverer discovery	*discover*	x x x x x
18 *weary*	weariness	weary	wearily
19 *long*	length	lengthen	x x x x x
20 insistent	insistence	*insist*	insistently
21 x x x x x	*slope*	slope	x x x x x
22 *high*	height heights	x x x x x	x x x x x
23 *suspicious*	*suspicion*	suspect	suspiciously
24 affectionate	affection	x x x x x	*affectionately*
25 x x x x x	proof	*prove*	x x x x x
26 x x x x x	distribution	*distribute*	x x x x x
27 separate	separation	*separate*	separately
28 lucky	luck	x x x x x	*luckily*
29 congratulatory	*congratulation*	congratulate	x x x x x
30 x x x x x	promotion	*promote*	x x x x x
31 *important*	importance	x x x x x	x x x x x
32 x x x x x	*claim*	claim	x x x x x

EXERCISE 43. Use the correct form of each italicized word in the sentence which follows. Notice the first two examples. Refer to the word form chart and examples whenever necessary.

1	*explain*	The leaders' *explanation* had no meaning to them.
2	*locate*	They found an excellent *location* for the camp.
3	*explore*	This _____ was important in American history.
4	*meaning*	Clark's words _____ nothing to the Indians.
5	*valuable*	The leaders _____ the Indian girl's assistance.
6	*plan*	They _____ to return by two different routes.
7	*lazy*	None of the men appreciated the guide's _____.
8	*long*	What was the _____ of the flatboat they used?
9	*dry*	They noticed the _____ of the air in the mountains.
10	*friend*	The girl helped them to win the Indians' _____.
11	*information*	The traders _____ them that the river was dangerous.
12	*luckily*	The men had a great deal of _____ on the journey.
13	*claim*	The government _____ the Oregon territory later.
14	*insist*	What was the reason for the Indian girl's _____?
15	*prove*	They found _____ that the stories had been true.
16	*high*	The great _____ of the mountains discouraged the men.
17	*loyal*	She showed her _____ to them on many occasions.
18	*familiar*	The girl's _____ with the region helped the men.
19	*important*	The president realized the _____ of the journey.
20	*distribute*	Was the _____ of gifts to the Indians helpful?
21	*birth*	The Indian girl's baby was _____ during the winter.
22	*weary*	The men's _____ was clear to their leaders.
23	*promote*	Clark received a _____ in rank from Congress.
24	*ready*	The men got _____ to leave the following day.
25	*affection*	The chief greeted the Indian girl _____.
26	*helpful*	They found their way with the _____ of the girl.
27	*separate*	The two groups of explorers traveled _____.
28	*separate*	What was the reason for the _____?
29	*hesitant*	The leaders _____ to take the Indian girl along.
30	*hesitant*	They had some _____ about taking the girl along.
31	*suspicious*	At first, the Indians were _____ of the men.
32	*suspicious*	The Indians tried not to show their _____.

EXERCISE 42. Study the following examples for the preceding word form chart. The numbers correspond to those on the word form chart.

1 **familiar, familiarity, familiarize, familiarly.** The man was *familiar* with their customs. Their customs were *familiar* to the man. The man's face was *familiar* to the Indians. He spoke to them *familiarly*. They traveled along a *familiar* route. His *familiarity* with their customs was helpful. The men *familiarized* themselves with the Indians' customs.

2 **exploratory, explorer, exploration, explore.** The men *explored* the entire region. The *explorers* traveled a great distance. Their *exploration* was important in American history. The *exploratory* journey was a success.

3 **friendly, friend, friendship.** Some of Clark's *friends* went on the expedition. Some of the men were *friends of his*. Most of the Indians were *friendly*. *Friendly* Indians met them along the river. They wanted to *win the friendship* of the Indians. They wanted to *gain their friendship*. Their *friendship* was important to the explorers.

4 **location, locate.** The men *located* their camp near the village. Their camp was *located* near the river. They chose the *location* carefully.

5 **informative, information, inform, informatively.** They got *information* from the traders. The traders *informed* them of the dangerous spots. The traders were very *informative*. The traders spoke about several areas *informatively*.

6 **dry, dryness.** They used *dry* grass for their fires. The *dryness* of the grass helped them. The sun had *dried* the grass completely.

7 **explanatory, explanation, explain.** The leaders *explained* everything to the Indians. Their *explanation* was very simple. His *explanatory* speech wasn't understood.

8 **meaningful, meaning, mean, meaningfully.** The explanation *had no meaning*. The Indians didn't know the *meanings* of the words. Their explanation *meant nothing* to the Indians. The explanation wasn't *meaningful*. The leaders didn't explain things *meaningfully*. What does that word *mean*? What is the *meaning* of that word?

9 **lazy, laziness, lazily.** They picked up a *lazy* guide. The guide's *laziness* wasn't helpful. The guide sat by the fire *lazily*.

10 **hesitant, hesitation, hesitate, hesitantly.** They were *hesitant* to take her along. They were *hesitant* about taking her along. Normally, they weren't *hesitant* men. They considered the matter *hesitantly.* They *hesitated* to take her along. Their *hesitation* worried the girl.

11 **planning, plan.** They *planned* to leave in the spring. They discussed the *plan* carefully. Their *plans* were complete. They made plans for the trip. The *planning* was important. They followed the *planned* route.

12 **birth, be born.** The *birth* of her baby occurred in the winter. She *gave birth* to a baby boy. The baby *was born* in the winter.

13 **ready, readiness.** The men were *ready* to leave. They *got ready* quickly. They were *ready* for the trip. They *readied* the boats for the trip. They reported their *readiness* to their leaders. Everything was *in readiness* for the trip.

14 **loyal, loyalty, loyally.** The girl was always *loyal* to the leaders. She was a *loyal* person. She protected the leaders *loyally.* Her *loyalty* was important to the expedition.

15 **helpful, help, helpfully.** Her *help* was important to the expedition. She *helped* the men in many ways. She was always *helpful.* She worked in the camp *helpfully.*

16 **valuable, value.** Her help was *valuable* to the expedition. She was *of great value* to them. They realized her *value.* They *valued* her help.

17 **discoverer, discovery, discover.** Lewis was the *discoverer.* He *discovered* the narrow canyon. The *discovery* was discouraging.

18 **weary, weariness, wearily.** The *weary* men stopped for a moment. They sat by the fire *wearily.* They stopped because of their *weariness.* The long journey had *wearied* the men.

19 **long, length, lengthen.** Clark and his men took the *long* route. They estimated the *length* of the route. By going to the north, they *lengthened* the route.

20 **insistent, insistence, insist, insistently.** The girl *insisted* that she had seen signals. She *insisted* on going ahead. Her *insistence* gave them courage. She was an *insistent* person. She mentioned the signals *insistently.*

21 **slope.** The banks of the river *sloped* steeply upward. The men couldn't walk on the *slopes.* The *sloping* banks gave them much trouble.

98

22 **high, height, heights.** The mountains were *high*. They saw *higher* mountains in the distance. The *highest* mountains were still ahead. They didn't know about the great *height* of the mountains. They had much trouble in the *heights*.

23 **suspicious, suspicion, suspect, suspiciously.** The Indians were *suspicious* of them. The Indians treated them *suspiciously*. The Indians showed their *suspicion* clearly. They *suspected* the men of stealing horses.

24 **affectionate, affection, affectionately.** The chief greeted the girl *affectionately*. They were *affectionate* to each other. Everyone noticed their *affection*.

25 **proof, prove.** They *proved* that the stories had been true. They *found proof* that the stories had been true. They *had proof* that the stories had been true. The *proof* was in front of them.

26 **distribution, distribute.** They *distributed* gifts to the Indians. The *distribution* of gifts was important.

27 **separate** (adjective), **separation, separate** (verb), **separately.** The groups *separated* in June. They planned the *separation* carefully. The groups traveled along *separate* routes. The groups traveled *separately*.

28 **lucky, luck, luckily.** They *had good luck* on the trip. Their *luck* continued on the return trip. They were *lucky* to meet as planned. The *lucky* travelers returned in six months. *Luckily,* they found each other again.

29 **congratulatory, congratulation, congratulate.** The president wrote a letter of *congratulation*. The men appreciated his *congratulations*. The president *congratulated* the men on their success. They appreciated his *congratulatory* letter.

30 **promotion, promote.** The government *promoted* him to the rank of general. He was *promoted* to the rank of general. The *promotion* was announced publicly.

31 **important, importance.** The discovery was *important* to the men. It was an *important* discovery. They realized the *importance* of the discovery.

32 **claim.** The United States *claimed* ownership of the territory. The expedition was the basis of the *claim*. The United States *made claims* of ownership.

EXERCISE 44. Select the correct way to complete each of the following sentences. Write each sentence in its correct form.

1 New Orleans in Louisiana was (a) the capital of the nation. (b) familiar to almost everyone. (c) unknown to white men. (d) known only to explorers and Indians.

2 President Jefferson sent out an expedition (a) to conquer the territory. (b) to explore the territory. (c) to buy the territory from the Indians. (d) to look for gold and silver.

3 Later the Lewis and Clark Expedition was the basis of (a) Jefferson's claim to a large farm west of the Mississippi. (b) the purchase of the entire area between the Mississippi and the Rocky Mountains. (c) the great civil war between the North and the South. (d) American claims of ownership of the Oregon territory.

4 Before starting their journey, Lewis and Clark purchased (a) the Louisiana Territory. (b) drawings and reports of the area. (c) the friendship of the Indians. (d) bright cloth and jewelry for the Indians.

5 When they saw the signal fires on the flat prairies, the Indians (a) sold their horses to the group. (b) loaded their boats with supplies. (c) came to meet the explorers. (d) collected information about the region.

6 The information that Spain no longer controlled the territory (a) bothered the Indian chiefs greatly. (b) gave the Indian chiefs great joy. (c) discouraged the tribe from which Sacajawea had been stolen. (d) had little significance to the Indian chiefs.

7 At the top of the Bitter Root Mountains in August of 1805, Lewis realized that they had to (a) wave flags above their heads in friendship. (b) find the Shoshone Indians or give up and return. (c) float to the west on rafts. (d) use nets to live on fish from the river.

8 After three weeks of traveling toward the Pacific along the great Columbia River, the men noticed (a) their leader was unable to move for several days. (b) Captain Clark was writing in his diary. (c) they had been traveling for a year and a half. (d) there were seagulls in the air and large salmon in the river.

9   When Clark made a detailed map of their journey to the Pacific coast, he discovered (a) their boats and supplies had been left with the Indians.   (b) he and his men had gone five hundred miles out of their way.   (c) the junction of the Snake River and a large river from the north formed a great waterway.   (d) they had proved that the traders' stories had been true.

10 On the return trip, the expedition had to wait at the foot of the mountains for one month (a) in order to cross the mountains in two groups.   (b) because they wanted to take the short route back. (c) so Clark could make a detailed map of the entire journey. (d) because the snow had not melted in the mountains.

11 In return for the Indians' assistance on the way back, Lewis and Clark (a) explained their good reputation to the Indians.   (b) gave them merchandise in place of money.   (c) acted as doctors for some of the sick Indians.   (d) built crude rafts and boats for them.

12 The men traveled quickly on the return trip because (a) they were anxious to reach their homes again.   (b) they were anxious to see the Pacific side of the huge mountains.   (c) they had little merchandise left to use as money.   (d) they wanted to make new clothes from animal skins.

13 The leaders of the expedition and their men reached St. Louis (a) on June 13, 1805.   (b) at noon on November 7, 1805.   (c) on March 23, 1806.   (d) in the fall of 1806.

14 When the expedition finally returned to St. Louis from the Pacific Coast, (a) they met wild and ferocious grizzly bears.   (b) the people led the men through the streets in joy.   (c) they were not even familiar to the Indians.   (d) all of the men spent money on guns and ammunition.

15 A year after the expedition, the Congress of the United States (a) sent a warm letter of congratulation to the two leaders.   (b) announced the success of the expedition.   (c) gave double pay and 300 acres of land to each of the men in the expedition.   (d) wanted complete notes and drawings of the plants and animals of the region.

Seeds for the Future

A. DAGOSTINO

PART ONE

AMONG THE hardy pioneers of America, there was a modest and gentle hero. The story of this gentle pioneer has survived because of his unusual qualities. He did everything voluntarily. His motives were always kind and creative, not violent or hostile. His name was Jonathan Chapman, but everyone remembers him as "Johnny Appleseed."

Johnny Appleseed was apparently born in Boston, Massachusetts in 1775. According to the first reliable report, Johnny was in the Territory of Ohio in 1801. At that time, Johnny had a horse and a load of apple seeds. He was planting these seeds in various places around the borders of Licking Creek. He probably followed the same strange occupation during the following five years. However, no one knows for sure.

seed	modest	survive	motive	hostile
hardy	gentle	quality	creative	apparent
pioneer	hero	voluntary	violent	

The next reliable account of his movements was made in the spring of 1806. A pioneer in Jefferson County noticed a peculiar boat on the Ohio River. The boat had a remarkable passenger and an odd cargo. The passenger was Johnny Appleseed. He was transporting a load of apple seeds. He wanted to create orchards on the farthest edge of settlements. His journey down the river took a great deal of time because he stopped at every pleasant spot to plant his seeds.

Johnny had two regular routes for his trips. One was over part of the old Indian trail from Fort Duquesne to Detroit. The other required

reliable	creek	remarkable	create	spot
load	occupation	odd	orchard	route
plant	for sure	cargo	far	trail
various	account	transport	settlement	require
border				

him to travel 166 miles northwest from Fort Duquesne to reach the Black Fork of the Mohican River. Today, the region which Johnny traveled through is densely populated. However, it still possesses great romantic beauty. It is a country of hills, forests, and green valleys. Numerous streams flow through this region on their way to the Ohio River. In Johnny's time, this area was a real wilderness. There were vast regions of small trees between the streams and the hills where the forests of tall trees began. There were innumerable bears, wolves, deer, and wild hogs. Wild flowers grew in the tall grass along the river. Willow and alder trees rose over the green river banks. The grass was full of poisonous snakes. The settlers were careful to protect their legs against the constant danger of these reptiles. But Johnny traveled through the entire region with bare feet. He used to plant his seeds and put a small enclosure around them. He was too busy to worry about accidents.

Later, when settlers came to the places Johnny had visited, they cleared small areas. Then they removed the small apple trees and re-planted them on their own cleared pieces of land. Many of the places which were chosen by Johnny are known today. He always chose these orchard sites carefully and with the inspiration of an artist or poet.

QUESTIONS FOR ORAL AND WRITTEN PRACTICE

(1) In what way was Johnny Appleseed different from other American pioneers? (2) Why has the story of Johnny Appleseed survived? (3) Were his motives violent or hostile? What were they? (4) By what name does everyone remember him? (5) What was his real name? (6) When and where was he born? (7) Where was Johnny in 1801? (8) What did he have at that time? (9) What was he doing with the seeds? (10) Where was he planting the seeds? (11) What did Johnny do during the following five years? (12) Who knows for sure? (13) When was the next reliable report of his movements made? (14) Who noticed Johnny in 1806? (15) What did the pioneer in Jefferson County notice? (16) What kind of passenger did the boat have? What kind of cargo? (17) What was Johnny Appleseed doing? (18) What did he want to do? (19) How many regular routes did Johnny have for his trips? (20) What was one of his routes?

dense	vast	alder tree	constant	remove
populate	innumerable	rise	danger	replant
romantic	bear	bank	reptile	site
numerous	wolf	snake	bare	inspiration
stream	deer	settler	enclosure	artist
flow	wild hog	protect	accident	poet
wilderness	willow tree			

(21) What did the other route require him to do? (22) What is this region like today? (23) What does the region still possess? (24) What was this area like in Johnny's time? (25) What was there between the streams and the hills where the forests began? (26) What kinds of animals were there? (27) Where did the wild flowers grow? (28) Where did the willow and alder trees rise? (29) What was the grass full of? (30) What were the settlers careful to do? (31) How did Johnny protect his feet and legs against snakes? (32) What did he put around the places where he had planted seeds? (33) Why didn't he worry about accidents? (34) What did the settlers do with the small apple trees later? (35) How did Johnny choose orchard sites?

PART TWO

In appearance, Johnny Appleseed was a small, thin man. He was full of restless energy. He had long, dark hair and a beard which he never shaved. He was always oddly dressed. In later years, his principal garment was made from a coffee sack. He cut holes in the sack for his head and his arms. His hats were equally peculiar. For a long time, he wore a tin pan. Later, he constructed a cardboard hat with an immense peak in front. He generally went barefooted even in the coldest weather, but he sometimes made himself a crude pair of sandals for his long journeys. His constant companion was a thin gray wolf. He had found the wolf nearly dead in a bear trap one day. He had nursed the wolf back to good health over a period of many months. The wolf never went far away from Johnny after that.

When he wandered into the settlements, Johnny was always treated with the greatest respect by the rude frontier men. Youngsters never made fun of him despite his appearance. His sympathy for youthful troubles made him the friend of young people wherever he went. He was shy with adults, but he was generous and affectionate with children, especially little girls. In the Indian villages, Johnny was also treated with great kindness. He was regarded as a great "medicine man" by these people. His strange appearance, odd actions, and ability to endure

appearance	equal	pair	respect	shy
restless	tin pan	sandals	frontier	adult
energy	construct	companion	youngster	generous
beard	cardboard	nearly	make fun of	affectionate
shave	immense	trap	sympathy	regard
principal	peak	nurse	youthful	ability
garment	barefooted	wander	wherever	endure
sack	crude	treat		

pain impressed the Indians greatly. He often stuck pins and needles into his body to prove his endurance. When the settlers were killed and tortured by the Indians during the War of 1812, Johnny was never harmed. This immunity often gave him a chance to warn the settlers before an Indian attack. On one occasion, he traveled along the border for several days without food or sleep in order to warn every settler of an approaching attack.

Thirty-seven years after his first appearance on Licking Creek, Johnny noticed that civilization, wealth, and population were appearing in the wilderness of Ohio. Before that, he had easily kept in advance of the wave of settlement. However, towns and churches were making their appearance. He felt that his work was done in that region. He had labored there long enough. He visited every house, and he said a solemn farewell to all the families. The little girls who had been delighted with his gifts were now mothers of large families. The boys who had wondered at his ability to bear pain were the heads of families.

During the following nine years, he continued his odd work along the western border of Ohio and Indiana. By the summer of 1847, the fruit of his work had covered a hundred thousand square miles of territory. One summer evening of that year, he entered the house of a settler in Allen County, Indiana. As usual, he was welcomed warmly. He refused to eat with the family but accepted some bread and milk which he ate on the doorstep. Later in the evening, he read the Bible to the family and delivered his usual sermon called "news right from heaven." As usual, he slept on the floor that night. In the early morning, he was found with a strange expression on his face. He could hardly speak. A doctor was called immediately, but old Johnny died only a few hours later. The doctor's statement to the family has been recorded through letters and diaries of the period. "Johnny was calm—even serene—at the approach of death."

impress	immunity	appear	bear	heaven
stick	chance	in advance	refuse	expression
pin	warn	wave	accept	hardly
needle	attack	labor	doorstep	record
prove	approach	solemn	the Bible	diary
endurance	civilization	farewell	deliver	calm
torture	wealth	delight	sermon	serene
harm	population	wonder		

(36) What did Johnny Appleseed look like? (37) What kind of hair did he have? (38) How often did he shave his beard? (39) How was he always dressed? (40) In later years, what was his principal garment made from? (41) Why did Johnny cut holes in the sack? (42) What were his hats like? (43) What kind of hat did he wear for a long time? (44) What kind of hat did he construct later? (45) What did he generally wear on his feet? (46) What kind of shoes did he sometimes make for his long journeys? (47) Who was his constant companion? (48) Where had he found the wolf? (49) Why didn't the wolf ever go very far away from Johnny? (50) How was Johnny treated by the rude frontier men? (51) Why didn't youngsters make fun of him? (52) How did he act with adults? (53) With whom was he generous and affectionate? (54) How was Johnny treated in the Indian villages? (55) What was he regarded as by the Indians? (56) What things impressed the Indians greatly? (57) Why did he often stick pins into his body? (58) What happened to Johnny during the War of 1812? (59) Why did he travel along the border without food or sleep on one occasion? (60) What did Johnny notice in 1838? (61) Why did Johnny feel that his work was done in that region? (62) What did he say to all the families? (63) What had happened to the little girls who had been delighted with his gifts? (64) What had happened to the boys who had wondered at his ability to bear pain? (65) What did Johnny do during the following nine years? (66) Where did he continue his odd work? (67) How much territory had his work covered by the summer of 1847? (68) Whose house did he enter one summer evening of that year? (69) How was he welcomed? (70) What did he accept from the family? (71) Where did Johnny eat the food the family gave him? (72) What did he do later in the evening? (73) Where did he sleep that night? (74) When did Johnny die?

SUMMARY SENTENCES FOR LABORATORY PRACTICE

(1) There was a modest and gentle hero among American pioneers. (2) The story has survived because of his unusual qualities. (3) His name was Jonathan Chapman. (4) But everyone remembers him as

"Johnny Appleseed." (5) He was apparently born in Boston in 1775. (6) He first appeared in Ohio in 1801. (7) He had a horse and a load of apple seeds. (8) He was planting these seeds in various places. (9) He followed the same occupation during the following five years. (10) The next reliable report was made in the spring of 1806. (11) A pioneer saw Johnny in a peculiar boat on the Ohio River. (12) He was transporting a load of apple seeds. (13) His journey down the river took a great deal of time. (14) He stopped at every pleasant spot to plant his seeds. (15) He had two regular routes for his trips. (16) The region Johnny traveled through is densely populated today. (17) It is a country of hills, forests, and green valleys. (18) In Johnny's time, this area was a real wilderness. (19) There were vast regions of small trees by the streams. (20) Forests of tall trees began near the hills. (21) There were bears, wolves, and deer. (22) The grass was full of poisonous snakes. (23) But Johnny traveled through the region with bare feet. (24) He used to plant his seeds and put an enclosure around them. (25) Later, settlers removed the small apple trees. (26) They replanted the trees on their own cleared pieces of land. (27) Johnny always chose these orchard sites carefully. (28) In appearance, he was a small, thin man. (29) He was full of restless energy. (30) He had long, dark hair. (31) He had a beard which he never shaved. (32) He was always oddly dressed. (33) For a long time, he wore a tin pan for a hat. (34) His constant companion was a thin gray wolf. (35) He had found the wolf nearly dead in a bear trap. (36) Johnny was always treated with respect by the frontier men. (37) Youngsters never made fun of him despite his appearance. (38) He was a friend of young people wherever he went. (39) He was shy with adults. (40) But he was generous and affectionate with children. (41) In the Indian villages, he was treated with great kindness. (42) He was regarded as a great "medicine man" by these people. (43) His ability to endure pain impressed the Indians greatly. (44) During the War of 1812, he was never harmed. (45) He warned settlers of approaching attacks. (46) Thirty-seven years later, he felt that his work was done. (47) He felt that he had worked there long enough. (48) He said a solemn farewell to all the families. (49) He continued his odd work along the western border. (50) He worked there until the summer of 1847.

EXERCISE 45. From the column at the left, select the best synonym for the italicized word in each sentence. Rewrite the sentence using the synonym.

whole
hostile
peaceful
almost
seriously
hurt
ridiculed
demonstrate
chief
uncovered
ahead
place
scarcely
tolerate
stiff paper
unfinished

1 He found the wolf *nearly* dead in a trap.
2 His feet were *bare* during the entire journey.
3 He was never *harmed* during the war.
4 He chose each *spot* with great inspiration.
5 He wanted to *prove* his ability to the Indians.
6 His *principal* garment was made from a sack.
7 He sometimes made himself *crude* sandals.
8 He had kept *in advance* of the settlements.
9 The boys and girls never *made fun of* him.
10 He was *calm* at the approach of death.
11 His ability to *endure* pain impressed them.
12 He could *hardly* speak before he died.
13 He spoke to all of the families *solemnly*.
14 He made a *cardboard* hat with a peak.
15 He traveled through the *entire* region slowly.

EXERCISE 46. From the column at the left, select the correct word for the blank space in each sentence. Do not change the form of any of these words.

border
stuck
affectionate
violent
rose
shy
densely
warn
flow
treat
tin pan
despite
trail
worry
protect
pain

1 Streams _____ through this region to the Ohio.
2 He traveled to Detroit over an old Indian _____.
3 He continued his work along the western _____.
4 Beautiful tall trees _____ over the river banks.
5 The region he lived in is _____ populated today.
6 Johnny used a _____ as a hat for a long time.
7 They never made fun of him _____ his appearance.
8 The settlers were careful to _____ their legs.
9 He often _____ pins and needles into his body.
10 His ability to endure _____ impressed the Indians.
11 He was _____ with children, especially girls.
12 How did the rude frontier men _____ Johnny?
13 Johnny was _____ with adults in the settlements.
14 He tried to _____ the settlers before attacks.
15 He was always too busy to _____ about accidents.

110

EXERCISE 47. Supply the correct preposition for each blank space.

1 Johnny was apparently born _____ Boston _____ 1775.
2 According _____ the report, he was _____ that region _____ 1801.
3 The next report was made _____ the spring _____ 1806.
4 Streams flow _____ that region _____ their way _____ the Ohio.
5 He stopped _____ every pleasant spot _____ the river.
6 The settlers removed the small trees _____ the enclosures.
7 He was treated _____ great respect _____ the frontier men.
8 _____ later years, his chief garment was made _____ a sack.
9 He cut holes _____ the coffee sack _____ his head and arms.
10 He made a cardboard hat _____ an immense peak _____ front.
11 The little girls were always delighted _____ Johnny's gifts.
12 _____ one occasion, he traveled _____ food _____ several days.
13 He continued his odd work _____ the following nine years.
14 Later _____ the evening, he read the Bible _____ the family.
15 Johnny was found _____ a strange expression _____ his face.

EXERCISE 48. From the column at the right, select the correct line to complete each of the numbered lines at the left. Write each sentence in its correct form.

1 The story has survived
2 His immunity gave him
3 He was transporting
4 They came to the places
5 Johnny was too busy
6 His river journey
7 He chose orchard sites
8 Numerous small streams
9 The region he traveled in
10 His garment was made
11 Johnny's odd actions
12 Johnny was never
13 He sometimes made
14 The tall grass was full
15 They protected their legs

(A) against the reptiles
(B) harmed by the Indians
(C) Johnny had cleared
(D) of poisonous snakes
(E) a load of apple seeds
(F) with artistic inspiration
(G) because of his qualities
(H) impressed the Indians
(I) is densely populated now
(J) flow through the region
(K) from a coffee sack
(L) to worry about accidents
(M) took a great deal of time
(N) a crude pair of sandals
(O) a chance to warn them

EXERCISE 49. Study the following word form chart carefully. The word forms which occurred in the preceding story are italicized.

	ADJECTIVE	NOUN	VERB	ADVERB
1	*modest*	modesty	x x x x x	modestly
2	x x x x x	survival	*survive*	x x x x x
3	voluntary	volunteer	volunteer	*voluntarily*
4	creative	creation	*create*	creatively
5	*violent*	violence	violate	violently
6	*hostile*	hostility	x x x x x	x x x x x
7	*reliable*	reliability	rely	reliably
8	*various*	variety	vary	x x x x x
9	*peculiar*	peculiarity	x x x x x	peculiarly
10	x x x x x	growth	*grow (irreg.)*	x x x x x
11	*vast*	vastness	x x x x x	vastly
12	protective	protection	*protect*	protectively
13	dangerous	*danger*	endanger	dangerously
14	apparent	*appearance*	*appear*	apparently
15	energetic	*energy*	x x x x x	energetically
16	constructive	construction	*construct*	constructively
17	x x x x x	*companion*	accompany	x x x x x
18	x x x x x	treatment	*treat*	x x x x x
19	respectful	*respect*	respect	respectfully
20	sympathetic	*sympathy*	sympathize	sympathetically
21	*generous*	generosity	x x x x x	generously
22	*affectionate*	affection	x x x x x	affectionately
23	kind	*kindness*	x x x x x	kindly
24	x x x x x	*endurance*	*endure*	x x x x x
25	painless / painful	*pain*	pain	painlessly / painfully
26	impressive	impression	*impress*	impressively
27	x x x x x	proof	*prove*	x x x x x
28	x x x x x	*warning*	*warn*	x x x x x
29	x x x x x	*attack*	attack	x x x x x
30	wealthy	*wealth*	x x x x x	x x x x x
31	warm	warmth	warm	*warmly*
32	*calm*	calmness	x x x x x	calmly

EXERCISE 50. Use the correct form of each italicized word in the sentence which follows. Notice the first two examples. Refer to the word form chart and examples whenever necessary.

1	*modest*	People always remember him for his *modesty*.
2	*sympathy*	He tried to *sympathize* with their troubles.
3	*respect*	They tried to show their _____ for him.
4	*affectionate*	He spoke to all of the young people _____.
5	*warmly*	The family gave Johnny a _____ welcome.
6	*create*	His motives were always kind and _____.
7	*various*	Johnny tried to _____ his method each time.
8	*survive*	What is the reason for the _____ of the story?
9	*appear*	He noticed the _____ of wealth and civilization.
10	*endure*	He proved his _____ to the Indians.
11	*attack*	The Indians had _____ the settlers two times.
12	*treat*	He always received good _____ from the Indians.
13	*warn*	Johnny's _____ saved the lives of the settlers.
14	*prove*	He gave them _____ of his ability to endure pain.
15	*impress*	Johnny made a strong _____ on the Indians.
16	*calm*	The doctor mentioned Johnny's _____.
17	*energy*	Johnny continued to be an _____ person.
18	*danger*	The snakes in the tall grass were _____.
19	*peculiar*	People often spoke about his many _____.
20	*grow*	He noticed the rapid _____ of the population.
21	*violent*	Johnny did not approve of any kind of _____.
22	*construct*	He used cardboard in the _____ of his old hat.
23	*vast*	He loved the _____ of the hills and forests.
24	*wealth*	Some of the people in the region became _____.
25	*hostile*	_____ was not one of Johnny's motives.
26	*kind*	He was treated with _____ in the settlements.
27	*pain*	The injury from the accident was very _____.
28	*protect*	The settlers needed _____ for their legs.
29	*voluntary*	Johnny had _____ to do all of these things.
30	*companion*	The gray wolf _____ Johnny constantly.
31	*generous*	People noticed his great _____ with children.
32	*reliable*	Can we _____ on this report of his activities?

EXERCISE 51. Study the following examples for the preceding word form chart. The numbers correspond to those on the word form chart.

1   **modest, modesty, modestly.**   He was a *modest* man. He spoke about himself *modestly*. *Modesty* is an unusual quality.

2   **survival, survive.**   The story of his life has *survived* through the years. His unusual qualities were responsible for the *survival* of the story.

3   **voluntary, volunteer, voluntarily.**   His work was *voluntary*. He worked *voluntarily*. He *volunteered* to do the work. He worked as a *volunteer*.

4   **creative, creation, create, creatively.**   He was a *creative* person. He worked *creatively*. He *created* apple orchards in pleasant spots. He was interested in the *creation* of beauty.

5   **violent, violence, violate, violently.**   He wasn't a *violent* person. He didn't speak *violently*. He didn't approve of *violence*. He didn't *violate* his religious beliefs.

6   **hostile, hostility.**   He wasn't a *hostile* person. He didn't approve of *hostility*.

7   **reliable, reliability, reliably.**   He was a *reliable* person. He always worked *reliably*. *Reliability* was one of his qualities.

8   **various, variety, vary.**   He planted his seeds in *various* places. He chose a *variety* of places. He always *varied* his selection of orchard sites.

9   **peculiar, peculiarity, peculiarly.**   He was a *peculiar* person. He always dressed *peculiarly*. People spoke about his *peculiarities*.

10   **growth, grow.**   Flowers *grow* in many places. Flowers *grew* along the river. Flowers have *grown* in this place for many years. The *growth* of the flowers was rapid. The population *grew* rapidly. The *growth* of the population was rapid.

11   **vast, vastness, vastly.**   There were *vast* regions of trees. The settlers discovered the *vastness* of the level areas. There was a *vast* improvement in the conditions. The conditions were improved *vastly*.

12   **protective, protection, protect, protectively.**   They *protected* their property from the Indians. *Protection* was important. They were very *protective* of their land. They took *protection* against the Indians. They kept watch over their land *protectively*.

13   **dangerous, danger, endanger, dangerously.**   There was constant *danger* in the forests. There were *dangerous* animals in the forests. He lived *dangerously*. He *endangered* his safety by trying to warn the settlers.

114

14 **apparent, appearance, appear, apparently.** His *appearance* surprised people. *In appearance,* he was small and thin. He *appeared* to be hungry. His endurance was *apparent*. *Apparently,* he felt little pain.

15 **energetic, energy, energetically.** He was an *energetic* person. He did his work *energetically*. He had a great deal of *energy*.

16 **constructive, construction, construct, constructively.** He *constructed* an unusual hat. He used cardboard in the *construction* of the hat. He was a *constructive* person. He worked *constructively*.

17 **companion, accompany.** A gray wolf was his constant *companion*. The wolf *accompanied* him everywhere.

18 **treatment, treat.** The Indians *treated* him kindly. He was *treated* kindly everywhere. He received kind *treatment* from the Indians.

19 **respectful, respect, respectfully.** He was treated with *respect*. He was treated *respectfully*. The Indians were *respectful* of him. They *respected* him.

20 **sympathetic, sympathy, sympathize, sympathetically.** His *sympathy* was apparent. He *had great sympathy* for people's troubles. He *sympathized* with them. He was *sympathetic* to their problems. He answered their questions *sympathetically*.

21 **generous, generosity, generously.** He was *generous* with children. He treated children *generously*. Children appreciated his *generosity*.

22 **affectionate, affection, affectionately.** He was *affectionate* with children. He treated children *affectionately*. He *had great affection* for children. His *affection* was apparent.

23 **kind, kindness, kindly.** The Indians were *kind* to him. The Indians treated him *kindly*. They treated him with *kindness*.

24 **endurance, endure.** He could *endure* great pain. He proved his *endurance*.

25 **painful, painless, pain, painfully, painlessly.** The *pain* didn't bother him. The wound didn't *pain* him. The wound wasn't *painful*. The wound was *painless*. He didn't cry *painfully*. The operation was performed *painlessly*.

26 **impressive, impression, impress, impressively.** His ability *impressed* everyone greatly. The *impression* was a strong one. His ability *made a strong impression* on everyone. Everyone *got the impression* that it was painless. His ability was *impressive*. He proved his ability *impressively*.

27 **proof, prove.** He *proved* his endurance. He *gave them proof* of his endurance. The *proof* was impressive.

28 **warning, warn.** He *warned* the settlers of the attack. The *warning* saved the settlers' lives. He *gave them warning* of the approaching attack.

29 **attack.** The Indians *attacked* the small village. The settlers knew about the *attack* in advance.

30 **wealthy, wealth.** There wasn't much *wealth* in the small village. A few people were *wealthy*. Not many *wealthy* people lived there.

31 **warm, warmth, warmly.** They were *warm* people. They welcomed him *warmly*. He appreciated the *warmth* of their welcome.

32 **calm, calmness, calmly.** He was always *calm*. He accepted things *calmly*. Everyone noticed his *calmness*.

EXERCISE 52. Select the correct way to complete each of the following sentences. Write each sentence in its correct form.

1 People remember the story of Johnny Appleseed because (*a*) he did everything voluntarily. (*b*) he had unusual qualities. (*c*) he was violent and hostile. (*d*) he wanted to create orchards.

2 Johnny's trip down the Ohio River in 1806 took a great deal of time because (*a*) he had two regular routes for his trips. (*b*) the boat had an odd cargo. (*c*) there was no reliable account of his movements. (*d*) he stopped at every pleasant spot to plant seeds.

3 The settlers were careful to protect their legs against (*a*) Johnny's small enclosures. (*b*) the vast regions of small trees. (*c*) bears, wolves, and deer. (*d*) the constant danger of reptiles.

4 Johnny was a friend of young people wherever he went because of (*a*) his unusual companion. (*b*) his sympathy for youthful troubles. (*c*) his ability to endure pain. (*d*) his odd garments and hats.

5 The rude frontier men always treated Johnny (*a*) oddly and violently. (*b*) with the inspiration of a poet. (*c*) calmly and serenely. (*d*) with great respect.

6 The Indians were greatly impressed by Johnny's (*a*) load of apple seeds. (*b*) kind and creative motives. (*c*) generosity and affection with children. (*d*) strange appearance and odd actions.

7   Once Johnny traveled along the border for several days without food or sleep (*a*) to warn every settler of an approaching attack. (*b*) to prove his endurance to the Indians. (*c*) to nurse the wolf back to good health. (*d*) to keep in advance of a wave of settlement.

8   Thirty-seven years after his first appearance on Licking Creek, Johnny noticed that (*a*) his work had covered a hundred thousand square miles. (*b*) settlers were killed and tortured by the Indians. (*c*) settlers had removed his trees and replanted them. (*d*) civilization, wealth, and population were appearing in the wilderness of Ohio.

9   In 1838, Johnny said a solemn farewell to all the families in that region because (*a*) the girls and boys were now mothers and heads of families. (*b*) there was no danger of another war. (*c*) he felt his work there was done. (*d*) the western border of Ohio and Indiana possessed great romantic beauty.

10   During the years 1838 to 1847, Johnny (*a*) refused to eat with families. (*b*) continued his odd work on the western border of Ohio and Indiana. (*c*) was a great "medicine man" in an Indian village. (*d*) traveled down the Ohio River in a peculiar boat.

Better Known
as Mark Twain

THIS REMARKABLE MAN went to a log-cabin school until he was twelve years old. That was the end of his formal education. In spite of this, he became the most famous literary figure of his generation. He received honorary degrees from Oxford University and Yale University. People speak of him as the best known humorous writer of all times. He also brought realism and western local color to American fiction. He made millions of dollars by writing articles, short stories, and books. His real name was Samuel Langhorne Clemens, but he is better known all over the world as Mark Twain.

Mark Twain was born in a small Missouri village near the Mississippi River in 1835. At that time, Andrew Jackson was the president of the country. Abraham Lincoln was still a young farm laborer in Illinois. The first railroad had been built seven years before. The Industrial Revolution was at hand. The economic collapse of American prosperity, called the Panic of 1837, still lay ahead. This was also the literary period later called the "New England Renaissance."

Mark Twain was not a healthy baby. In fact, he was not expected to live through the first winter. But with his mother's tender care, he managed to survive. He had been born in a tiny two-room cabin. Eight people lived together there. He had four brothers and sisters. A slave girl lived with them too.

As a boy, Mark Twain caused much trouble for his parents. He used to play practical jokes on all of his friends and neighbors. The nature of his jokes often led to violence. He hated to go to school, and

remarkable	generation	fiction	renaissance	survive
log cabin	honorary	laborer	tender	tiny
formal	degree	railroad	manage	slave
education	humorous	industrial	collapse	practical joke
in spite of	of all times	revolution	prosperity	nature
literary	realism	at hand	panic	lead
figure	local color	economic	lay ahead	violence

he constantly ran away from home. He always went in the direction of the nearby Mississippi. He was fascinated by that mighty river. He liked to sit on the bank of the river for hours at a time and just gaze at the mysterious islands and the passing boats and rafts. He was nearly drowned nine different times. He learned many things about the river during those days. He learned all about its history and the unusual people who rode up and down it. He never forgot those scenes and those people. He later made them part of the history of America in his books *Tom Sawyer* and *Huckleberry Finn*.

Mark Twain inherited his genius for humor from his mother. Obviously, he did not inherit it from his father. He once stated that he had never seen a smile on his father's face. On the other hand, his mother had the rare ability to say humorous things with perfect innocence. This same ability made Mark Twain an extremely humorous public speaker.

After his father's death in 1847, Mark Twain left school and became a printer's apprentice. His mother felt that he would make a living and get some education in this way. He worked for the printer as an apprentice for two years. During that time, he received only his board and clothes as pay.

By 1853, Mark Twain was tired of Missouri. He got an urge to see the world and started out with empty pockets. He worked as a printer in St. Louis, Chicago, New York, and Philadelphia. Then, as a result of reading a book, he decided to go to the upper part of the Amazon River. He planned to make a fortune by collecting and selling cocoa. His only problem was money for the trip. That problem was solved in an unusual way. He found a fifty-dollar bill on the sidewalk and left for Brazil the next day. He got as far as the Mississippi River and then ran out of money.

Next Mark Twain decided to become a river-boat pilot on the Mississippi. He followed his new profession for fifteen months. He memorized all the turns, shallow spots, and dangerous rocks in the 1200 miles from St. Louis to New Orleans. He learned about the pride and responsibilities of the pilots. He became an excellent pilot. However,

constantly	scene	extremely	make a fortune	memorize
run away	inherit	public	cocoa	turn
nearby	genius	apprentice	solve	shallow
fascinate	humor	make a living	bill	spot
gaze	obviously	board	sidewalk	dangerous
mysterious	on the other hand	urge	run out	rock
raft	rare	empty	pilot	pride
drown	innocence	as a result	profession	responsibility

his life as a pilot came to a sudden end. The river was closed to navigation at the outbreak of the Civil War. Then he joined the Confederate Army, but shortly after that, his company was disbanded. He did not join the army again.

He followed his brother Orion to Nevada in 1861 and consequently took up his next profession. He became a miner in this frontier region. During this period, he started to write short articles. The publisher of the *Enterprise* in Virginia City, Nevada recognized Mark Twain's ability and offered him a job as an editor with a salary of $25 a week. He walked 125 miles over bad roads and rough country to accept the job. It was at this time that he adopted the pen name "Mark Twain."

Later Mark Twain worked in San Francisco for a while and then became a miner again. In his spare time, he wrote a short story called "The Celebrated Jumping Frog of Calaveras County." This story made him known all over the country, and he decided to become a full-time writer and lecturer. He went to New York in 1867 and published his first book that year. His next book, *Innocents Abroad*, was published in 1869. It was a report of his European tour as a Westerner saw it. It was a completely new kind of travel book. It gave him a national reputation.

In 1870, Mark Twain was married to Olivia Langdon in Elmira, New York. It was an extremely successful marriage. They were devoted to each other throughout their lives. His wife Olivia had a strong and lasting influence on his writing. She edited almost all of his manuscripts. Among other things, she was always careful to remove all of the bad words. He always accepted her changes without argument. In the years following his marriage, he wrote the books for which he is most famous: *Tom Sawyer* in 1876, *Huckleberry Finn* in 1884, and *A Connecticut Yankee in King Arthur's Court* in 1889.

Unfortunately, Mark Twain had no business ability at all. He made vast profits from writing and lecturing, but time after time, he lost money in bad investments. He finally lost his entire fortune in the publishing business in 1895. He took the responsibility for all of his

come to an end	frontier	spare time	reputation	remove
navigation	region	celebrate	successful	argument
outbreak	period	frog	marriage	Yankee
join	publisher	county	devote	court
army	editor	full time	throughout	vast
disband	salary	lecturer	last	profit
consequently	rough	innocent	influence	time after time
take up	adopt	abroad	edit	investment
miner	pen name	tour	manuscript	

debts. He wrote large numbers of stories in order to pay those debts. He made a successful tour around the world. He was finally able to pay. Despite the tremendous effort this had required, he had been able to keep his health. His life had worse tragedies than the financial ones, however. His wife Olivia died in 1904. Three of his children had died previously.

At the age of seventy, his hair was completely white. He decided to buy fourteen white suits and a hundred white neckties. He wore nothing but white from head to foot until his death in Redding, Connecticut on April 21, 1910.

| debt | tremendous | require | financial | from head to foot |
| despite | effort | tragedy | previously | |

QUESTIONS FOR ORAL AND WRITTEN PRACTICE

(1) What kind of school did Mark Twain go to? (2) How long did he go to school? (3) What did he become? (4) From whom did he receive honorary degrees? (5) How do people speak of him? (6) What did he bring to American fiction? (7) How much money did he make? (8) How did he make this money? (9) What was his real name? (10) By what name is he known all over the world? (11) Where was he born? (12) When was he born? (13) What kind of house was he born in? (14) How many people lived in the cabin? (15) Who were those people? (16) How did he manage to survive his first winter? (17) Did he cause his parents much trouble? How? (18) Where did he always go? (19) Why did he always go toward the

Mississippi River? (20) What did he like to do when he sat on the bank of the river? (21) What did he learn during those days? (22) How did he use those Mississippi River scenes later? (23) Where did Mark Twain get his genius for humor? (24) Why did he obviously not inherit it from his father? (25) What rare ability did his mother have? (26) Why was Mark Twain an extremely humorous public speaker? (27) What did he do after his father's death? (28) How did his mother feel about this? (29) How long did he work for the printer as an apprentice? (30) What did he receive as pay during that time? (31) What happened to Mark Twain in 1853? (32) Where did he work as a printer? (33) Where did he decide to go as a result of reading a book? (34) What did he plan to do there? (35) What was his only problem? (36) How was that problem solved? (37) How far did he get? (38) What did he decide to become next? (39) How long did he follow that profession? (40) How many miles did he travel from St. Louis to New Orleans? (41) What did he memorize? (42) Why did his life as a pilot come to a sudden end? (43) When did he follow his brother to Nevada? (44) Who first recognized Mark Twain's ability as a writer? (45) What kind of job did the publisher offer him? (46) What did Mark Twain do in order to accept the job? (47) When did Mark Twain go to New York and publish his first book? (48) What was the name of his next book? (49) What was the book about? (50) Whom did Mark Twain marry in 1870? (51) What kind of influence did his wife have on his writing? (52) How did his wife help him? (53) What are the names of some of his most famous books? (54) When were they published? (55) What happened to all the profits he made from writing and lecturing? (56) How did he lose his entire fortune in 1895? (57) What did he do in order to pay his debts? (58) What other tragedies did his life have? (59) What did Mark Twain decide to do at the age of seventy? (60) When did Mark Twain die?

SUMMARY SENTENCES FOR LABORATORY PRACTICE

(1) He only went to school until he was twelve. (2) That was the end of his formal education. (3) He became famous in spite of this. (4) He became a famous humorous writer. (5) He made millions of dollars by writing. (6) His real name was Samuel Clemens. (7) But everyone remembers him as "Mark Twain." (8) He was born in Missouri in 1835. (9) He led an interesting and unusual life. (10) He was born in a tiny two-room cabin. (11) He was not ex-

pected to live through the winter. (12) But he managed to survive. (13) He caused his parents much trouble. (14) He used to play jokes on everyone. (15) He hated to go to school. (16) He often ran away from home because of school. (17) He loved to sit on the banks of the Mississippi. (18) He was fascinated by the river. (19) He was nearly drowned many times. (20) He learned many things about the river. (21) He never forgot the scenes or the people. (22) Later, he wrote about them in his books. (23) He became an extremely humorous public speaker. (24) He inherited his sense of humor from his mother. (25) He had never seen a smile on his father's face. (26) He left school after his father's death. (27) He became a printer's apprentice. (28) He worked on this job for two years. (29) He received only his board and clothes as pay. (30) But he got some education. (31) He also made a living. (32) Then he got an urge to see the world. (33) He worked as a printer in many big cities. (34) Once he decided to go to South America. (35) He planned to make a fortune. (36) But he didn't have any money for the trip. (37) Then he found fifty dollars on the street. (38) He left for Brazil the next day. (39) But he ran out of money very soon. (40) Then he took a trip down the Mississippi. (41) He decided to become a river-boat pilot. (42) He became an excellent pilot. (43) He learned all the turns and dangerous spots. (44) He was a pilot for fifteen months. (45) Then he followed his brother to Nevada. (46) He became a miner in the frontier region. (47) He started to write articles. (48) A publisher recognized his ability. (49) He got a job as a newspaper editor. (50) He walked 125 miles to accept the job. (51) He went to New York in 1867. (52) He published his first book that same year. (53) Then he took a European tour. (54) He wrote a book about this tour. (55) The book gave him a national reputation. (56) He got married in 1870. (57) It was a successful marriage. (58) His wife had a strong influence on his writing. (59) He accepted her changes without argument. (60) He wrote many books and made much money. (61) But he had no business ability at all. (62) He lost much money in bad investments. (63) He lost all of his money in the publishing business. (64) He took the responsibility for his debts. (65) He traveled around the world and wrote many stories. (66) He was finally able to pay his debts. (67) Three of his children died before 1904. (68) He lived to be seventy years old. (69) He wore nothing but white until his death.

EXERCISE 53. From the column at the left, select the best synonym for the italicized word in each sentence. Rewrite the sentences using the synonyms.

dispute
continuing
rough
pay
uncommon
took out
free
whole
amazing
almost
loving
stare
clearly
desire
very small
great

1 He was born in a *tiny* cabin near the river.
2 His mother's *tender* attention saved his life.
3 His mother had a *rare* ability for humor.
4 *Obviously*, he inherited his ability from her.
5 He was interested in the *mighty* Mississippi.
6 He liked to *gaze* at the passing boats.
7 He was *nearly* drowned nine different times.
8 He felt an *urge* to travel around the world.
9 As an editor, his *salary* was $25 per week.
10 He wrote a story in his *spare* time.
11 Olivia had a *lasting* influence on his work.
12 She *removed* things from his manuscripts.
13 He accepted her changes without *argument*.
14 He finally lost his *entire* fortune.
15 He was a *remarkable* lecturer and humorist.

EXERCISE 54. From the column at the left, select the correct word for each blank space in the sentences at the right. Use each word only once. Do not change the forms of the words.

shallow
ran out
vast
fascinated
violence
debts
managed
constantly
recognized
realism
rafts
took up
degrees
genius
devoted
pride

1 Despite his health, he _____ to survive.
2 He inherited his _____ for humor.
3 His practical jokes often led to _____.
4 Young Sam _____ ran away from home.
5 He was _____ by the mighty Mississippi.
6 He liked to gaze at the passing _____.
7 He _____ of money before reaching Brazil.
8 He memorized the _____ spots in the river.
9 The river-boat pilots had much _____.
10 He _____ mining as a profession in 1861.
11 A publisher _____ Mark Twain's ability.
12 He was _____ to his wife Olivia.
13 He made _____ profits from his stories.
14 He took the responsibility for his _____.
15 Mark Twain brought _____ to American fiction.

EXERCISE 55. Supply the correct preposition for each blank space.

1 He made millions _____ dollars _____ writing stories.
2 He inherited his genius _____ humor _____ his mother.
3 He lost his money _____ bad investments time _____ time.
4 He found $50 _____ the sidewalk and left _____ Brazil.
5 He wrote many stories _____ order to pay his debts.
6 He learned many things _____ the river and its history.
7 He brought realism _____ American fiction.
8 He worked _____ a printer _____ an apprentice.
9 He worked _____ San Francisco _____ a while.
10 He became a miner _____ the frontier region.
11 He made a successful tour _____ the world.
12 He started his trip _____ empty pockets.
13 He was married _____ Olivia Langdon _____ 1870.
14 He wore nothing but white _____ head _____ foot.
15 He died _____ Connecticut _____ April 21, 1910.

EXERCISE 56. From the column at the right, select the correct line to complete each of the numbered lines at the left. Write each sentence in its correct form.

1	The publisher offered him	(A)	closed to navigation
2	He used to play	(B)	the turns and shallow spots
3	The story made him	(C)	to accept the job
4	The Mississippi River was	(D)	was published in 1869
5	With his mother's care	(E)	known all over the country
6	In his spare time	(F)	a job as an editor
7	He wore nothing	(G)	came to a sudden end
8	He walked 125 miles	(H)	a full-time writer
9	He decided to become	(I)	by that mighty river
10	He took the responsibility	(J)	for all of his debts
11	He memorized all	(K)	he wrote a short story
12	His life as a pilot	(L)	he managed to survive
13	He lost his fortune	(M)	jokes on his friends
14	A report of his tour	(N)	in the publishing business
15	He was fascinated	(O)	but white until his death

EXERCISE 57. Study the following word form chart carefully. The word forms which occurred in the preceding story are italicized.

	ADJECTIVE	NOUN	VERB	ADVERB
1	*humorous*	*humor*	x x x x x	humorously
2	prosperous	*prosperity*	prosper	prosperously
3	*tender*	tenderness	x x x x x	tenderly
4	x x x x x	fascination	*fascinate*	x x x x x
5	*mysterious*	mystery	x x x x x	mysteriously
6	historical	*history*	x x x x x	historically
7	x x x x x	inheritance	*inherit*	x x x x x
8	*perfect*	perfection	perfect	perfectly
9	innocent	*innocence*	x x x x x	innocently
10	dead	*death*	die	x x x x x
11	*empty*	emptiness	empty	x x x x x
12	decisive	decision	*decide*	decisively
13	solvable	solution	*solve*	x x x x x
14	professional	*profession*	x x x x x	professionally
15	x x x x x	memory	*memorize*	x x x x x
16	responsible	*responsibility*	x x x x x	responsibly
17	proud	*pride*	x x x x x	proudly
18	*dangerous*	danger	endanger	dangerously
19	*excellent*	excellence	excel	excellently
20	*sudden*	suddenness	x x x x x	suddenly
21	complete	completion	complete	*completely*
22	*national*	nation	x x x x x	nationally
23	*successful*	success	succeed	successfully
24	x x x x x	marriage	*marry*	x x x x x
25	x x x x x	devotion	devote	x x x x x
26	influential	*influence*	influence	x x x x x
27	x x x x x	acceptance	*accept*	x x x x x
28	argumentative	*argument*	argue	argumentatively
29	profitable	*profit*	profit	profitably
30	x x x x x	*investment*	invest	x x x x x
31	tragic	*tragedy*	x x x x x	tragically
32	x x x x x	requirement	*require*	x x x x x

128

EXERCISE 58. Use the correct form of each italicized word in the sentence which follows. Notice the first two examples. Refer to the word form chart and examples whenever necessary.

1	*innocence*	He told the story with an *innocent* expression.
2	*solve*	He found an easy *solution* to his problem.
3	*pride*	He was _____ of his ability as a pilot.
4	*empty*	The _____ of his pockets did not frighten him.
5	*mysterious*	He described the _____ in some of his books.
6	*decide*	He made a _____ to leave his home.
7	*completely*	He _____ his first book in 1867.
8	*dangerous*	He did not try to avoid the _____.
9	*profession*	He became a _____ writer and lecturer.
10	*humor*	People appreciated his _____ stories.
11	*tender*	He survived because of her _____ care.
12	*perfect*	He was _____ serious when he said it.
13	*fascinate*	There was a strange _____ about the islands.
14	*excellent*	During that time, he became an _____ writer.
15	*profit*	He made great _____ by writing books.
16	*tragedy*	His wife's death was a _____ event.
17	*successful*	He finally _____ in paying all of his debts.
18	*prosperity*	Everyone was _____ during that period.
19	*influence*	His wife had an _____ on his writing.
20	*require*	The payment of his debts _____ all his effort.
21	*death*	His father _____ when he was twelve years old.
22	*investment*	What did he _____ his entire fortune in?
23	*sudden*	He made a _____ change in his plans.
24	*argument*	He seldom _____ with his wife about her changes.
25	*memorize*	His good _____ helped him in his writing.
26	*marry*	Why was their _____ so successful?
27	*inherit*	He _____ no money at all from his father.
28	*responsibility*	His friends knew he was a _____ person.
29	*national*	His stories made him famous _____.
30	*devote*	He wrote about his _____ to his wife.
31	*history*	Later, he wrote several _____ novels.
32	*accept*	He wrote a letter of _____ to the editor.

EXERCISE 59. Study the following examples for the preceding word form chart. The numbers correspond to those on the word form chart.

1 **humorous, humor, humorously.** He was a *humorous* writer. He wrote about people *humorously*. People appreciated his *humor*.

2 **prosperous, prosperity, prosper, prosperously.** It was a period of *prosperity*. Everyone *prospered* because of business. People were *prosperous* because of business. They spent their money *prosperously*.

3 **tender, tenderness, tenderly.** His mother treated him with *tenderness*. His mother treated him *tenderly*. His mother gave him *tender* care.

4 **fascination, fascinate.** The river *fascinated* him. It was a *fascinating* sight. He couldn't resist the *fascination* of the river.

5 **mysterious, mystery, mysteriously.** He gazed at the *mysterious* islands. The islands attracted him *mysteriously*. Later he wrote about the *mystery* of the islands. People usually enjoy *mysteries*.

6 **historical, history, historically.** He enjoyed studying *history*. He read about *historical* events. Certain events were important *historically*.

7 **inheritance, inherit.** He *inherited* this ability from his mother. This *inheritance* made him a wonderful speaker.

8 **perfect (adj.), perfection, perfect (verb), perfectly.** He gave a *perfect* answer. He gave the answer *perfectly*. He did everything with great *perfection*. He *perfected* his style of writing.

9 **innocent, innocence, innocently.** He gave an *innocent* answer. He gave the answer *innocently*. He spoke with great *innocence*.

10 **dead, death, die.** His father *died* when he was away. His father was *dead* when he returned. His father's *death* caused problems.

11 **empty, emptiness.** He looked at the *empty* drawer. The *emptiness* of the drawer surprised him. He *emptied* his suitcase looking for money.

12 **decisive, decision, decide, decisively.** He *decided* to leave his home. Was his *decision* a good one? He *made the decision* after his father had died. He *reached a decision* after much consideration. It was a *decisive* event. He spoke *decisively*.

13 **solvable, solution, solve.** The problem was *solvable*. He *solved* the problem easily. The *solution* to the problem was simple. He *found the solution* easily.

14 **professional, profession, professionally.**   Writing was his *profession*. He was a *professional* writer. He was a *professional*. He wrote stories and articles *professionally*.

15 **memory, memorize.**   His *memory* was good. He *had a good memory*. He *memorized* all the turns in the river.

16 **responsible, responsibility, responsibly.**   He was a very *responsible* person. He always acted *responsibly*. He *had a responsibility* to help his mother. He *felt a responsibility* to pay his debts. Some people never *take responsibilities*. His *responsibility* was a great one.

17 **proud, pride, proudly.**   He was *proud* of his ability as a pilot. He spoke about his work *proudly*. His *pride* was obvious. He *took pride in* his work.

18 **dangerous, danger, endanger, dangerously.**   There were many *dangerous* situations along the way. Once the boat moved from side to side *dangerously*. The movement of the boat *endangered* the passengers. The *danger* didn't frighten him. He *was in danger* many times during his trip.

19 **excellent, excellence, excel, excellently.**   He was an *excellent* lecturer. He told jokes *excellently*. He *excelled* in lecturing. Everyone recognized his *excellence*.

20 **sudden, suddenness, suddenly.**   There was a *sudden* explosion. The boat stopped *suddenly*. The *suddenness* surprised everyone.

21 **complete, completion, completely.**   He *completed* a book of short stories. He returned after the *completion* of his work. The *completed* book was sent to the publisher. The *complete* edition contained all of the stories. The stories were *completely* original. He described childhood scenes *completely*. The publisher sold his stock of books *completely*.

22 **national, nation, nationally.**   His stories were read all over the *nation*. His books were distributed *nationally*. His stories gave him a *national* reputation.

23 **successful, success, succeed, successfully.**   His books were *successful*. He became a *successful* author. He published his books *successfully*. He *succeeded* in making a fortune. His *success* in writing brought many problems.

24 **marriage, marry.**   He *married* Olivia Langdon. They *married* in 1870. He *got married* to her in Elmira, New York. Their *marriage* was successful.

25 **devotion, devote.** He *devoted* much time to his work. They were *devoted* to each other. She was a *devoted* wife. People noticed their *devotion* to each other.

26 **influential, influence.** She *had an influence* on his writing. Her *influence* on his writing was noticeable. She *influenced* him in his writing. His wife was *influential* in his success.

27 **acceptance, accept.** He *accepted* his wife's advice. She was pleased by his *acceptance* of her advice.

28 **argumentative, argument, argue, argumentatively.** He *had an argument* with his friend. It was an *argument* about politics. He seldom *argued* with his wife about anything. He was an *argumentative* person. He wrote about many subjects *argumentatively*.

29 **profitable, profit, profitably.** He *made a profit* every year. He *profited* from writing and lecturing. His *profit* from his investment was small. Publishing wasn't a *profitable* business for him. He didn't invest his money *profitably*.

30 **investment, invest.** He *invested* his money in the publishing business. He lost his money in that *investment*.

31 **tragic, tragedy, tragically.** He wrote a *tragic* story. The story ended *tragically*. The *tragedy* occurred at the end of the story.

32 **requirement, require.** His work *required* much time. He spent the *required* amount of time on his writing. The *requirement* in time was very great.

EXERCISE 60. Select the correct way to complete each of the following sentences. Write each sentence in its correct form.

1 Mark Twain inherited his genius for humor (*a*) as a result of reading a book. (*b*) by learning the history of the Mississippi River. (*c*) because he was born during a period of economic collapse. (*d*) from his mother.

2 He became a printer's apprentice because his mother felt (*a*) he would make a living and get some education. (*b*) he would learn all about the unusual people who rode on river boats. (*c*) he would become a full-time writer and lecturer. (*d*) he would make a fortune as a miner.

3 Mark Twain started to write short articles (*a*) while he was a miner in the frontier region. (*b*) after he had written his two most famous books. (*c*) after he had lost his entire fortune in the publishing business. (*d*) during the Panic of 1837.

4   He decided to go to the upper part of the Amazon (*a*) because he memorized all the turns, shallow spots, and dangerous rocks in the river.   (*b*) as a result of reading a book.   (*c*) after a short story made him known all over the country.   (*d*) because time after time, he made bad investments.

5   He published his first book (*a*) in 1853.   (*b*) in 1861.   (*c*) in 1867.   (*d*) in 1870.   (*e*) in 1876.

6   He was an extremely humorous public speaker because (*a*) of his urge to see the world.   (*b*) he knew about the pride and responsibilities of river-boat pilots.   (*c*) of his ability to say humorous things with perfect innocence.   (*d*) he adopted the pen name "Mark Twain."

7   His book *Innocents Abroad,* published in 1869, was (*a*) about his life as a miner in the frontier region.   (*b*) a report of his European tour as a Westerner saw it.   (*c*) written while Andrew Jackson was the president of the country.   (*d*) the worst tragedy in his life.

8   He wrote the books for which he is most famous (*a*) during the Civil War.   (*b*) after his marriage to Olivia Langdon.   (*c*) after the death of his wife.   (*d*) before his first trip.

9   He lost his money time after time (*a*) from writing and lecturing. (*b*) because his wife had a strong and lasting influence on his writing.   (*c*) because of his tours.   (*d*) through lack of business ability.

10   In order to pay all of his debts, (*a*) he wrote large numbers of stories.   (*b*) he was careful to remove all of the bad words from his manuscripts.   (*c*) he followed his brother to Nevada.   (*d*) he decided to become a river-boat pilot.

THOMAS A. EDISON

The Wizard
of Menlo Park

By Marshall C. Harrington

ALTHOUGH TODAY he is considered one of the greatest inventors in the memory of man, Thomas Alva Edison failed to complete even his first year in elementary school! At the age of twelve, he decided that he disliked mathematics. As a practical and self-educated man, he cared little about theory and abstraction. He was often wrong, especially in his explanations of the scientific principles on which his inventions were based. Nevertheless, he introduced thousands of devices which enriched the industrial, economic, and social life of the entire world.

Thomas Edison was born in Ohio on February 11, 1847. At the

wizard	fail	educate	principle	enrich
although	elementary	theory	invention	industrial
consider	dislike	abstraction	base	economic
inventor	mathematics	explanation	nevertheless	social
memory	practical	scientific	device	

usual age, he was sent to school, but his mother removed him from school after only three months. His mother had been a school teacher before her marriage. With this experience, she was able to continue her son's education at home. At the age of ten, Thomas was able to read rather difficult books. Although he continued to read throughout his life, he had no use for the ancient classics, and he made fun of the educational procedures of schools and colleges. After he left home, he learned through his own efforts.

Edison's interest in science began when he read a textbook of general science at the age of ten or eleven. It is typical of his personality that he often found incorrect conclusions in the work of others even at this age!

Edison's family was not poor. However, his interest in experiments led to considerable expense, and he asked for permission to earn money by selling newspapers on a train. After getting a little experience in this work, he organized his own newspaper business and employed boys to sell papers on other trains. All of his earnings went into chemicals and supplies. He appropriated an empty baggage car on the train for his laboratory. In this way, he could spend all the spare time on each trip usefully.

Edison began experiments in electricity during his years as a paper boy on the train. The telegraph interested him particularly, and he studied to be a telegraph operator. During the Civil War, the demand for telegraph operators increased, and at the age of fifteen, Edison secured a position at Port Huron, Michigan as a night operator. Because he used his days for experiments, he needed sleep at night. However, he was required to send a signal every hour during the night to show that he was on duty. This led to Edison's first invention. He invented a device to send the signal for him while he slept!

In 1868, Edison obtained a position in the Western Union office in Boston. However, his inventions were taking more and more of his

remove	educational	experiment	appropriate	the Civil War
marriage	procedure	lead	baggage	secure
experience	effort	considerable	laboratory	position
education	science	expense	spare time	require
rather	textbook	permission	usefully	signal
throughout	typical	organize	electricity	on duty
have no use for	personality	employ	telegraph	invent
ancient	incorrect	earnings	particularly	obtain
classic	conclusion	chemical	operator	take time
make fun of	however	supplies		

time. In 1868, he received his first patent for an automatic vote recorder for the House of Representatives. Edison thought that it would save much time and confusion. However, it was rejected for this same reason. The legislators did not wish to lose the effective weapon of roll-calls which consumed much time. Edison made a decision then and there. In the future, he would work on only those inventions for which there was a definite need.

Edison lost all of his money on the experiments on the automatic vote recorder, and in 1869, he arrived in New York penniless and hungry. Within a few days, he had a job at three hundred dollars a month as the supervisor of an electric device for indicating the price of gold in brokers' offices in Manhattan. Shortly after that, he left the Gold Indicator Company in order to devote his entire time to his own inventions. Improvements in stock tickers, telegraph repeaters, and automatic and duplex telegraphy soon followed. Very much to his surprise, his first sale of an invention brought him forty thousand dollars. The invention was an improved stock ticker.

Edison soon started manufacturing stock tickers to meet the demand. He employed fifty men in two shifts, and he was the foreman for both shifts! Workers found it difficult to satisfy Edison because he expected them to be as tireless as he. They called him the "old man" before he was thirty!

The quadruplex telegraph in 1874 was Edison's first major achievement. His next important production was the carbon microphone. Probably Edison's most original invention was the phonograph in 1877.

It is easy to see that Edison had many interests. At one time, he was working on fifty inventions simultaneously. Because of his excellent memory, he was able to keep the details clearly in mind. Without hesitation, he went from one assistant to another and plunged immediately into involved technical problems.

patent	consume	devote	satisfy	phonograph
automatic	make a decision	improvement	expect	at one time
recorder	then and there	stock ticker	tireless	simultaneously
representative	in the future	repeater	quadruplex	excellent
save time	definite	duplex telegraphy	major	keep in mind
confusion	penniless	to his surprise	achievement	hesitation
reject	supervisor	manufacture	production	assistant
legislator	electric	meet the demand	carbon microphone	plunge
effective	indicate	foreman	probably	involve
weapon	broker	shift	original	technical
roll-call	indicator			

QUESTIONS FOR ORAL AND WRITTEN PRACTICE

(1) How many years of school did Edison complete? (2) What did he decide that he disliked at the age of twelve? (3) How did he feel about theory and abstraction? Why? (4) In what things was he often wrong? (5) How many devices did Edison introduce? (6) What effect did these devices have on the world? (7) When was Edison born? (8) Where was he born? (9) When was he sent to school for the first time? (10) What had his mother been before her marriage? (11) With this experience, what was she able to do? (12) How did Edison feel about the ancient classics? (13) How did he feel about the educational procedures of schools and colleges? (14) In what way did he continue to learn after he left home? (15) When did his interest in science begin? (16) Why did he ask his parents for permission to earn money? (17) How did he earn money? (18) What kind of business did he organize? (19) What did all of his earnings go into? (20) What did he appropriate for his laboratory? (21) When did he begin experiments in electricity? (22) Why did he study to be a telegraph operator? (23) What increased during the Civil War? (24) What kind of position did Edison secure at the age of fifteen? Where? (25) Why did he need sleep at night? (26) What was he required to do every hour during the night? Why? (27) What was Edison's first invention? (28) Where did Edison obtain a position in 1868? (29) What did he receive his first patent for? (30) What did Edison think it would save? (31) Why was it rejected? (32) What didn't the legislators wish to lose? Why? (33) What type of inventions did Edison decide to work on in the future? (34) How did Edison lose all of his money? (35) In what condition did he arrive in New York? (36) What happened within a few days? (37) Why did he leave the Gold Indicator Company? (38) What improvements soon followed? (39) How much did his first sale of an invention bring him? (40) Why did the workers find it difficult to satisfy Edison? (41) What was he called before he was thirty? (42) What was Edison's first major achievement? (43) What was probably his most original invention? When was it invented? (44) What was he able to do because of his excellent memory? (45) What did he do without hesitation?

PART TWO

Thomas Alva Edison had workshops in Newark and later in Menlo Park. The latter is well-known as the birthplace of the incandescent lamp, perhaps Edison's greatest contribution to civilization. At the time he began to work on the problem, he realized that much more was involved than the invention of the lamp itself. In those days, arc lights provided the only practical kind of electric illumination, but they were not suitable for use in homes. Gas lights were much more satisfactory. Edison wanted to provide electric light that would be better than gas. Without going into technical details, here are the things which Edison had to do: (1) to invent a small source of light that would be safe, would need little attention, and would have a reasonably long life; (2) to devise circuits so that each light would be independent of others; (3) to provide a suitable system of conductors and feeders for bringing

workshop	civilization	suitable	attention	independent
the latter	realize	satisfactory	reasonably	system
well-known	arc light	detail	devise	conductor
incandescent lamp	provide	source	circuit	feeder
contribution	illumination			

the electricity to the home; (4) to develop efficient electric generators and high-speed steam engines to drive them; (5) to invent suitable regulating, protective, and measuring devices.

Naturally, not all the principles and devices that went into Edison's system were original with him. Others had worked on the incandescent lamp, the generator, and distribution systems. However, none of these were in practical form. Edison produced the whole system in actual working condition in about three years. Interestingly enough, Edison received practically nothing for the great achievement of the electric light!

Edison married his first wife, Mary Stillwell, in 1871 while he was still at Newark. Mrs. Edison died in 1884 at Menlo Park, and Edison left for Orange, New Jersey soon afterwards. His second wife was Mina Miller, whom he married in 1886. Edison built elaborate research laboratories in Orange. He also bought a large house near the laboratory and lived there comfortably.

Edison's brilliant eyes were his most striking physical feature. He was of medium height and rather stocky. He was fond of tea and coffee and particularly liked strong cigars and chewing tobacco. He was careless in his grammar and caustic in his comments. He took no exercise and continually neglected his health. For example, Edison's resistance to fatigue is well-known. He began giving up sleep early in his life. From the age of sixteen to sixty-five, he secured an average of about four hours of sleep a night! When he was developing the phonograph, he once worked five days and nights without resting! Deafness cut Edison off from normal social activities to a large extent. He avoided public affairs and almost never made speeches. He tried to avoid the honors that were showered upon him in his later years.

The inventions of the latter part of Edison's life were not as important or successful as those of his earlier years. The motion picture camera and projector in 1891 are perhaps the most important inventions

efficient	elaborate	particularly	resistance	avoid
generator	research	chew	fatigue	public
steam engine	brilliant	tobacco	give up	affair
regulate	strike	careless	average	make a speech
protective	physical	grammar	deafness	honor
measure	feature	caustic	cut off	shower
distribution	medium	comment	normal	successful
actual	height	continually	social	motion picture
working condition	stocky	neglect	activity	projector
practically	fond of	health	to a large extent	perhaps

of this period. The first commercial motion picture on flexible film was made in his studio.

Edison secured over one thousand patents and developed innumerable trade secrets that were not patented. Among these were many minor inventions that have not been mentioned here. Two important discoveries that he did not use resulted from his work. One was the antenna for wireless telegraphy. Edison anticipated only the earlier work of Hertz and Marconi and sold his patent to the latter. The second was the "Edison effect"—the emission of electricity from heated bodies. This is the principle of the modern radio tube and is indispensable for modern radios, phonographs, talking motion pictures, and the long-distance telephone. Edison patented it, but others put it to practical use.

Edison's health was not seriously affected until about 1929. His last illness began in June, 1931, and he passed away at the age of eighty-four on October 18 of that year.

QUESTIONS FOR ORAL AND WRITTEN PRACTICE

(46) Where did Edison have shops? (47) What is Menlo Park well-known for? (48) What provided the only practical kind of illumination in those days? (49) What were they not suitable for? (50) What was much more satisfactory? (51) What did Edison want to provide? (52) What kind of small source of light did Edison have to invent? (53) What circuits did he have to devise? (54) What did he have to provide in order to bring the electricity to the home? (55) What did he have to develop? (56) What devices did Edison have to invent? (57) How much of the work that went into Edison's systems was original with him? (58) What did Edison produce in about three years? (59) How much did he receive for the achievement of the electric light? (60) When did Edison marry his first wife? Where? (61) What was her name? (62) What did he do when his first wife died in 1884? (63) Whom did he marry in 1886? (64) What did Edison build in Orange, New Jersey? (65) What were his most striking physical features? (66) What did he look like? (67) What was he fond of? (68) On the average, how much sleep did he secure

commercial	trade secret	wireless telegraphy	radio tube	seriously
flexible	minor	anticipate	indispensable	affect
film	mention	effect	long-distance	illness
studio	result	emission	put to use	pass away
innumerable	antenna	body		

from the age of sixteen to sixty-five? (69) How long did Edison work without resting when he was developing the phonograph? (70) What effect did deafness have on Edison? (71) What did Edison try to avoid in his later years? (72) Were the inventions of the latter part of Edison's life important? (73) What were the most important inventions of this period? (74) What was made in his studio? (75) To whom did Edison sell his patent for the antenna for wireless telegraphy? (76) What is the "Edison effect?" (77) What is this principle indispensable for? (78) When was Edison's health seriously affected? (79) How old was he when he died? When did he die?

SUMMARY SENTENCES FOR LABORATORY PRACTICE

(1) Edison is considered one of the greatest inventors. (2) He failed to complete even his first year in school. (3) He was a practical and self-educated man. (4) He cared little about theory and abstraction. (5) He introduced thousands of devices. (6) They enriched the industrial and social life of the world. (7) Edison was born in Ohio in 1847. (8) He was sent to school at the usual age. (9) His mother removed him from school after three months. (10) She had been a teacher before her marriage. (11) She continued her son's education at home. (12) Edison made fun of colleges. (13) After he left home, he learned through his own efforts. (14) His interest in science began at the age of ten. (15) He read a textbook of general science. (16) His family wasn't poor. (17) But his experiments led to considerable expense. (18) He asked for permission to earn money. (19) Then he organized his own newspaper business. (20) He employed boys to sell papers on trains. (21) His earnings went into chemicals and supplies. (22) He began experiments in electricity.

(23) The telegraph interested him particularly. (24) He studied to be a telegraph operator. (25) The demand for telegraph operators increased. (26) He secured a position as a night operator. (27) He used his days for experiments. (28) And he needed sleep at night. (29) But he was required to send a signal. (30) He had to send it every hour during the night. (31) This led to his first invention. (32) His device sent the signal while he slept. (33) He obtained a position in Boston. (34) He received his first patent in 1868. (35) His invention was a vote recorder. (36) He thought his device would save time. (37) But the legislators didn't want to save time. (38) He lost all of his money on the recorder. (39) He decided to make only practical things in the future. (40) He got a job in New York. (41) He was the supervisor of an electric device. (42) He decided to devote his entire time to inventions. (43) His first invention brought him forty thousand dollars. (44) The invention was an improved stock ticker. (45) He soon started manufacturing the device. (46) He employed fifty men in two shifts. (47) He was the foreman for both shifts. (48) Workers found it difficult to satisfy him. (49) He expected them to work as hard as he did. (50) They called him the "old man" before he was thirty. (51) His first major achievement was made in 1874. (52) His next important production was the carbon microphone. (53) His most original invention was the phonograph. (54) The incandescent lamp was his greatest contribution. (55) In those days, there were only arc lights. (56) But they weren't suitable for use in homes. (57) Gas lights were much more satisfactory. (58) Edison wanted to produce satisfactory electric light. (59) He had to do many things in order to provide an electric light. (60) Not all the principles were original with him. (61) But he produced the whole system in working condition. (62) He received practically nothing for this great achievement. (63) It's easy to see that he had many interests. (64) Once he was working on fifty inventions simultaneously. (65) He had an excellent memory. (66) He was able to keep details clearly in mind. (67) His brilliant eyes were very striking. (68) He was of medium height and rather stocky. (69) He liked strong cigars and chewing tobacco. (70) He continually neglected his health. (71) Deafness cut him off from normal social activities. (72) He tried to avoid public affairs. (73) His health wasn't seriously affected until 1929. (74) His last illness began in June 1931. (75) He passed away at the age of eighty-four.

EXERCISE 61. From the column at the left, select the best synonym for the italicized word in each sentence. Rewrite the sentences using the synonyms.

consent
countless
turned down
involving
characteristic
weariness
endeavor
sarcastic
hired
essential
appropriate
delay
remember
outstanding
disregarded
especially

1. His eyes were his most *striking* feature.
2. It was *typical* of Edison's personality.
3. He learned through his own *efforts*.
4. He *employed* boys to sell papers for him.
5. His first patented invention was *rejected*.
6. Gas light was more *suitable* for home use.
7. He started the work without any *hesitation*.
8. This principle is *indispensable* for radio.
9. He developed *innumerable* trade secrets.
10. Edison *particularly* liked strong cigars.
11. He could *keep* details clearly *in mind*.
12. He was often *caustic* in his comments.
13. His resistance to *fatigue* is well-known.
14. He continually *neglected* his health.
15. He asked for his parents' *permission*.

EXERCISE 62. From the column at the left, select the correct word for each blank space in the sentences at the right. Use each word only once. Do not change the forms of the words.

indicated
considered
avoided
resulted
affected
devoted
consumed
based
neglected
employed
removed
required
disliked
realized
rejected
failed

1. He _____ to complete even one year in school.
2. His mother _____ him from school after that.
3. He was _____ to send a signal every hour.
4. At twelve, he decided that he _____ mathematics.
5. Many important discoveries _____ from his work.
6. That kind of work _____ much time and effort.
7. He _____ his entire time to his inventions.
8. His first patented invention was _____.
9. The device _____ the changing price of gold.
10. His inventions were _____ on scientific principles.
11. He _____ fifty men in two shifts after that.
12. He _____ social activities and public affairs.
13. His health was not seriously _____ until 1929.
14. He _____ there were difficulties in this work.
15. He _____ his health by not sleeping enough.

EXERCISE 63. Supply the correct preposition for each blank space.

1 Edison was often wrong _____ his explanations.
2 _____ the age _____ ten, he read difficult books.
3 He earned money _____ selling newspapers _____ a train.
4 _____ this way, he could spend his spare time usefully.
5 The demand _____ operators increased _____ the war.
6 He had to send a signal every hour _____ the night.
7 There was a definite need _____ certain inventions.
8 He worked _____ devices which were practical.
9 He received his first patent _____ a device _____ 1868.
10 He began to devote his time _____ his own inventions.
11 He got a job _____ a supervisor _____ $300 per month.
12 Arc lights weren't suitable _____ use _____ homes.
13 Edison cared very little _____ theoretical matters.
14 Everyone noticed his carelessness _____ grammar.
15 This carelessness was not typical _____ his personality.

EXERCISE 64. From the column at the right, select the correct line to complete each of the numbered lines at the left. Write each sentence in its correct form.

1 Edison failed to complete   (A) from social activities
2 He had no use   (B) a striking physical feature
3 As a boy, his earnings   (C) but others put it to use
4 His early experiments led   (D) his first year in school
5 His most original invention   (E) to considerable expense
6 He manufactured stock tickers   (F) went into his experiments
7 At one time time, he was working   (G) was the phonograph in 1877
8 Arc lights were not   (H) his greatest achievement
9 Edison had to invent   (I) on fifty inventions at once
10 The whole system was   (J) produced in three years
11 His brilliant eyes were   (K) to meet the demand
12 He received little for   (L) for the ancient classics
13 He patented the "Edison effect"   (M) suitable for use in homes
14 Deafness cut him off   (N) him forty thousand dollars
15 His first sale brought   (O) a small source of light

145

EXERCISE 65. Study the following word form chart carefully. The word forms which occurred in the preceding story are italicized.

ADJECTIVE	NOUN	VERB	ADVERB
1 *practical*	practicality	x x x x x	practically
2 theoretical	*theory*	theorize	theoretically
3 *industrial*	industry	industrialize	industrially
4 *social*	society	socialize	socially
5 *educational*	*education*	*educate*	x x x x x
6 x x x x x	*procedure*	proceed	x x x x x
7 conclusive	*conclusion*	conclude	conclusively
8 expensive	*expense*	x x x x x	expensively
9 x x x x x	employment	*employ*	x x x x x
10 useful	usefulness	x x x x x	*usefully*
11 *electric*	electricity	x x x x x	electrically
12 operative	operation *operator*	operate	x x x x x
13 secure	security	*secure*	securely
14 x x x x x	requirement	*require*	x x x x x
15 supervisory	supervision *supervisor*	supervise	x x x x x
16 indicative	*indicator* indication	indicate	x x x x x
17 x x x x x	*demand*	demand	x x x x x
18 *satisfactory*	satisfaction	*satisfy*	satisfactorily
19 expectant	expectation	*expect*	expectantly
20 productive	producer *production*	*produce*	productively
21 *excellent*	excellence	excel	excellently
22 x x x x x	provision	*provide*	x x x x x
23 *independent*	independence	x x x x x	independently
24 *elaborate*	elaborateness	x x x x x	elaborately
25 comfortable	comfort	x x x x x	*comfortably*
26 *brilliant*	brilliance	x x x x x	brilliantly
27 *fond*	fondness	x x x x x	fondly
28 *careless*	carelessness	x x x x x	carelessly
29 neglectful	neglect	*neglect*	neglectfully
30 resistant	*resistance*	resist	x x x x x
31 deaf	*deafness*	deafen	deafly
32 *flexible*	flexibility	x x x x x	flexibly

EXERCISE 66. Use the correct form of each italicized word in the sentence which follows. Notice the first two examples. Refer to the word form chart and examples whenever necessary.

1	*produce*	The *production* of devices brought him a fortune.
2	*electric*	He began experiments in *electricity* as a boy.
3	*industrial*	His inventions aided the growth of _____.
4	*conclusion*	After some research, he _____ that it was possible.
5	*neglect*	He was continually _____ of his health.
6	*deaf*	How did his _____ affect his social life?
7	*elaborate*	Later he built _____ laboratories for research.
8	*operator*	He was responsible for the _____ of the device.
9	*employ*	Many men were _____ in his laboratories.
10	*expense*	The _____ of building a laboratory was great.
11	*educational*	As a child, he continued his _____ with his mother.
12	*practical*	In his opinion, _____ was an important thing.
13	*usefully*	He worried about the _____ of his inventions.
14	*require*	He found a way to take care of the _____.
15	*independent*	All of the lights in the circuit operated _____.
16	*flexible*	He knew that the _____ of film was important.
17	*fond*	People knew about his _____ for coffee and tea.
18	*brilliant*	Everyone noticed the _____ of his eyes.
19	*provide*	The _____ of independent circuits was important.
20	*secure*	The job which Edison obtained gave him _____.
21	*theory*	He wasn't interested in _____ things at all.
22	*indicate*	The device _____ the changing price of gold.
23	*satisfy*	Edison felt that their work wasn't _____.
24	*satisfy*	Edison's work gave him a great deal of _____.
25	*supervisor*	As the foreman, he always _____ the men's work.
26	*supervisor*	He always felt that careful _____ was important.
27	*excellent*	He profited from the _____ of his memory.
28	*excellent*	During his lifetime, he produced _____ devices.
29	*careless*	Was there much _____ in Edison's laboratories?
30	*careless*	Did the workers use the instruments _____?
31	*resistance*	When Edison was working, he _____ fatigue.
32	*resistance*	Edison seemed to be _____ to most diseases.

EXERCISE 67. Study the following examples for the preceding word form chart. The numbers correspond to those on the word form chart.

1 **practical, practicality, practically.** He was a *practical* inventor. He tried to invent *practical* things. The *practicality* of his inventions was important to him. He always worked *practically*.

2 **theoretical, theory, theorize, theoretically.** *Theory* didn't interest him. He didn't like *theoretical* things. He didn't work *theoretically*. He never *theorized* about things.

3 **industrial, industry, industrialize, industrially.** New York City has a large *industrial* area. *Industry* is important for the growth of a nation. The nation *industrialized* its production of metals. The area was developed *industrially*.

4 **social, society, socialize, socially.** *Social* activities weren't important to him. His *social life* wasn't important to him. He didn't often meet people *socially*. He didn't enjoy the *society* of other people. He didn't *socialize* very much.

5 **educational, educator, education, educate, educationally.** He didn't complete his formal *education*. He didn't admire *educators*. He was *educated* at home as a young boy. He didn't like the *educational* methods of the times. His inventions were important *educationally*.

6 **procedure, proceed.** He knew the *procedure* well. He *proceeded* with great caution.

7 **conclusive, conclusion, conclude, conclusively.** His tests were *conclusive*. At the *conclusion* of the experiment, he was satisfied. He *concluded* that the theory was correct. He came to the *conclusion* that he was correct. He proved his point *conclusively*.

8 **expensive, expense, expensively.** His experiments were *expensive*. The *expense* of his experiments was great. He discovered things *expensively*.

9 **employment, employ.** He *employed* many men in his laboratory. The *employment* of assistants was important to him. During bad times, many men were *out of employment*.

10 **useful, usefulness, usefully.** He invented *useful* devices. He always thought about the *usefulness* of his devices. He tried to spend his time *usefully*.

148

11 **electric, electrical, electricity, electrically.** He invented an *electric* device. He invented an *electrical* device. The device was operated by *electricity*. The device was operated *electrically*.

12 **operative, operation, operate.** He *operated* the machine. The *operation* of the machine was easy. He had to *keep the machine in operation*. He had to *keep the machine operative*. The machine was *out of operation*. The machine wasn't *operative*.

13 **secure, security, securely.** He *felt secure* in his new position. It was a *secure* position. *Security* is important to all nations. He *secured* a position at Port Huron. He tied the knot *securely*.

14 **requirement, require.** His boss *required* him to send a signal. He was *required* to send a signal every hour. He sent the *required* signal. The *requirement* was a difficult one for him. He was able to *satisfy the requirement*.

15 **supervisory, supervisor, supervision, supervise.** His new position was a *supervisory* one. He was the factory *supervisor*. The *supervision* of the work went well. The men did the work *under his supervision*. He *supervised* the work carefully.

16 **indicative, indicator, indication, indicate.** The machine was an *indicator*. The machine *indicated* the changing prices. People read the *indicated* prices carefully. The *indication* of prices was important. The prices were *indicative* of the value of gold.

17 **demand.** Industry *demanded* more stock tickers. The *demand* was great. He manufactured machines to *meet the demand*.

18 **satisfactory, satisfaction, satisfy, satisfactorily.** He required *satisfactory* work from everyone. His *satisfaction* depended on the quality of the work. It *gave him satisfaction* to invent things. He *got satisfaction* from producing new devices. Good work *satisfied* him. The workers found it difficult to *satisfy* him. The workers did the job *satisfactorily*.

19 **expectant, expectation, expect, expectantly.** He *expected* the men to work hard. He *expected* to receive money for his invention. He *expected* money for his invention. He waited *expectantly*. He was *expectant* of receiving money. His *expectations* were incorrect.

20 productive, production, producer, produce, productively. He was a very *productive* person. His next important *production* was a microphone. New methods increased the *production* of the factory. He wasn't the *producer* of all his inventions. He *produced* some of his inventions. He worked *productively* for over 50 years.

21 excellent, excellence, excel, excellently. He had an *excellent* memory. He recalled things *excellently*. The *excellence* of his memory helped him in his work. He *excelled* in many different things. His second model *excelled* the first.

22 provision, provide. He wanted to *provide* an electric light. The *provision* of electric lights helped everyone. He *made provisions* for independent circuits.

23 independent, independence, independently. He wanted each light to be *independent* of the others. The *independence* of each light in the circuit was important. He wanted each light to function *independently*.

24 elaborate, elaborateness, elaborately. He built an *elaborate* house. He furnished the house *elaborately*. The *elaborateness* of the house was impressive.

25 comfortable, comfort, comfortably. He enjoyed the *comfort* of his office. His office was *comfortable*. His office was furnished *comfortably*.

26 brilliant, brilliance, brilliantly. Everyone noticed his *brilliant* eyes. Everyone noticed the *brilliance* of his eyes. His eyes flashed *brilliantly*.

27 fond, fondness, fondly. He was *fond* of coffee. He drank both coffee and tea *fondly*. He had a great *fondness* for coffee.

28 careless, carelessness, carelessly. He was *careless* in some things. But he wasn't a *careless* man. He was never *careless* with delicate instruments. He didn't use instruments *carelessly*. The *carelessness* he showed about grammar didn't concern him. *Carelessness* often annoyed him.

29 neglectful, neglect, neglectfully. He was *neglectful* of his health. His health suffered because of his *neglect*. He *neglected* his health continually. He didn't work *neglectfully*.

THE YEARS OF HIS GENIUS

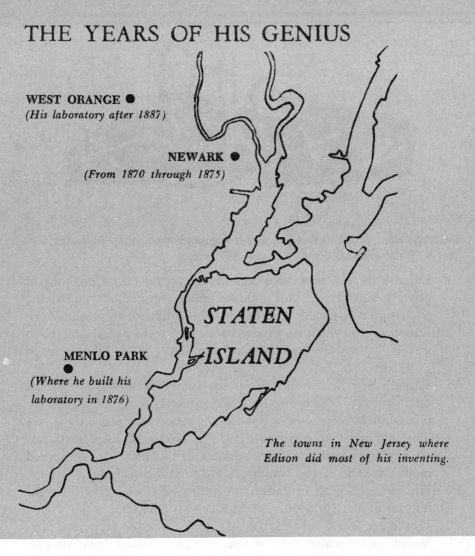

WEST ORANGE ●
(His laboratory after 1887)

NEWARK ●
(From 1870 through 1875)

STATEN ISLAND

MENLO PARK
●
(Where he built his laboratory in 1876)

The towns in New Jersey where Edison did most of his inventing.

30 **resistant, resistance, resist.** His system was *resistant* to bad weather. His *resistance* to fatigue is well-known. He *resisted* sickness until old age.

31 **deaf, deafness, deafly.** He *became deaf. Deaf* people have special problems. His *deafness* caused many problems. He turned his head toward the speaker *deafly.*

32 **flexible, flexibility, flexibly.** The first *flexible* film was made in his studio. The *flexibility* of the new film was remarkable. The film could be moved *flexibly.*

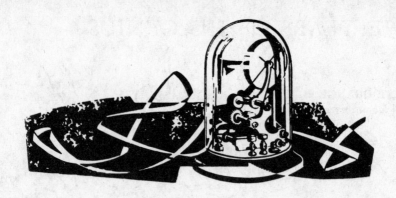

EXERCISE 68. Select the correct way to complete each of the following sentences. Write each sentence in its correct form.

1   Edison's interest in science began when (*a*) he read a textbook of general science. (*b*) his mother taught him about electricity. (*c*) he sold newspapers. (*d*) he started manufacturing stock tickers.

2   Edison sold newspapers to earn money (*a*) to buy clothes. (*b*) to travel. (*c*) to buy chemicals and supplies. (*d*) to be able to go to college.

3   Edison's first invention was (*a*) the incandescent light. (*b*) the phonograph. (*c*) a device for sending hourly telegraph signals for him while he slept. (*d*) a textbook of general science.

4   The automatic vote recorded for the House of Representatives (*a*) was acclaimed. (*b*) was Edison's first patent. (*c*) consumed much time and caused confusion. (*d*) is still used today.

5   His first sale of an invention, an improved stock ticker, brought him (*a*) $100. (*b*) $400. (*c*) $3,000. (*d*) $40,000.

6   Workers found it difficult to satisfy Edison because (*a*) he was careless in his grammar. (*b*) he wanted to do all the work himself. (*c*) he expected them to work as hard as he did. (*d*) deafness cut him off from normal activities.

7   Edison wanted to provide an electric light that (*a*) would be better than gas. (*b*) would be cheaper than candles. (*c*) would make a lot of money. (*d*) would be completely original.

8   He wanted to devise a circuit for electrical illumination (*a*) so that each light would work separately. (*b*) that would need much supervision. (*c*) without a suitable system of conductors. (*d*) that would send a signal every hour during the night.

9 The "Edison effect" is (a) his most striking physical feature.
(b) his resistance to fatigue.   (c) the principle of the modern radio
tube.   (d) the flexibility of motion picture film.

10 When Edison was developing the phonograph, (a) he secured over
one thousand patents.   (b) he sold his patent to Marconi.   (c) he
built elaborate research laboratories in Orange, New Jersey.
(d) he once worked five days and nights without resting.

11 As a practical and self-educated man, Edison (a) did not wish to
lose the effective weapon of roll-calls.   (b) cared little about theory
and abstraction.   (c) arrived in New York penniless and hungry.
(d) was able to keep details clearly in mind.

The story "The Wizard of Menlo Park" was adapted from "Thomas Alva Edison"
by Marshall C. Harrington as it appeared in *Vocations and Professions,* edited by
Phillip Henry Lotz, published by the Association Press, New York, 1940. Permission
for the rewriting of this section of the book was kindly granted by the Director
of the Association Press.

The illustrations by William Barss on pages 138 and 142 and the map on page 151
of "The Wizard of Menlo Park" originally appeared in *Young Tom Edison* by
Sterling North, published by Houghton Mifflin Company, Copyright 1958. The
illustrations have been reproduced with the permission of the publisher.

FROM
SLAVE
TO
TEACHER

THIS FAMOUS EDUCATOR and humanitarian started his life as a slave. "Booker" was his only name. He was not even sure of the exact place or date of his birth! This man later became the undisputed leader of all the Negroes in the United States. He was responsible for the success of the largest Negro school in the country. He wrote many important and successful books. He received an honorary degree from Harvard University. He was a friend and advisor of two presidents and hundreds of business, religious, and educational leaders.

Booker was apparently born near a small post office at Hale's Ford in Franklin, Virginia in 1858 or 1859. He lived in a little log cabin about fourteen by sixteen feet square. The cabin had no glass windows. There were only openings in the walls. There was no floor. Booker and his brother and sister slept on dirty rags on the ground. He knew almost nothing about his ancestry. He later heard reports that his father was a white man at a nearby plantation, but he never found out the man's

educator	undisputed	honorary	log cabin	report
humanitarian	Negro	degree	opening	nearby
slave	responsible	advisor	rag	plantation
exact	success	educational	ancestry	find out
birth	successful	apparent		

BOOKER T. WASHINGTON

name. His mother was a cook at a plantation. She had little time to train her children. Every slave was expected to work long hours. Even as a small child, Booker had no time to play.

The Civil War started in 1861. It lasted for four long years. Those were difficult times for everyone but especially for slaves. During that time, Booker was growing up.

Little by little, the Southern Confederacy weakened. The wounded and discouraged white masters began to come home. After four years of war within its borders, the Confederacy finally admitted its defeat. The slaves were free, but their situation was still bad. The whole way of southern life was in ruins. Large parts of the land were devastated. Confiscation and stealing made things even worse. Banks were closed, and factories were idle. There were few jobs. Like everyone else, Booker's family needed work and money to live. In 1866, his mother and stepfather took him to Malden, West Virginia, a small town several hundred miles away. Booker found work at a salt mine there.

Booker's mother could not read or write, but she wanted her son to learn. She found an old spelling book for him. This increased his interest in education. Then he went to a night school for a while. At this school, the teacher asked him his name. "Booker" was the only name he had ever known, but all of the other boys had two names. He thought quickly and chose the most important name he knew. He chose the name of the first president of the United States. "My name is Booker Washington," he answered. From then on, that was his name. Later he found out that his mother called him Booker Taliaferro as a child. He decided to use this name too, and he became Booker T. Washington.

One day in 1873, Booker heard about a school for Negroes. Some miners were talking about Hampton Institute. "The students are allowed to pay for their room and board by working," one of the men told the other. "It's the best Negro school in the country." Booker did not forget this conversation. Shortly after that, he heard that the wife of the mine owner, Mrs. Ruffner, needed a servant. Booker was ambitious, and he wanted to earn more money. He applied for the job and

train	Confederacy	defeat	stepfather	allow
expect	weaken	situation	mine	board
Civil War	wound	in ruins	spelling	ambitious
last	discourage	devastate	increase	earn
grow up	border	confiscation	from then on	apply
little by little	admit	idle	miner	

got it. Mrs. Ruffner was very strict, and the work was hard. Booker learned to be neat and clean. Mrs. Ruffner also encouraged him to study. All this time, Booker carefully saved part of his pay each week. Finally, he thought he had enough money. He gave up his job and set out for Hampton Institute.

The school was 500 miles away, and he had enough money to ride only a short distance. Therefore, he walked most of the way. He often slept beside the road or under porches. Many times, he had little or nothing to eat. When he arrived at the school, he was tired, dirty, and hungry.

Naturally, Booker was in no condition to make an impressive appearance at the school the next day. He was not accepted as a student immediately. After an interview, the assistant principal, Miss Mackie, was still doubtful about Booker. Finally, she gave Booker a broom and told him to sweep the room. Booker could clearly see that this was his entrance examination. He later wrote, "I knew I could sweep because Mrs. Ruffner had taught me that art well." He swept the room three times and then dusted it four times. He even dusted each book on the shelves. The teacher looked over the room carefully. She even looked at the closet shelves. Finally, she said to Booker, "I think you will be a good student." He became a student and a janitor the next day.

He got his room, board, and tuition at the school, but he had no money. He borrowed books from his classmates. Part of the time, he had only one pair of socks. His clothes always got dirty quickly because of his work, and this was a constant problem for him. But Booker learned to take a bath every day. He also learned to use a toothbrush for the first time at Hampton Institute.

In spite of his hardships at Hampton Institute, Booker was happy. He spent three busy years there. He received high marks in his classes. He enjoyed debating, and he never missed one meeting of the Debating Society during those three years. He also organized a speaker's club. Later in his life, this training helped Booker very much.

strict	condition	broom	janitor	in spite of
neat	impressive	sweep	tuition	hardship
encourage	appearance	entrance	borrow	mark
give up	accept	art	classmate	debate
set out	interview	dust	pair	miss
distance	assistant	shelf	socks	society
therefore	principal	look over	constant	organize
porch	doubtful	closet	bath	club

After his graduation with honors in 1875, Booker returned to Malden, his hometown. He became a teacher in the public school. In addition to his regular work there, he organized a night school and taught at a Sunday school. Not long after that, the principal of Hampton Institute invited him to come back to the school as a teacher. He was given an unusual job at Hampton. He was put in charge of a group of Indian boys. Booker was very successful in his work with these boys. He also took part in several other experiments in education at the school. In all, he stayed at Hampton for two years. During that time, he realized that his future was in the field of education. He worked eagerly and prepared for the future. This was his training period for the difficult work that was still ahead.

QUESTIONS FOR ORAL AND WRITTEN PRACTICE

(1) How did this famous educator start his life? (2) What was his only name? (3) What did this man later become? (4) What was he responsible for? (5) What did he write? (6) From what university did he receive an honorary degree? (7) Whom was he a friend

graduation	in addition to	in charge of	in all	prepare
honors	come back	Indian	field	period
hometown	unusual	take part	eager	ahead

and advisor of? (8) Where was he apparently born? (9) In what year was he born? (10) What kind of house did he live in? (11) What kind of windows did the cabin have? (12) What kind of floor did the cabin have? (13) What did the children sleep on? (14) What did Booker know about his ancestry? (15) What did he later hear about his father? (16) What was his father's name? (17) What did his mother do? (18) Why didn't she have much time to train her children? (19) How much time did Booker have to play as a child? (20) When did the Civil War start? (21) How long did the Civil War last? (22) For whom were those difficult times? (23) What happened to the Southern Confederacy during the four years of the war? (24) Who began to come home? (25) When did the Confederacy finally admit its defeat? (26) How was the situation after the defeat of the Confederacy? (27) In what condition was the whole way of southern life? (28) In what condition were large parts of the land? (29) What made things even worse? (30) Why were there few jobs? (31) Like everyone else, what did Booker's family need? (32) Where did Booker go in 1866? (33) How far away was Malden? (34) Who took him there? (35) What kind of work did Booker find there? (36) What did Booker's mother want him to learn? (37) What did she find for him? (38) What effect did this have on Booker? (39) What kind of school did he go to for a while? (40) What did the teacher at this school ask Booker? (41) Why did Booker need another name? (42) What name did he choose? (43) Why did he choose that name? (44) Why did he add the name Taliaferro later? (45) What did Booker hear about one day in 1873? (46) What school were the miners talking about? (47) What did one of the men say about the school? (48) When did he hear that Mrs. Ruffner needed a servant? (49) Why did he apply for the job? (50) What kind of person was Mrs. Ruffner? (51) What did Booker learn from Mrs. Ruffner? (52) What did Mrs. Ruffner encourage him to do? (53) What did Booker do with his pay all this time? (54) Why did Booker finally give up his job? (55) How far away was Hampton Institute? (56) Why did Booker walk most of the way? (57) Where did he often sleep along the way? (58) What did he have to eat? (59) In what condition was he when he arrived at the school? (60) Why wasn't he accepted as a student immediately? (61) What did Miss Mackie finally tell Booker to do? (62) What could Booker clearly see? (63) Why did he know that he could do that job well? (64) How many times did he sweep and dust the room? (65) What did the teacher finally say to Booker? (66) What did he become the next day? (67) What did he receive for his work at the school? (68) How much money did he receive? (69) How did he get books? (70) Why did his clothes get dirty quickly? (71) What did Booker learn to do at the school in order to be clean? (72) How many years did he spend there? (73) What subject did Booker especially enjoy? (74) What kind of club did he organize? (75) Why was this important? (76) When did he graduate from Hampton Institute? (77) What did he do after his graduation? (78) What did he become? (79) What did he do in addition to his regular work? (80) Who invited him to come back to Hampton Institute? (81) What kind of job was he given at the school? (82) Whom was he put in charge of? (83) What was the result of his work? (84) What else did he take part in at the school? (85) In all, how long did he stay there? (86) What did he realize during that time? (87) Why did he work eagerly?

PART TWO

Around the year 1880, a few people were beginning to see the wisdom of educating Negroes. At the request of a white merchant in Tuskegee, Alabama, the state legislature granted $2000 for a training school for Negroes. Some people felt that the principal of the school should be a white man. However, Booker T. Washington was strongly recommended by the officials of Hampton Institute. After much debate, he was finally accepted as the principal. Booker was an excellent choice. He had graduated from Hampton Institute with honors in 1875, and he had taught at Malden and later at Hampton Institute. He had worked hard for everything in his life. He understood his people, and he knew their problems. He had started life as a slave on a plantation. As a child, "Booker" was the only name he had known. He had not even known his father's name or the date of his birth. He had grown up during the terrible years of the Civil War. He had worked in a mine as a common laborer. He had worked his way through school as a janitor. He was accustomed to facing and overcoming hardships of every kind.

Booker left for Tuskegee in June, 1881. Naturally, he was eager

wisdom	legislature	official	terrible	face
request	grant	choice	laborer	overcome
merchant	recommend	graduate	accustom	

to start his new work. At Tuskegee, he was surprised. There was no school. "It hasn't been built yet," the people told him. This did not discourage Booker. He had solved many difficult problems before. He started by visiting all the people in the county—both Negroes and white people. He spoke to everyone about the importance of a normal school. He made many friends. He also invited many young Negroes to come to the school. Next, he rented a small cabin next to a Negro church. Then he got permission to use part of the church. He named the school "Tuskegee Normal and Industrial Institute." The school was opened on July 4, 1881.

On the first day, there were 30 students. He taught them very practical things. He felt that book knowledge was a waste of time for these students. The discipline at the school was strict. Professor Washington felt that this would develop character. His students were also taught correct manners and speech. He knew that this would help them very much later in their lives.

Within a few weeks, there were 50 students at the school, and another teacher was hired. Soon the small school needed more space. Professor Washington borrowed $500 from friends, and the school bought an old plantation with four small buildings just outside the town. The school needed another building, but there was practically no money left. Therefore, the students and the teachers built Porter Hall themselves. After that, they built a dormitory for girls called Alabama Hall. Each student spent part of his time on studies and part in physical labor. No student was turned away from the school for lack of money.

Although he loved his home, he spent only half of the year with his family. He traveled around the country the rest of the year. He made thousands of speeches and tried to interest people in Tuskegee in every way possible. He was always tactful and patient. He wanted the people of both races to understand each other and to live in harmony. This was his goal.

In 1895, Professor Washington was invited to speak at the Cotton States Exposition in Atlanta, Georgia. Governor Bullock of Georgia

surprise	industrial	manners	dormitory	tactful
solve	practical	speech	physical	patient
importance	knowledge	hire	turn away	race
normal school	waste	space	for lack of	harmony
invite	discipline	practically	although	goal
rent	develop	left	the rest	exposition
permission	character			

introduced him to an audience of several thousand Negroes and white people. This was the first time that an important white official had introduced a Negro leader to an audience of Southerners. He spoke about his educational objectives. He also asked for help and cooperation. His speech at Atlanta made him famous all over the United States.

| introduce | Southerner | objective | cooperation | all over |
| audience | | | | |

It was printed in many newspapers, and President Cleveland congratulated him in a letter.

Professor Washington worked night and day for his school. He went to wealthy people and asked them to help in any way possible. His gentle manners and his great faith in his plans convinced these people. Many of them gave large amounts for buildings, equipment, books, and scholarships.

In 1896, Professor Washington asked the Alabama legislature to create an agricultural experiment station at Tuskegee. He explained the importance of training Negro students in scientific agriculture. The legislature approved his plan. Professor Washington knew about the soil experiments of George Washington Carver, another former slave. He immediately invited Carver to Tuskegee to be in charge of the station. In his experiments, Professor Carver found hundreds of uses for the few things that could be planted in the poor southern soil. These experiments improved the standard of living for millions of people in the South. Next Professor Washington and Professor Carver started a "traveling school." They wanted to show these new products and ideas to farmers. They drove a wagon around the country and gave demonstrations. Their traveling school was very successful. As a result of their work, many farms produced three times as much as before.

By that time, Booker T. Washington's name was known all over the United States. He was recognized as the leader of his race in the country. In 1900, he wrote the story of his life in a book called *Up From Slavery*. He received honors from everywhere. In June 1896, he received the honorary degree of Master of Arts from Harvard University. This was the first time Harvard had honored a Negro in this way. At this ceremony, the President of Harvard, Charles W. Eliot, called Professor Washington a wise helper of his race and a good servant of his country. President Theodore Roosevelt admired Professor Washington's vigorous determination, and these two men became good friends.

print	convince	station	plant	recognize
congratulate	amount	scientific	standard	slavery
wealthy	equipment	agriculture	product	ceremony
gentle	scholarship	approve	idea	admire
faith	create	soil	wagon	vigorous
plan	agricultural	former	produce	determination

Business, religious, and educational leaders all came to Professor Washington for advice and assistance.

His constant hard work weakened his heart. His family and friends begged him to retire and rest, but he refused. He said he still had many important things to do. When he was in New York in November 1915, he became violently ill. He probably knew that the end was near because he asked his friends to take him back to Tuskegee. He died just a few hours after arriving at the Institute.

Today Tuskegee has a staff of 369 people and more than 2000 students. The school is justifiably proud of its 157 buildings and 5,189 acres of campus and farms. Although people everywhere have paid tribute to the memory of Booker T. Washington, at Tuskegee, his life is a continuing source of inspiration.

QUESTIONS FOR ORAL AND WRITTEN PRACTICE

(88) What were a few people beginning to see around the year 1880? (89) At whose request did the state legislature of Alabama grant $2000? (90) What was this money granted for? (91) What did some people feel about the principal of the school? (92) By whom was Booker T. Washington strongly recommended? (93) Why was Booker an excellent choice? Give the two most important reasons. (94) How had he started life? (95) During what years had he grown up? (96) What was Booker accustomed to doing? (97) When did Booker leave for Tuskegee? (98) Why was he surprised at Tuskegee? (99) What did the people tell him? (100) Why didn't this discourage him? (101) Whom did Booker visit? (102) What did he speak to everyone about? (103) What did he invite many young Negroes to do? (104) What did he rent? (105) What did he get permission to use? (106) What did he name the school? (107) When was the school opened? (108) How many students were there on the opening day? (109) What kind of things did he teach them? (110) Why did he teach the students practical things? (111) Why was the discipline at the school strict? (112) Why were his students also taught correct manners and speech? (113) How many students were there at the

advice	retire	probable	proud	memory
assistance	refuse	take back	acre	source
heart	violent	staff	campus	inspiration
beg	ill	justifiable	tribute	

164

school within a few weeks? (114) What did the small school soon need? (115) From whom did Professor Washington borrow $500? (116) What did the school buy with this money? (117) Where was the old plantation? (118) Why did the students and teachers build Porter Hall themselves? (119) How did each student spend his time? (120) How many students were turned away from the school for lack of money? (121) What part of each year did Professor Washington spend with his family? (122) What did he do the rest of the year? (123) How many speeches did he make? (124) What did he try to interest people in? (125) What did he want the people of both races to do? (126) What was Professor Washington invited to do in 1895? (127) What kind of audience was he introduced to? (128) Who introduced him to the audience? (129) Why was this a very significant event? (130) What did Professor Washington speak about? (131) What did Professor Washington ask for in his speech? (132) What was the result of his speech at Atlanta? (133) Where was his speech printed? (134) Who congratulated him in a letter? (135) To whom did he go for help? (136) What convinced these people? (137) What did many of them give large amounts for? (138) What did he ask the Alabama legislature to create in 1896? (139) Why did he invite George Washington Carver to be in charge of the station? (140) What did Professor Carver find in his experiments? (141) What was the result of these experiments? (142) What kind of school did Professors Washington and Carver start? (143) Why did they start this kind of school? (144) How did they demonstrate their new products and ideas to farmers? (145) What happened as a result of their work? (146) What was Booker T. Washington recognized as by that time? (147) What did he write in 1900? (148) What was the book called? (149) What kind of degree did he receive from Harvard University? (150) When did he receive the degree? (151) What did President Eliot call Booker T. Washington at the ceremony? (152) What did President Theodore Roosevelt admire? (153) Who came to Professor Washington for advice? (154) How did his constant hard work affect him? (155) What did his family and friends beg him to do? (156) Why did Professor Washington refuse to retire and rest? (157) When did he become violently ill? Where? (158) Why did he probably know that the end was near? (159) When did Booker T. Washington die? (160) Who has paid tribute to the memory of Booker T. Washington?

SUMMARY SENTENCES FOR LABORATORY PRACTICE

(1) He started his life as a slave. (2) "Booker" was his only name. (3) He was not even sure of the date of his birth. (4) He became the leader of all American Negroes. (5) He wrote many important and successful books. (6) He was a friend and advisor of two presidents. (7) He was probably born in a log cabin in Virginia. (8) There were openings in the walls for windows. (9) The children slept on dirty rags on the ground. (10) He knew almost nothing about his ancestry. (11) His mother was a cook at a plantation. (12) She had little time to train her children. (13) Every slave was expected to work long hours. (14) Booker grew up during the Civil War. (15) Finally the slaves were free. (16) But their situation was still bad. (17) Banks were closed, and factories were idle. (18) There were few jobs. (19) Booker found work at a salt mine. (20) His mother found an old spelling book for him. (21) This increased his interest in education. (22) He went to a night school for a while. (23) He was ambitious and wanted to earn more money. (24) He saved part of his pay each week. (25) He set out for Hampton Institute. (26) He arrived at the school tired, dirty, and hungry. (27) He became a student and a janitor the next day. (28) He got his room, board, and tuition at the school. (29) He borrowed books from his classmates. (30) He graduated from the school with honors. (31) He became a public school teacher. (32) Money was granted for a training school for Negroes. (33) Booker was accepted as the principal. (34) When he arrived in Tuskegee, there was no school. (35) This did not discourage him. (36) He rented a small cabin and part of a church. (37) The school was opened in 1881. (38) He taught the students very practical things. (39) Another teacher was hired. (40) Booker borrowed money from friends. (41) He bought an old plantation. (42) Each student helped to build the school. (43) Booker went to wealthy people for help. (44) His faith in his plans convinced these people. (45) He created an agricultural experiment station. (46) Then he started a "traveling school." (47) His name was known all over the country. (48) In 1900, he wrote the story of his life. (49) His constant hard work weakened his heart. (50) He died at the school in November 1915.

EXERCISE 69 (Part One). From the column at the left, select the best synonym for the italicized word in each sentence. Rewrite the sentence using the synonym.

1 Didn't he know the date of his birth *precisely?*

idle

exactly

impressive

organize

choose

last

clearly

allow

eagerly

find out

give up

neat

look over

doubtful

take part

constant

2 Why couldn't he *discover* his father's name?

3 What name did he *select* at his first school?

4 How long after that did the war *continue?*

5 Why were the factories *not operating?*

6 From whom did Booker learn to be *tidy?*

7 When did he *quit* his job at the salt mine?

8 Why did they *permit* the students to work?

9 Why was the teacher *uncertain* about Booker?

10 Why did the teacher *examine* the room?

11 What could he *plainly* see at that moment?

12 When did Booker *form* a speaker's club?

13 What was his *continual* problem at the school?

14 When did he *participate* in an experiment?

15 Why did he work *enthusiastically* at Hampton?

EXERCISE 70 (Part One). From the column at the left, select the correct word for the blank space in each sentence. Do not change the forms of the words.

1 The children slept on dirty _____ on the ground.

birth

strict

rags

swept

train

debate

in spite of

earn

defeat

ruins

board

eagerly

doubtful

field

pair

marks

2 He was not sure of the exact date of his _____.

3 His mother had no time to _____ her children.

4 The southern army finally admitted its _____.

5 The whole way of southern life was in _____.

6 Booker wanted to _____ more money by working.

7 The work was hard, and his boss was _____.

8 The assistant principal was _____ about him.

9 Booker _____ the school room three times.

10 He was happy at the school _____ his hardships.

11 Part of the time he had only one _____ of socks.

12 He always received high _____ in his classes.

13 He got his room, _____, and tuition at the school.

14 He worked _____ and prepared for the future.

15 Booker's future was in the _____ of education.

EXERCISE 71 (Part One). Supply the correct preposition for each blank space.

1 He was responsible _____ the success _____ the school.
2 The cabin was about fourteen _____ sixteen feet square.
3 The war started _____ 1861 and lasted _____ four years.
4 Those were very difficult times _____ everyone.
5 Booker was interested _____ the field _____ education.
6 Booker went _____ a night school _____ Malden _____ a while.
7 _____ 1873, he heard _____ a good school _____ Negroes.
8 He borrowed books _____ his classmates _____ Hampton.
9 Part _____ the time, he had only one pair _____ socks.
10 Later _____ his life, this training helped him very much.
11 He organized a club _____ addition _____ his regular work.
12 He was put _____ charge _____ a group _____ Indian boys.
13 He was successful _____ his work _____ these boys.
14 He took part _____ other experiments _____ education.
15 He worked eagerly and prepared _____ the future.

EXERCISE 72 (Part One). From the column at the right, select the correct line to complete each of the numbered lines at the left. Write each sentence in its correct form.

1 He was responsible   (A) him to study
2 He was put in charge   (B) he had ever known
3 His employer encouraged   (C) as a student immediately
4 His clothes got dirty   (D) from his classmates
5 He was not accepted   (E) in his work with them
6 He took part in   (F) for the school's success
7 Later in his life, this   (G) neat and clean
8 The teacher looked over   (H) read or write
9 He was successful   (I) because of his work
10 He learned to be   (J) training helped him
11 It was the only name   (K) made things worse
12 His mother could not   (L) of a group of Indians
13 He borrowed books   (M) he had enough money
14 Confiscation and stealing   (N) the room carefully
15 Finally, he thought   (O) several other experiments

168

EXERCISE 73 (Part Two). From the column at the left, select the best synonym for the italicized word in each sentence. Rewrite the sentence using the synonym.

retire
help
almost
useful
yield
ordinary
severely
purchase
give
intelligence
remainder
argument
objective
employ
belief
consent

1 The school had *practically* no money at first.
2 Did the state *grant* money for the school?
3 After much *debate*, he was finally accepted.
4 He had worked as a *common* laborer.
5 He taught the students very *practical* things.
6 He got *permission* to use another building.
7 When did he *hire* another teacher?
8 Why did he *buy* the old plantation?
9 He stayed at home the *rest* of the year.
10 His great *faith* in his plans convinced people.
11 He spoke to the audience about his *goal*.
12 Why did farms *produce* more than before?
13 Leaders came to Booker for *assistance*.
14 He became *violently* ill in November 1915.
15 His *wisdom* became apparent to everyone.

EXERCISE 74 (Part Two). From the column at the left, select the correct word for the blank space in each sentence. Do not change the forms of the words.

tuition
last
condition
solve
soil
hardships
retire
create
weaken
discipline
allow
wealthy
borrow
admire
audience
miss

1 How long did the Civil War _____?
2 He was in no _____ to appear at the school.
3 Why didn't he have to pay any _____?
4 Why did they _____ the students to work?
5 Did he _____ books from his classmates?
6 Did he ever _____ any of the club meetings?
7 He overcame _____ of almost every kind.
8 He was able to _____ most of the problems.
9 The _____ at the school was very strict.
10 He gave a speech to a very large _____.
11 He went to _____ people for assistance.
12 Did they _____ an agricultural station there?
13 They could plant few things in the poor _____.
14 Why did President Roosevelt _____ him?
15 People begged him to _____ and rest.

EXERCISE 75 (Part Two). Supply the correct preposition for each blank space.

1 Booker was accustomed _____ facing hardships.
2 Once he applied _____ a job at a salt mine.
3 He was hungry when he arrived _____ the school.
4 The principal finally accepted him _____ a student.
5 He prepared _____ the future by working eagerly.
6 He spoke _____ everyone _____ the importance of this.
7 It was granted _____ the request _____ a merchant.
8 He rented a small cabin next _____ a Negro church.
9 He believed _____ his educational plans and goals.
10 He tried to interest everyone _____ the new school.
11 He asked people to help _____ any way possible.
12 Many leaders came _____ Booker _____ assistance.
13 The school at Tuskegee was opened _____ July 4, 1881.
14 He received a degree _____ Harvard _____ June 1896.
15 He wrote the story _____ his life _____ a book _____ 1900.

EXERCISE 76 (Part Two). From the column at the right, select the correct line to complete each of the numbered lines at the left. Write each sentence in its correct form.

1 He asked them to help
2 His speech made him
3 He had worked his way
4 He got permission
5 There was practically
6 The traveling school
7 His constant hard work
8 He taught his students
9 He had solved
10 He was eager to
11 He had started life
12 He was accustomed
13 They drove a wagon
14 He had not even known
15 His gentle manners

(A) the date of his birth
(B) no money left
(C) in any way possible
(D) weakened his heart
(E) to use part of a church
(F) famous almost everywhere
(G) start his new work
(H) to overcoming hardships
(I) through school
(J) very practical things
(K) convinced many people
(L) around the country
(M) difficult problems before
(N) as a slave
(O) was very successful

EXERCISE 77. Study the following word form chart carefully. The word forms which occurred in the preceding story are italicized.

	ADJECTIVE	NOUN	VERB	ADVERB
1	*wise*	wisdom	x x x x x	wisely
2	*strong*	strength	strengthen	strongly
3	*patient*	patience	x x x x x	patiently
4	x x x x x	*choice*	choose (irreg.)	x x x x x
5	x x x x x	acceptance	*accept*	x x x x x
6	*eager*	eagerness	x x x x x	eagerly
7	x x x x x	invitation	*invite*	x x x x x
8	introductory	introduction	*introduce*	x x x x x
9	wasteful	*waste*	waste	wastefully
10	x x x x x	development	*develop*	x x x x x
11	*tactful*	tact	x x x x x	tactfully
12	harmonious	*harmony*	x x x x x	harmoniously
13	faithful	*faith*	x x x x x	faithfully
14	creative	creation	*create*	creatively
15	*scientific*	science scientist	x x x x x	scientifically
16	x x x x x	approval	*approve*	x x x x x
17	x x x x x	improvement	*improve*	x x x x x
18	successful	*success*	succeed	successfully
19	x x x x x	recognition	*recognize*	x x x x x
20	admirable	admiration	*admire*	admirably
21	*vigorous*	vigor	invigorate	vigorously
22	advisable	*advice*	advise	advisably
23	*ill*	illness	x x x x x	x x x x x
24	*proud*	pride	x x x x x	proudly
25	*difficult*	difficulty	x x x x x	x x x x x
26	decisive	decision	*decide*	decisively
27	*ambitious*	ambition	x x x x x	ambitiously
28	preparatory	preparation	*prepare*	x x x x x
29	x x x x x	surprise	*surprise*	x x x x x
30	*clean*	cleanliness	clean	cleanly
31	productive	production	*produce*	productively
32	solvable	solution	*solve*	x x x x x

EXERCISE 79. Use the correct form of each italicized word in the sentence which follows. Notice the first two examples. Refer to the word form chart and examples whenever necessary.

1	*wise*	A few people saw the *wisdom* of this idea.
2	*strong*	His work required great *strength* and courage.
3	*patient*	His work also required a great deal of _____.
4	*choice*	Why did the officials _____ him for the position?
5	*accept*	When did he announce his _____ of the position?
6	*eager*	He explained the reason for his _____.
7	*invite*	The governor sent Booker a formal _____.
8	*introduce*	The _____ was made by the governor himself.
9	*waste*	He felt it was _____ to spend time on books.
10	*develop*	His first goal was the _____ of character.
11	*tactful*	He knew that much _____ was necessary.
12	*harmony*	He wanted people to live together _____.
13	*faith*	All of the teachers were _____ to Booker.
14	*create*	The _____ of a new station was important.
15	*scientific*	Later Tuskegee offered new courses in _____.
16	*approve*	The state legislature finally gave its _____.
17	*improve*	This caused an _____ in the standard of living.
18	*success*	Did he _____ in getting money for the school?
19	*recognize*	He received _____ all over the United States.
20	*admire*	The president expressed his _____ of Booker.
21	*vigorous*	All his life he worked with great _____.
22	*advice*	Why was he able to _____ business leaders?
23	*ill*	What was the cause of his violent _____?
24	*proud*	He always spoke about the school with _____.
25	*difficult*	In the beginning, he faced many _____.
26	*decide*	He explained the importance of the _____.
27	*ambitious*	His first employer recognized his great _____.
28	*prepare*	He had good _____ for this kind of work.
29	*surprise*	He tried hard not to show his _____.
30	*clean*	He explained to them that _____ was important.
31	*produce*	They showed these new _____ to the farmers.
32	*solve*	Booker finally found a _____ to the problem.

EXERCISE 78. Study the following examples for the preceding word form chart. The numbers correspond to those on the word form chart.

1 **wise, wisdom, wisely.** He was a *wise* man. He always spoke and acted *wisely*. Everyone admired his *wisdom*. *Wisdom* is important in life.

2 **strong, strength, strengthen, strongly.** He was a *strong* man. He used *strong* words. He spoke about the subject *strongly*. He had great *strength* physically and mentally. He wanted to *strengthen* the position of the school.

3 **patient, patience, patiently.** He was a *patient* man. He waited for an opportunity very *patiently*. Everyone admired his *patience*. *Patience* is an important quality.

4 **choice, choose, chose, chosen.** His *choice* of names was unusual. What name did he *choose?* He *chose* the name of the first president. His mother had *chosen* his first name.

5 **acceptance, accept.** The principal *accepted* him as a student. He *accepted* the offer gratefully. He was happy about the *acceptance*. He sent his *letter of acceptance* immediately.

6 **eager, eagerness, eagerly.** He was *eager* to start his work. He started his work *eagerly*. His *eagerness* was easy to understand.

7 **invitation, invite.** The governor *invited* him to speak at a conference. He was *invited* by the governor. He received *a formal invitation*. He accepted the *invitation* at once.

8 **introductory, introduction, introduce.** The governor *introduced* him to the audience. He was *introduced* by the governor. The *introduction* was short. The governor *made the introduction*. His *introductory* comments were complimentary.

9 **wasteful, waste, wastefully.** He felt this was *a waste of time*. He tried to eliminate any *waste* of effort. Please put the *waste* in the wastebasket. He didn't want to *waste* time. He didn't *waste* the money. He wasn't a *wasteful* person. He wasn't *wasteful* with money. He didn't use his time *wastefully*.

10 **development, develop.** He wanted to *develop* personality in his students. Things *developed* very rapidly. He observed the *developments* carefully.

11 **tactful, tact, tactfully.** He was a *tactful* man. He discussed the subject *tactfully*. He *used great tact* when he discussed things. *Tact* is a useful quality.

12 **harmonious, harmony, harmoniously.** *Harmony* between races was important to him. He wanted both races to *live in harmony*. He felt that a *harmonious* relationship was important. He felt that both races could live *harmoniously*.

13 **faithful, faith, faithfully.** The teachers were *faithful* to their leader. They worked for the school *faithfully*. Their *faith* in him was apparent. They *expressed their faith* in their leader.

14 **creative, creation, create, creatively.** He *created* a new department in the school. He felt that the *creation* of a new department was important. He was a *creative* person. He always thought about education *creatively*.

15 **scientific, science, scientist, scientifically.** He knew that *science* was important in agriculture. A *scientist* came to the school. The students studied *scientific* agriculture. They studied agriculture *scientifically*.

16 **approval, approve.** His plan was *approved* by the legislature. They *expressed their approval* of the plan. Their *approval* was important.

17 **improvement, improve.** The experiments helped to *improve* the standard of living. The *improvement* was easy to see. They *made improvements* everywhere.

18 **successful, success, succeed, successfully.** He wrote many *successful* books. He finished school *successfully*. He was responsible for the *success* of the school. *Success* is an important thing to many people. He *succeeded* in his work.

19 **recognition, recognize.** *Recognition* came slowly. He *received recognition* from everyone. People *recognized* him as the leader of his race. I could not *recognize* that man in the darkness of the night. *Recognition* was impossible in the darkness.

20 **admiration, admire.** The president *admired* the professor's determination. The president expressed his *admiration* to many people.

21 **vigorous, vigor, invigorate, vigorously.** He was a *vigorous* worker. He always worked *vigorously*. His *vigor* for that kind of work was apparent. Hard work seemed to *invigorate* him.

22 **advisable, advice, advise, advisably.** Many people asked him for *advice*. He *gave advice* to many educators. He *advised* many educators. He felt that strong action was *advisable*. He was *advisably* careful.

23 **ill, illness.** He became very *ill*. His *illness* was serious.

24 **proud, pride, proudly.** He was *proud* of his students' accomplishments. He spoke about their accomplishments *proudly*. His *pride* was apparent. He *expressed his pride* in their accomplishments. He *took pride in* speaking about the school.

25 **difficult, difficulty.** The work was *difficult*. Those were *difficult* times for everyone. Everyone *had difficulty* with the work. He mentioned his *difficulties* to his friends.

26 **decisive, decision, decide, decisively.** The *decision* was important. He had to *make a decision* quickly. He *decided* to ask for help. He was a *decisive* person. He spoke about the subject *decisively*.

27 **ambitious, ambition, ambitiously.** He was an *ambitious* student. He always worked *ambitiously*. He always *worked with great ambition*. His *ambition* was to help people.

28 **preparation, prepare.** He *prepared* his lessons carefully. He *prepared* for the conference by reading the reports carefully. He was *prepared* to answer questions. His *preparation* for the job was excellent. He *made preparations* for the visitors.

29 **surprise.** His answer *surprised* everyone. Their *surprise* was apparent.

30 **clean, cleanliness, cleanly.** He *cleaned* the room carefully. His clothes were *clean*. He always dressed neatly and *cleanly*. He knew that *cleanliness* was important.

31 **productive, production, produce, productively.** The farmers were able to *produce* better crops. The amount of *production* was also increased. Farms became more *productive*. The land was used more *productively*.

32 **solvable, solution, solve.** The problem was *solvable*. The problem was *solved* by him. He *solved* the problem easily. The *solution* was simple. He *found the solution* very easily.

EXERCISE 80. Select the correct way to complete each of the following sentences. Write each sentence in its correct form.

1 According to the story, Booker's mother wanted him (*a*) to be the president of Harvard University. (*b*) to learn how to read and write. (*c*) to find an old spelling book. (*d*) to choose the name of the first president.

2 The wife of the mine owner encouraged Booker (*a*) to get a job in the salt mine. (*b*) to organize a speaker's club. (*c*) to become a janitor at a university. (*d*) to be neat and clean and to study.

3 Booker was not accepted as a student at Hampton Institute immediately because (*a*) he was in no condition to make an impressive appearance after his 500-mile trip. (*b*) he was ambitious and wanted to earn more money. (*c*) he enjoyed debating too much. (*d*) he swept and dusted the room several times.

4 During the time he was at Hampton Institute as a teacher, Booker realized that (*a*) he could sweep because Mrs. Ruffner had taught him well. (*b*) his future was in the field of education. (*c*) he knew almost nothing about his ancestry. (*d*) the Confederacy had finally admitted its defeat.

5 Among other reasons, Booker T. Washington was a good choice for the job of principal in the new school at Tuskegee because (*a*) he understood his people and knew their problems. (*b*) he didn't know his father's name or the date of his birth. (*c*) the state legislature had granted $2000 for a training school. (*d*) people were beginning to see the wisdom of educating Negroes.

6 Professor Washington taught the first students at Tuskegee very practical things because (*a*) he was strongly recommended by the officials of Hampton Institute. (*b*) he was eager to start his new work. (*c*) each student spent part of his time in physical labor. (*d*) he felt that book knowledge was a waste of time for them.

7 Professor Washington's speech in Atlanta in 1895 was significant because this was the first time that (*a*) a Negro had received an honorary degree. (*b*) the Alabama legislature had granted a large amount of money for a speaker. (*c*) an important white official had introduced a Negro leader to an audience of Southerners. (*d*) a speech had made someone famous all over the United States.

8 Many wealthy people gave money to Tuskegee because of (a) a dormitory for girls called Alabama Hall. (b) President Cleveland's letter of congratulation. (c) Booker's successful work with a group of Indian boys. (d) Booker's gentle manners and his great faith in his plans.

9 Professors Washington and Carver started a "traveling school" in order (a) to show farmers new ideas and new products that could be grown in poor soil. (b) to explain the importance of training Negro students in scientific agriculture. (c) to convince people that the school needed another building. (d) to create an agricultural experiment station.

10 Professor Washington's family and friends begged him to retire and rest, but he said that (a) he was writing a book about his life called *Up From Slavery*. (b) Theodore Roosevelt admired his vigorous determination. (c) he still had many important things to do. (d) business leaders needed advice and assistance.

MAN IN FLIGHT

By Bernard Jaffe

SAMUEL P. LANGLEY was a successful architect and civil engineer in Chicago in the mid-nineteenth century. At the age of thirty, he became a professional astronomer and earned an international reputation.

Langley worked out a system of regulating clocks in railroad stations. In his system, he used astronomical measurements. For the first time, every station had uniform and correct time. The system in use today is based on Langley's original plan.

He made many contributions in the field of solar research. He suggested a new concept on the nature of sunspots. Several years later, he was proved to be correct. He invented a sensitive heat-measuring instrument to study unknown parts of the sun's spectrum. His invention

flight	astronomer	measurement	research	sensitive
successful	earn	uniform	suggest	measure
architect	international	in use	concept	instrument
civil engineer	reputation	base	nature	unknown
mid-nineteenth	system	original	sunspot	spectrum
century	regulate	contribution	prove	invention
professional	astronomical	solar	invent	

was extremely sensitive. For example, it could detect the body heat of a cow a quarter mile away. Langley was one of the first people to suggest a definite relationship between solar heat and the weather on earth. He was one of the first to see the possibility of predicting the weather.

Langley became Assistant Secretary and then Secretary of the Smithsonian Institution. As Secretary, he entered the field of aeronautics. He made many experiments. After these experiments, he built a large model airplane that flew three quarters of a mile. It was named the Aerodrome No. 6, from the Greek words meaning "air runner." Langley had shown that mechanical flight was possible. He felt that his work was done. He stopped his experiments with the following prediction: "The great universal highway overhead is now soon to be opened."

Several years later, the United States War Department asked Langley to design and build a flying machine. Military officials wanted a machine large enough to carry a pilot. Langley designed the aircraft and started construction of the frame in the shops at the Smithsonian. He felt that he needed a very powerful but light motor. Therefore, he tried to find a motor which weighed less than ten pounds per horsepower. Manufacturers in Europe and the United States stated that this was impossible. In the meantime, he had practically completed his flying machine. Therefore, there was only one thing for Langley to do. He designed and built his own motor. In a short time, he produced a water-cooled gasoline engine of 52 horsepower which weighed less than five pounds per horsepower!

After five years of planning and working, Langley's machine was ready to take off from a boat in the Potomac River. Langley felt that his motor could keep the machine in the air but could not lift it from the ground. Therefore, he planned to use a movable launching car on the deck of the boat. On the first trial on October 7, 1903, the flying machine caught on the launching car. Both the pilot and the machine fell into the river, and the watching crowd was disappointed. Langley's

extremely	institution	overhead	shop	produce
detect	aeronautics	department	powerful	take off
quarter	experiment	design	therefore	lift
definite	model	military	weigh	movable
relationship	mechanical	official	horsepower	launch
possibility	possible	pilot	manufacturer	deck
predict	prediction	aircraft	impossible	trial
assistant	universal	construction	in the meantime	disappoint
secretary	highway	frame		

machine was repaired for a second test flight two months later. Again it fell into the water, and the crowd lost patience. Newspapers reported the complete failure of "Langley's Folly." The inventor was widely criticized. A heavier-than-air flying machine, they said, was just a madman's dream.

Langley, now almost seventy years old, returned to his solar research. His seventeen years' work with flying machines was over. Exactly nine days later, Langley's dream came true only one hundred air miles away.

QUESTIONS FOR ORAL AND WRITTEN PRACTICE

(1) What was Samuel P. Langley's profession in Chicago. (2) What did he do at the age of thirty? (3) What kind of reputation did he earn? (4) What kind of system did Langley work out? (5) What kind of measurements did he use? (6) What did every railroad station have for the first time? (7) What is the system in use today based on? (8) In what field did he make many contributions? (9) What new concept did he suggest? (10) When was he proved to be correct? (11) Why did he invent a heat-measuring instrument? (12) How sensitive was his invention? (13) What did he suggest about the weather on earth? (14) What possibility did he see? (15) At the Smithsonian, what field did he enter? (16) When did he build a large model airplane? (17) How far did the model airplane fly? (18) What was the model named? (19) Where did the name come from? (20) How did Langley feel then? Why? (21) What did he predict when he stopped his experiments? (22) What did the War Department ask Langley to do? (23) When did they ask him? (24) How large a machine did the military officials want? (25) What did Langley do after he had designed the aircraft? (26) What kind of motor did he need? (27) What kind of motor did he try to find? (28) What did the manufacturers in Europe and the United States say? (29) Where did Langley find the motor he needed? (30) What kind of engine did he produce? (31) How much did his motor weigh per horsepower? (32) When was Langley's machine ready to take off? (33) What did he feel that his motor could do? (34) What did he feel that his motor couldn't do? (35) How did he plan to launch the machine? (36) When was the first trial? (37) What happened on the first trial?

| repair | failure | inventor | criticize | come true |
| lose patience | folly | widely | exactly | |

(38) How did the watching crowd feel?   (39) When was the machine ready for a second test flight?   (40) After the second test flight, what did newspapers report?   (41) How did newspapers describe Langley's flying machine?   (42) What did Langley do after that?   (43) When and where was Langley's dream realized?

PART TWO

The successful conquerors of the air were two brothers, Wilbur and Orville Wright of Dayton, Ohio. As the owners of a bicycle company which they had established in 1888, the brothers had considerable experience with all sorts of mechanical devices. Their attention had been attracted to the problem of human flight by a newspaper story about the death of Otto Lilienthal in 1896 during a gliding flight.

Wilbur and Orville Wright had been encouraged by Samuel Langley's achievements. They had corresponded with Langley and had carefully read the books and articles which he had recommended. They had made careful experiments of their own, first with kites and then with a homemade wind tunnel. These experiments had confirmed two facts for them. First, any inclined surface will receive a lift when it moves through the air. Second, a curved surface will receive a greater lift than a flat one.

With the help of the United States Weather Bureau, the Wright brothers found an ideal location for their gliding experiments. They decided on a narrow sandy beach along the coast of North Carolina at Kitty Hawk. The strong and steady winds at Kitty Hawk supplied the most suitable atmospheric conditions for their efforts. There, in September 1902, they made more than a thousand flights with a glider. They were making tests and trying to solve the many problems of flight. One of these was the problem of equilibrium. In the beginning, the Wrights solved this problem in a peculiar way. The pilot changed his position as he moved through the air! On May 23, 1903, the Wrights patented a wing bending device for better lateral control of the machine while it was in flight. During their tests, they also learned

conquerer	human	wind tunnel	narrow	effort
owner	glide	confirm	sandy	glider
bicycle	encourage	fact	beach	solve
establish	achievement	incline	steady	equilibrium
considerable	correspond	surface	supply	in the beginning
experience	recommend	curve	suitable	peculiar
all sorts of	kite	bureau	atmospheric	patent
device	homemade	ideal	condition	lateral

SAMUEL P. LANGLEY

to land their glider more safely. Their accident rate began to drop. Finally, they put in a four-cylinder twelve-horsepower engine.

A twenty-one-mile-per-hour wind was blowing on the morning of December 17, 1903. At 10:30 A.M., Orville Wright crawled onto the bottom wing, and the motor was started. The twin propellers were set in motion in opposite directions. The wire holding the airplane was untied, and the plane went forward along a track into the wind. Finally, as Orville moved the controls, it left the ground. It flew perfectly for

accident	put in	twin	opposite	untie
rate	cylinder	propeller	wire	track
drop	crawl	set in motion		

about 120 feet before landing safely. The first human flight in a pow-ered heavier-than-air machine lasted 12 seconds. History was made.

Three more flights were made that day. In the last one, the ma-chine flew for 59 seconds and went 852 feet in the air. The Wrights were very excited, but the public did not give it much importance. There were no newspapermen at Kitty Hawk that morning. Only three news-papers printed any account of the event. Only five people were actually present when this new method of travel was born.

The Wrights built a new machine. Over a year later, they made a twenty-four-mile flight near Dayton, Ohio. They received a patent for their flying machine in 1906. They looked around for customers, but no one was interested. In late 1907, the United States Government be-came interested in planes, and the Wrights built one for the Army. It carried two men and enough fuel for a 125-mile flight. This was the first plane ever bought by the United States Army.

Less than three months before they received their airplane patent, Samuel P. Langley died, at the age of seventy-two.

Some of Langley's friends felt that he had built the first plane able to carry a man. They felt that the launching car, and not Langley's plane, had caused the failure of the trials. They asked Glen Curtiss to rebuild Langley's original machine. In 1914, after many changes, it flew successfully for 150 feet. This led the public to believe that Langley, and not the Wright brothers, was the real pioneer. The aerodrome was returned to Washington, repaired, and placed in the National Museum with the inscription:

THE FIRST MAN-CARRYING AEROPLANE IN THE HISTORY OF THE WORLD CAPABLE OF SUSTAINED FREE FLIGHT

Of course, Orville Wright was hurt by this action. Many years of argu-ment over the right to the invention followed. If he had lived, Langley would never have approved of these arguments. He had always avoided such things during his lifetime. Langley was a scrupulously honest man. He was always shy and made friends with great difficulty. He

power	actually	successfully	sustain	lifetime
excite	customer	pioneer	argument	scrupulously
public	fuel	repair	rights	honest
importance	cause	inscription	approve	shy
newspaperman	rebuild	capable	avoid	difficulty
account				

never married and had no close family ties. Nevertheless, he was an active worker in the field of science and was a member of many scientific organizations.

In 1920, the new Secretary of the Smithsonian Institution asked Orville Wright to turn over his original Kitty Hawk plane to the Smithsonian. Wright answered that a "correction of history" was essential first. In 1942, the Smithsonian Institution publicly acknowledged that "Wilbur and Orville Wright made the first sustained flights in a heavier-than-air machine in 1903, and the 1914 flights of Langley's machine, as reconditioned and altered, did not prove that it could have been flown in 1903 before them." This satisfied Orville, and today the original Kitty Hawk plane is in the Smithsonian Institution.

Today, Samuel P. Langley is not forgotten. Through his efforts, the National Zoological Park, the National Gallery of Art and the Astrophysical Observatory, all in Washington, were built. Many people think of these as his monuments. In 1922, he received official recognition of his vital work when the first United States airplane carrier was named after him. In addition, Langley Field in Norfolk, Virginia, will always carry the name of this pioneer in aviation.

QUESTIONS FOR ORAL AND WRITTEN PRACTICE

(44) Who were the successful conquerors of the air? (45) What kind of company did they own? (46) When had they established the company? (47) What did they have experience with? (48) How was their attention attracted to the problem of human flight? (49) What had the brothers been encouraged by? (50) With whom had they corresponded? (51) What had they carefully read? (52) What had they made careful experiments with? (53) What two facts had their experiments confirmed for them? (54) What did the brothers find with the help of the Weather Bureau? (55) What location did they decide on? (56) Why did they decide on Kitty Hawk? (57) When did they make their first glider flights at Kitty Hawk? (58) How many flights did they make there? (59) Why did they make these flights? (60) What was one of these problems? (61) How did they solve the

family ties	organization	acknowledge	astrophysical	vital
active	turn over	recondition	observatory	carrier
science	correction	alter	monument	in addition
member	essential	gallery	recognition	aviation
scientific	publicly			

- Barberis -

WILBUR WRIGHT

problem of equilibrium in the beginning? (62) What device did they patent in 1903, and what was it for? (63) What else did they learn to do during their tests? (64) What happened to their accident rate? (65) What kind of engine did they finally put in? (66) How strong was the wind on the morning of December 17? (67) Who crawled onto the bottom wing, Orville or Wilbur? (68) In what directions did the propellers go? (69) What happened when the wire holding the airplane was untied? (70) What happened as Orville moved the controls? (71) How many feet did it fly, and how long did the flight last? (72) How many flights were made that day? (73) How long was the last flight, in seconds and in feet? (74) How many newspapermen were there at Kitty Hawk that morning? (75) How many people were actually present at this first flight? (77) When did they receive a

ORVILLE WRIGHT

patent for their flying machine? (78) Who became interested in late 1907? (79) How many men and how much fuel did the first Army plane carry? (80) How old was Langley when he died? (81) What did some of Langley's friends feel had caused the failure of the trials? (82) Who was asked to rebuild Langley's original machine? (83) What did the 1914 flight lead the public to believe? (84) Why did many arguments follow? (85) Why didn't Langley make friends easily? (86) What family ties did he have? (87) What did the new Secretary of the Smithsonian ask Orville Wright in 1920? (88) What did Wright answer? (89) Where is the Kitty Hawk today? (90) What was built in Washington through Langley's efforts? (91) When and how did Langley receive official recognition of his work? (92) What airfield will always carry his name?

SUMMARY SENTENCES FOR LABORATORY PRACTICE

(1) Langley was a successful architect and civil engineer. (2) At the age of thirty, he became a professional astronomer. (3) He earned an international reputation. (4) He worked out a system of regulating clocks. (5) The system in use today is based on his plan. (6) He made many contributions in the field of science. (7) Then he entered the field of aeronautics. (8) He made many experiments. (9) He built a large model airplane. (10) It flew three quarters of a mile. (11) He had shown that mechanical flight was possible. (12) He felt that his work was done. (13) He stopped his experiments. (14) The government asked him to build a flying machine. (15) He designed the aircraft and started construction. (16) He needed a very powerful but light motor. (17) Manufacturers said this was impossible. (18) He designed and built his own motor. (19) He produced a gasoline engine of 52 horsepower. (20) After five years, his machine was ready to take off. (21) On the first trial, the machine fell into the river. (22) The watching crowd was disappointed. (23) Newspapers reported complete failure. (24) The inventor was widely criticized. (25) Exactly nine days later, Langley's dream came true. (26) The Wright brothers became interested in building an airplane. (27) They read books and articles Langley had recommended. (28) They made careful experiments of their own. (29) They found an ideal location for their experiments. (30) They decided on a beach along the coast. (31) The strong, steady winds supplied suitable conditions. (32) They made more than a thousand flights with a glider. (33) They tried to solve the many problems of flight. (34) They learned to land their glider safely. (35) Finally, they put in a four-cylinder engine. (36) Their first trial was on the morning of December 17, 1903. (37) Orville moved the controls and the plane left the ground. (38) It flew perfectly for about 120 feet. (39) The first flight in a powered machine lasted 12 seconds. (40) In the last flight, the machine flew for 59 seconds. (41) It went 852 feet in the air. (42) The two brothers were very excited. (43) But the public did not give it much importance. (44) Only five people were there when this first flight was made. (45) Over a year later, the brothers made a twenty-four-mile flight. (46) They received a patent for their flying machine in 1906. (47) In 1907, the government became interested in planes. (48) The brothers built one for the Army. (49) It carried enough fuel for a 125-mile flight. (50) The government finally bought it.

EXERCISE 81. From the column at the left, select the best synonym for the italicized word in each sentence. Rewrite the sentences using the synonyms.

built
finished
connection
lifted
essential
fulfilled
standard
timid
report
controversy
forecast
test
proved
appropriate
balance
constant

1 For the first time, stations had *uniform* time.
2 He saw a *relationship* between the two things.
3 He felt it was possible to *predict* the weather.
4 Langley was too *shy* to have many friends.
5 He *constructed* a large model airplane.
6 He *completed* the frame in the Smithsonian shops.
7 On the first *trial,* the airplane failed to fly.
8 These experiments had *confirmed* two facts.
9 One of the big problems was *equilibrium.*
10 The conditions at Kitty Hawk were *suitable.*
11 The *steady* winds along the beach were helpful.
12 Nine days later, Langley's dream was *realized.*
13 Only three newspapers printed an *account* of it.
14 Many years of *argument* over the rights followed.
15 He received official recognition of his *vital* work.

EXERCISE 82. From the column at the left, select the correct word for each blank space in the sentences at the right. Use each word only once. Do not change the forms of the words.

public
deck
avoid
failure
sensitive
surfaces
rights
kites
solve
ideal
active
patent
rate
wire
fuel
repair

1 Langley was a very _____ worker in his field.
2 His heat-measuring device was _____.
3 He tried to _____ arguments during his lifetime.
4 The newswapers criticized Langley's _____.
5 Langley didn't plan to _____ the plane again.
6 The two brothers made experiments with _____.
7 Curved _____ get more lift than flat ones.
8 They were trying to _____ many problems.
9 Their accident _____ began to drop.
10 They found the _____ location for their tests.
11 The _____ holding the plane was untied.
12 The _____ did not think the flight was important.
13 It carried enough _____ for a 125-mile flight.
14 There was an argument over the _____ to the invention.
15 They received a _____ for their airplane.

EXERCISE 83. Supply the correct preposition for each blank space.

1 He became an astronomer _____ the age _____ thirty.
2 Langley made friends _____ great difficulty.
3 He saw the possibility _____ predicting weather.
4 Later the government became interested _____ airplanes.
5 Langley's motor could keep his plane _____ the air.
6 But the motor could not lift the plane _____ the ground.
7 The machine fell _____ the river _____ the first trial.
8 The Wrights experimented _____ a homemade wind tunnel.
9 They solved the problem _____ an unusual way.
10 The brothers made flights _____ gliders _____ the beginning.
11 They made a thousand flights there _____ September 1902.
12 The plane went forward _____ a track and _____ the wind.
13 They made the first powered flight _____ December 17, 1903.
14 The plane carried enough fuel _____ a long flight.
15 They argued _____ the rights _____ the invention.

EXERCISE 84. From the column at the right, select the correct line to complete each of the numbered lines at the left. Write each sentence in its corrct form.

1	Langley was proved	(A)	caught on the launching car
2	He made many contributions	(B)	widely criticized
3	He needed a very powerful	(C)	it much importance
4	There was only one thing	(D)	as his monuments
5	The twin propellers were	(E)	with great difficulty
6	The public did not give	(F)	experiments of their own
7	They asked Glen Curtiss	(G)	for Langley to do
8	Langley would never have	(H)	to rebuild his airplane
9	Langley made friends	(I)	to see this possibility
10	Many people think of these	(J)	but light motor
11	He was one of the first	(K)	to be correct
12	Langley's flying machine	(L)	for their experiments
13	The inventor was	(M)	set in motion
14	The brothers had made	(N)	approved of arguments
15	The location was ideal	(O)	in solar research

EXERCISE 85. Study the following word form chart carefully. The word forms which occurred in the preceding story are italicized.

ADJECTIVE	NOUN	VERB	ADVERB
1 *professional*	profession professional	x x x x x	professionally
2 systematic	*system*	systematize	systematically
3 regulatory	regulator regulation	*regulate*	x x x x x
4 x x x x x	*measurement*	measure	x x x x x
5 *uniform*	uniformity	x x x x x	uniformly
6 *original*	origin original originality	originate	originally
7 x x x x x	*contribution*	contribute	x x x x x
8 x x x x x	suggestion	*suggest*	x x x x x
9 inventive	*inventor* *invention*	invent	inventively
10 *sensitive*	sensitivity	sensitize	sensitively
11 predictable	*prediction*	predict	predictably
12 experimental	*experiment*	experiment	experimentally
13 *mechanical*	mechanic mechanics *machine*	mechanize	mechanically
14 x x x x x	*flight*	*fly* (irreg.)	x x x x x
15 x x x x x	design	*design*	x x x x x
16 x x x x x	*construction*	construct	x x x x x
17 x x x x x	weight	*weigh*	x x x x x
18 x x x x x	*lift*	lift	x x x x x
19 movable	*motion* movement	*move*	x x x x x
20 patient	*patience*	x x x x x	patiently
21 critical	critic criticism	*criticize*	critically
22 achievable	*achievement*	achieve	x x x x x
23 x x x x x	correspondent correspondence	*correspond*	x x x x x
24 x x x x x	recommendation	*recommend*	x x x x x
25 x x x x x	confirmation	*confirm*	x x x x x
26 *steady*	steadiness	steady	steadily

ADJECTIVE	NOUN	VERB	ADVERB
27 *suitable*	suitability	suit	suitably
28 x x x x x	*patent*	*patent*	x x x x x
29 x x x x x	*device*	devise	x x x x x
30 *opposite*	opposite opposition	oppose	x x x x x
31 perfect	perfection	perfect	*perfectly*
32 x x x x x	*recognition*	recognize	x x x x x

EXERCISE 86. Study the following examples for the preceding word form chart. The numbers correspond to those on the word form chart.

1 **professional, profession, professionally.** He became a *professional* astronomer. He was a *professional*. He did the work *professionally*. Astronomy became his *profession*.

2 **systematic, system, systematize, systematically.** He worked out a *system* of regulating clocks. He regulated clocks *systematically*. He worked out a *systematic* method of regulating clocks. He *systematized* things.

3 **regulatory, regulator, regulation, regulate.** His measurements *regulated* the clocks. The *regulation* of clocks is important. He used a *regulatory* device. The *regulator* worked perfectly.

4 **measurement, measure.** The *measurement* of time is important. His *measurements* were correct. He *measured* the distance.

5 **uniform, uniformity, uniformly.** Every station had *uniform* time. The clocks showed the time *uniformly*. All the clocks operated with *uniformity*.

6 **original, origin, originality, originate, originally.** The *original* airplane was a model. Where is the *original* now? His plan was *original*. His *original* plan is used today. He always tried to think *originally*. *Originally*, he planned to do something different. He *originated* the plan. What is the *origin* of the plan? People realized the *originality* of the plan.

7 **contribution, contribute.** His *contribution* to solar research was important. He made *contributions* in his field. He *contributed* greatly.

8 **suggestion, suggest.** He *suggested* the idea to several people. His *suggestion* was important. He made *suggestions* to several people.

9 **inventive, inventor, invention, invent, inventively.** His *inventions* were important. He was an *inventor*. He had an *inventive* mind. He always worked *inventively*. He *invented* many things.

10 **sensitive, sensitivity, sensitively.** He invented a *sensitive* instrument. The instrument measured heat *sensitively*. The *sensitivity* of the machine was surprising. The machine had great *sensitivity*.

11 **predictable, prediction, predict.** He *predicted* the development of aviation. He *predicted* that aviation would be important. He *made a prediction*. His *prediction* was accurate. He felt that weather was *predictable*.

12 **experimental, experiment, experimentally.** He *experimented* with a model airplane. His *experiments* with the model were important. He *made experiments* with a model. He *conducted experiments* with a model. He built an *experimental* airplane. He flew the model *experimentally*.

13 **mechanical, mechanic, mechanics, machine, mechanize, mechanically.** He had shown that *mechanical* flight was possible. It was possible to fly *mechanically*. He hired a *mechanic* to help him. The brothers studied *mechanics* through books. It was possible to fly in a *machine*. He *mechanized* flight.

14 **flight, fly.** They wanted to *fly* as far as possible. The airplane *flew* three quarters of a mile. No airplane had *flown* before that time. The first *flight* was short. The plane *made a flight* of three quarters of a mile. People said that a *flying* machine was impossible.

15 **design.** He *designed* an aircraft for the army. The *design* was original.

16 **construction, construct.** The *construction* of the frame was important. He *constructed* the frame in a short time.

17 **weight, weigh.** His motor *weighed* five pounds. The *weight* was five pounds.

18 **lift.** The motor and the wings *lifted* the airplane from the ground. The wing received a *lift* when it moved. The wings had great *lifting* power.

19 **movable, movement, motion, move.** He used a *movable* launching car. The launching car *moved* forward. The forward *movement* of the car was important. The propellers were *set in motion*. The forward *motion* was stopped.

20 **patient, patience, patiently.** *Patience* was necessary. The crowd *lost patience*. The crowd wasn't *patient*. The crowd didn't observe his failure *patiently*.

21 **critical, critic, criticism, criticize, critically.** The invention was *criticized* by almost everyone. His *critics* called the airplane "Langley's Folly." There was much *criticism* of the invention. They were *critical* of his work. They spoke about his work *critically*.

22 **achievable, achievement, achieve.** The *achievement* of flight was important. The brothers were encouraged by his *achievements*. He *achieved* many things during his life. He *achieved* success with his model. He felt that flight was *achievable*.

23 **correspondent, correspondence, correspond.** The brothers *corresponded* with Langley. The *correspondence* was helpful to them. They *carried on correspondence* for several years. Their *correspondent* helped them.

24 **recommendation, recommend.** He *recommended* things to them. He *recommended* books for them to read. He *recommended* that they study certain things. They read the *recommended* books. His *recommendations* were helpful. He made *recommendations* to them.

25 **confirmation, confirm.** Their experiments *confirmed* several facts. There were several *confirmed* facts. The *confirmation* of these facts was important. They *got confirmation* through their experiments.

26 **steady, steadiness, steadily.** The *steady* winds were helpful. The winds blew across the beach *steadily*. The *steadiness* of the winds was helpful. The winds *steadied* the wings of the airplane.

27 **suitable, suitability, suit, suitably.** They considered the *suitability* of the location. The strong winds supplied *suitable* conditions for their efforts. The beach was *suitably* located for their efforts. The location *suited* the brothers because of the strong winds.

28 **patent.** The brothers *patented* the new device. They *applied for a patent*. They *received a patent* later. The *patent* was an important one.

29 **device, devise.** They *devised* a way to give the pilot better control. The *device* gave the pilot better control.

30 **opposite** (adj., noun, prep.), **opposition, oppose.** The two propellers moved in *opposite* directions. The motors were *opposite* each other. Did the left motor turn clockwise?—No, just *the opposite*. The motors *opposed* each other. The *opposition* of the motors caused certain problems.

31 **perfect** (adj.), **perfection, perfect** (verb), **perfectly.** The airplane made a *perfect* flight. The airplane flew *perfectly* for 120 feet. *Perfection* of the wing was important. They *perfected* the device later.

32 recognition, recognize. People finally *recognized* him as an important scientist. They finally *recognized* the importance of his work. He finally *received recognition* for his work. *Recognition* wasn't important to him.

EXERCISE 87. Use the correct form of each italicized word in the sentence which follows. Notice the first two examples. Refer to the word form chart and examples whenever necessary.

1	*original*	Langley's plans showed much *originality*.
2	*machine*	He showed that *mechanical* flight was possible.
3	*sensitive*	His instrument was _____ to the heat of the sun.
4	*achieve*	The Wright brothers heard of Langley's _____.
5	*fly*	The machine was repaired for another _____.
6	*device*	The Wright brothers patented a bending _____.
7	*suggest*	They listened to his _____ carefully.
8	*uniform*	All clocks operated _____ with his regulator.
9	*regulate*	Was the _____ of clocks an important thing?
10	*system*	The two brothers made their experiments _____.
11	*contribution*	Langley _____ many things to the field of science.
12	*measurement*	He knew that careful _____ were very important.
13	*experiment*	Langley built an _____ model to test carefully.
14	*recommend*	He made many important _____ to the brothers.
15	*patience*	People did not listen to the scientist _____.
16	*correspond*	What was the exact nature of their _____?
17	*confirm*	Their experiments gave them _____ of two facts.
18	*recognition*	Later people _____ him as a great scientist.
19	*perfectly*	They finally announced the_____of the machine.
20	*perfectly*	After many months, they _____ the wing device.
21	*invent*	Many of his _____ are in practical use today.
22	*invent*	Langley was always an _____ person.
23	*suitable*	The narrow beach was _____ for the experiment.
24	*suitable*	They discussed the _____ of the sandy beach.
25	*steady*	The _____ of the winds was important to them.
26	*steady*	The winds moved across the sandy beach _____.
27	*move*	The two propellers were carefully set in _____.
28	*move*	He planned to use a _____ launching car.
29	*predict*	He realized the _____ of weather was possible.
30	*predict*	He felt that the weather was _____.
31	*criticize*	The newspapers _____ him for his failure.
32	*criticize*	The newspapers were _____ of his experiments.

EXERCISE 88. Select the correct way to complete each of the following sentences. Write each sentence in its correct form.

1 Samuel P. Langley earned an international reputation as (a) an architect and builder. (b) a civil engineer. (c) an astronomer and inventor. (d) an airplane pilot.

2 Langley invented a heat-measuring instrument (a) to study sunspots. (b) to study the sun's spectrum. (c) because he wanted to measure the body heat of a cow. (d) to regulate railroad clocks.

3 Several years after Langley had suggested a new concept on the nature of sunspots, (a) he received a patent for a military aircraft. (b) he led the public to believe that he was the original pioneer. (c) he returned to civil engineering. (d) he was proved to be correct.

4 One large model airplane flew (a) a quarter mile. (b) three quarters of a mile. (c) 120 feet. (d) one mile.

5 Langley felt that his work was done (a) when he had proved that weather could be predicted. (b) because he had finished his solar research. (c) when he had worked out his system for regulating railroad clocks. (d) when he had shown that mechanical flight was possible.

6 The War Department asked Langley to design and build an aircraft that (a) would be lighter than air. (b) would be large enough to carry a pilot. (c) would be efficient for predicting weather. (d) would have a motor which weighed less than ten pounds per horsepower.

7 After he had constructed the frame, Langley looked for a motor that (a) weighed at least 10 pounds per horsepower. (b) was easy to find. (c) weighed less than 10 pounds per horsepower. (d) was water-cooled.

8 On its first trial on October 7, 1903, Langley saw his machine (a) land safely. (b) fly 150 feet. (c) fall into the Potomac River. (d) take off from the ground.

9 Langley had worked with flying machines (a) for seventeen years. (b) all his life. (c) for seventy years. (d) for five years.

10 The Wright brothers' experiments confirmed for them that (a) a heavier-than-air flying machine was a madman's dream. (b) a curved surface will receive a greater lift than a flat one. (c) they needed a very powerful but light motor. (d) they needed a wind tunnel.

11 The wing bending device they patented solved the problem of (*a*) landing safely. (*b*) launching the glider. (*c*) the high accident rate. (*d*) equilibrium.

12 The first human flight in a powered heavier-than-air machine (*a*) was made by the five people who were actually present. (*b*) caused Langley's death at the age of seventy-two. (*c*) lasted only twelve seconds. (*d*) was made by Curtiss in Langley's original machine.

13 Langley was (*a*) loud and moody. (*b*) married and the father of two girls. (*c*) one of a large family. (*d*) extremely honest and shy.

14 In 1920, Orville Wright said (*a*) he would gladly turn over the original Kitty Hawk plane to the Smithsonian. (*b*) "a correction of history" was needed before turning over the Kitty Hawk plane. (*c*) he refused to turn over the Kitty Hawk plane. (*d*) he would build a monument to Langley.

15 Langley's vital work was recognized (*a*) in a special citation from the United States Government. (*b*) by placing his name on several buildings in Washington. (*c*) when the United States' first airplane carrier was named after him in 1922. (*d*) by Orville Wright, when he built the Langley monument.

The story "Man in Flight" had its origin in Bernard Jaffe's *Men of Science in America,* Chapter Fourteen, "Samuel Pierpont Langley (1834-1906)" by permission of Simon and Schuster, Publishers, Copyright 1944 by Bernard Jaffe. Because of the special considerations involved in preparing readings for students of English as a second language, the section dealing with Langley and the Wright brothers in Mr. Jaffe's book was freely rewritten and is not representative of the author's professional writing technique.

The illustration by Jacob Landau on page 179 originally appeared in *The Wright Brothers, Pioneers of American Aviation* by Quentin Reynolds, New York, Landmark Books, Random House, Copyright 1950. The illustrations have been reproduced with the permission of the publisher.

THE END OF THE SHENANDOAH

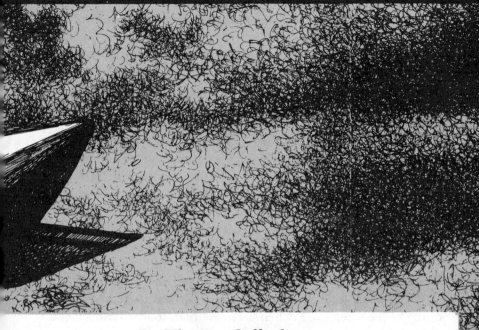

By Thomas Gallagher

PART ONE

IT WAS SEPTEMBER 1925. Lieutenant Commander Zachary Lansdowne and his wife were standing beneath the Shenandoah, a giant navy dirigible. People called it "the strongest dirigible ever built." Commander Lansdowne was in command of the Shenandoah which was ready for a trip from Lakehurst, New Jersey, to Detroit, Michigan. "There'll be storms in Ohio," he said, "but I think I can avoid them."

Mrs. Lansdowne was worried. Her husband had often told her that storms over the Ohio Valley in September could break the frame of a dirigible. It was cloudy and windy as the Shenandoah started its trip west. There were 41 officers and men aboard.

Everything went well until after midnight of the next day. Then over Ohio, the Shenandoah ran into strong winds. For several hours,

lieutenant	giant	in command	worry	windy
commander	navy	there'll	frame	aboard
beneath	dirigible	avoid	cloudy	run into

the dirigible made little progress despite the roaring power of all its engines. Lightning flashed around the huge airship and thunder seemed to knock it sideways.

Commander Lansdowne and 13 other men were in the control car under the front part of the ship. They were trying to keep the Shenandoah under control. A strong vertical air current was pushing the giant upward. This was extremely dangerous. Above the height of 3,800 feet, the ship's gas bags which were distributed throughout the interior could easily expand and break. Everybody in the control car realized the extreme danger.

Although he was reluctant to do it, Lansdowne decided to release some of the gas. In comparison with hydrogen, the cost of helium was enormous. The Shenandoah contained $150,000 worth of helium gas. But he knew this would prevent the airship from rising; it would also prevent the gas bags from breaking. The men released gas for five minutes, but the ship still rose. At 7,000 feet, they succeeded in getting the ship level again. Their chances of survival seemed better.

Just then, a layer of cold air descended on the ship, and the Shenandoah swayed and turned almost on end. Then the giant began to plunge rapidly. Cook John T. Hahn had just lowered the flame under some boiling coffee when the kitchen utensils began to fly over his head. Everywhere men hesitated for only a moment and then grabbed for girders in alarm. Blood rushed to their heads as the pressure of the atmosphere and the acceleration increased.

It was like riding down a waterfall. The giant dirigible fell 4,500 feet, almost four times the height of the Empire State Building! At 2,500 feet, the Shenandoah suddenly stopped falling. The air became hot and sticky again. Another air current was forcing the ship upward again! There was no doubt about it now. They were in trouble. Huge

progress	vertical	although	chance	girder
despite	current	reluctant	survival	in alarm
roar	upward	release	layer	pressure
power	extremely	in comparison	descend	atmosphere
engine	dangerous	hydrogen	sway	acceleration
lightning	height	helium	turn on end	increase
flash	bag	enormous	plunge	waterfall
huge	distribute	contain	lower	suddenly
airship	throughout	worth	flame	sticky
thunder	interior	prevent	boil	force
knock	expand	rise	utensils	doubt
sideways	realize	succeed	hesitate	invisible
control	extreme	level	grab	piston
under control	danger			

invisible pistons of hot and cold air were going up and down all around the ship at different speeds and with unequal force.

The Shenandoah was too big to avoid the approaching disaster. Unlike a small ship, the Shenandoah could not ascend or descend as it passed from one force to another. The giant dirigible was two city blocks long! The force which was exerted at the front and rear of the ship was often the exact opposite of the force which was exerted at the middle of the ship. It was like bending a pencil downward at both ends.

Lieutenant Commander Rosendahl, second in command, had just climbed the ladder from the control cabin when the frame began to vibrate strangely. His ears were filled with a thunderous metallic sound as the ship's frame began to crack. Everything became very confused.

Chief Rigger Tobin was on his way to the control car. Suddenly he started to step into thousands of feet of space. It was an astonishing sight. The part of the ship that had been in front of him was drifting away! He and Rosendahl had been only 200 feet apart. Now they were completely separated from each other. *The ship had broken in two!*

QUESTIONS FOR ORAL AND WRITTEN PRACTICE

(1) What was the Shenandoah? (2) What did people call the Shenandoah? (3) Who was in command of the Shenandoah? (4) What was the Shenandoah ready for? (5) What did the commander say about the weather? (6) Why was Mrs. Lansdowne worried? (7) How was the weather as the dirigible started its trip? (8) How many officers and men were there aboard the Shenandoah? (9) How did everything go until midnight of the next day? (10) What did the ship run into over Ohio? (11) How much progress did the ship make with the power of its engines? (12) How did the thunder and lightning affect the ship? (13) Where were Commander Lansdowne and 13 other men? (14) What were they trying to do? (15) What was pushing the Shenandoah upward? (16) Where were the ship's gas bags located? (17) What could happen to the ship's gas bags above 3,800 feet? (18) What did everybody in the control car realize?

speed	block	downward	crack	sight
unequal	exert	climb	confuse	drift
avoid	rear	ladder	rigger	apart
approach	exact	vibrate	step	separate
disaster	opposite	thunderous	space	break in two
ascend	bend	metallic	astonish	

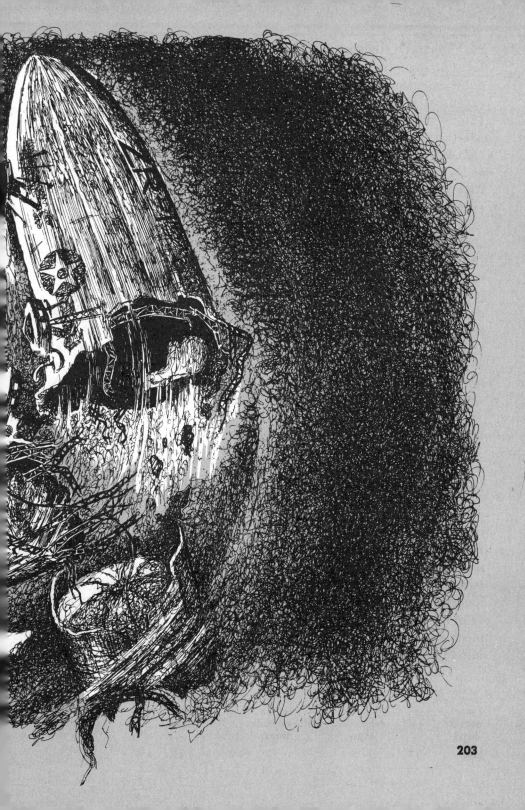

(19) What did Commander Lansdowne decide to do? (20) Why was he reluctant to do it? (21) How many dollars' worth of helium gas did the Shenandoah contain? (22) Why did he decide to release the expensive helium? (23) For how long did the men release gas? (24) What happened when the men released gas? (25) What happened at 7,000 feet? (26) How did their chances of survival seem then? (27) What descended on the ship just then? (28) What did the Shenandoah begin to do rapidly? (29) What had the cook just done? (30) What did the kitchen utensils begin to do? (31) What did men everywhere do? (32) Why did blood rush to their heads? (33) What was it like? (34) How many feet did the giant dirigible fall? (35) What happened at 2,500 feet? (36) How did the air become? (37) What was going up and down all around the ship? (38) How long was the Shenandoah? (39) Why couldn't the ship avoid the approaching disaster? (40) What had Lieutenant Commander Rosendahl just done? (41) What did the frame begin to do? (42) What were his ears filled with? (43) How did everything become at that moment? (44) Where was the chief rigger going? (45) What did he suddenly start to do? (46) What astonishing sight was in front of him? (47) How far apart had he and Rosendahl been? (48) Why were they now separated from each other?

PART TWO

The framework of the Shenandoah was twisted into peculiar shapes, and cables ripped through light metal sheets. Empty oil drums collided violently with pieces of the framework. There were cries of dismay and absolute disbelief as the Shenandoah broke in two. Two men immediately fell out of the open ends to their deaths. At the same time, the control car broke away from the front part of the ship. A few seconds before, Colonel Hall, an army observer on the trip, and Lieutenant Anderson had left the control car. One of the men saw Lt. Anderson disappear through a hole in the ship. Commander Lansdowne and 11 of his men were killed when the control car, which now looked very much like a bus in mid-air, crashed to the earth. He had been born just a hundred miles away where his mother was still living.

The most frightening part of the disaster was just beginning for

framework	cable	drum	absolute	disappear
twist	rip	collide	disbelief	crash
peculiar	sheet	violently	death	frighten
shape	empty	dismay		

the 27 men who were still alive. The two parts of the ship were tossed around violently by the storm. The men held tightly to anything they could find. They were in extreme danger of falling to their deaths. It was like a horrible dream!

The back part of the ship fell to the earth first. The men inside waited until they were fifteen feet from the ground. Then they started to jump. Some men broke their ankles, but everybody survived. From the ground, they saw the front part of the ship. The wind was tossing it around at an altitude of 5,000 feet!

There were six men inside the front part of the Shenandoah. In addition, Lt. Anderson, who had disappeared through a hole in the ship, was still hanging from two wires with both hands and swinging beneath the ship. One of the men threw a rope to Anderson. Somehow he tied the rope around his body. Then, while the other men shouted encouragement, the man pulled Anderson back into the ship inch by inch.

Finally, to bring the Shenandoah to earth, the men began to release the rest of the gas. The crippled ship came downward rapidly. The men tried desperately to slow down the ship as they came closer to the ground. They lowered 200-foot ropes. They hoped these would get caught in the tops of trees and stop the ship. Somehow the ropes failed to get caught in any of them. Two miners on the ground, Ode Gorden and Herb Poling, saw the ropes and did their best to help. They grabbed the ropes firmly, but the crippled ship dragged them along the ground and knocked them against trees.

Meanwhile, a farmer named Ernest Nichols was getting an urgent telephone call from a friend. "Something is coming your way, Ernie! I don't know what it is, but you had better take a look!"

Nichols ran outside. Something was coming straight toward his house. He did not know what it was either. Because of the ropes, it looked like a flying octopus. He glanced over his shoulder and saw his oldest son looking out the upstairs window. He knew that in another minute his wife and six children would be crushed to death.

Just then, he heard the men inside the thing. "Grab hold! Grab

---

toss around	altitude	inch by inch	get caught	take a look
tightly	in addition	cripple	fail	octopus
horrible	hang	desperately	do one's best	glance
dream	swing	slow down	drag	crush
ankle	shout	ropes	urgent	grab hold
survive	encouragement			

hold!" they yelled. "Turn it south!" Nichols reacted quickly. He grabbed one of the ropes and wrapped it around a fence post. The post broke in two. He grabbed the rope again and tied it around an old tree stump. This did not stop the ship either, but it did turn it away from the house. The front part of the ship was now coming straight at him, and he had to run for his life. Then he grabbed the rope again and this time he wrapped it around a strong tree. The remains of the Shenandoah came down to the ground at last! Fourteen men had died and there were 27 survivors.

Nichols' six children were up by the time the men began climbing out of the remains, and they all helped to tie down the nose section of the dirigible.

In the meantime, the cook, who had been the first to reach the ground, had telephoned the news of the disaster from a farmhouse. This call had multiplied into the thousands. Farmers and workers were getting into their Model-T cars and searching all around the area for the fallen "Daughter of the Stars." When they found the remains of the unlucky giant, the most outrageous case of souvenir hunting in American history began. Hundreds of people pulled away practically enough silk covering, metal sheets, and gauges to start stores.

It was the beginning of the end of a brave chapter in aviation history. Ten years later, the disaster of the German dirigible Hindenburg at Lakehurst, New Jersey, made the verdict final. The big bags were too slow, too expensive, and too fragile. In every way, they were less efficient than the airplane, which was just beginning to write a new chapter in the history of flight.

QUESTIONS FOR ORAL AND WRITTEN PRACTICE

(49) What kinds of shapes was the framework twisted into? (50) What did cables do? (51) What did empty oil drums do? (52) What kind of cries were there? (53) What happened to the Shenandoah? (54) What happened to two men immediately? (55) What happened to the control car? (56) Who had left the control car a few seconds before? (57) What happened to Lieutenant Anderson? (58) What happened to Commander Lansdowne and 11 of his men? (59) Where had the commander been born? (60) How many men

yell	remains	area	covering	verdict
wrap	survivor	star	gauge	make final
fence	in the meantime	unlucky	brave	fragile
post	multiply	outrageous	chapter	efficient
stump	Model-T	souvenir	aviation	flight

were still alive?   (61) What was happening to the two parts of the ship?   (62) What did the men do?   (63) What were the men in extreme danger of?   (64) Which part of the ship fell to the earth first?   (65) What did the men do fifteen feet from the ground?   (66) What did they see from the ground?   (67) How many men were inside the front part of the Shenandoah?   (68) Where was Lieutenant Anderson?   (69) What did one of the men do?   (70) What did the man do next?   (71) What did the men do to bring the Shenandoah to earth?   (72) How did the men try to slow down the ship?   (73) Who did their best to help?   (74) What happened when they grabbed the ropes?   (75) What was Ernest Nichols getting from a friend?   (76) What did the friend say?   (77) What did Nichols do?   (78) What did the Shenandoah look like?   (79) What did he see when he glanced over his shoulder?   (80) What did he know would happen in another minute?   (81) What did the men inside the Shenandoah yell?   (82) What did Nichols wrap the rope around first?   (83) What happened?   (84) What did he tie the rope around next?   (85) Why did he have to run for his life?   (86) How did he finally stop the Shenandoah?   (87) How many men had died?   (88) When did the disaster of the Hindenburg occur?   (89) What was wrong with dirigibles?   (90) What was just beginning to write a new chapter in the history of flight?

SUMMARY SENTENCES FOR LABORATORY PRACTICE

(1) It was September 1925.   (2) Commander Lansdowne was in command of a giant navy dirigible.   (3) It was named the "Shenandoah."   (4) People called it "the strongest dirigible ever built."   (5) The dirigible was ready for a trip from New Jersey to Detroit, Michigan.   (6) The commander said there would be storms in Ohio.   (7) But he thought he could avoid them.   (8) The Shenandoah started its trip west.   (9) It was cloudy and windy.   (10) There were 41 officers and men aboard.   (11) Everything went well for a while.   (12) The ship was over Ohio after midnight of the next day.   (13) Then the ship ran into strong winds.   (14) For several hours, the dirigible made little progress.   (15) The power of its engines didn't help.   (16) Lightning flashed around the huge ship.   (17) Thunder seemed to knock it sideways.   (18) The commander and 13 other men were in the control car.   (19) They were under the front part of the ship.   (20) They were trying to keep the ship under control.   (21) A strong air current was pushing the ship upward.   (22) This was extremely dangerous.   (23) The ship's gas bags could expand and break.

(24) Everybody realized the extreme danger. (25) The commander decided to release some of the gas. (26) But he was reluctant to do it. (27) The cost of helium gas was enormous. (28) The men released gas for five minutes. (29) Then the ship rose and became level again. (30) Just then, a layer of cold air descended on the ship. (31) The dirigible fell 4,500 feet. (32) At 2,500 feet, the ship suddenly stopped falling. (33) Another air current was forcing the ship upward again. (34) The ship was too big to avoid the approaching disaster. (35) It was like bending a pencil downward at both ends. (36) The frame began to vibrate strangely. (37) Everything became very confused. (38) The ship broke in two. (39) Two men immediately fell out of the open ends. (40) The control car broke away from the front part of the ship. (41) It crashed to the earth. (42) The commander and 11 men were killed. (43) Twenty-seven men were still alive. (44) The two parts of the ship were tossed around by the storm. (45) The men held tightly to anything they could find. (46) They were in extreme danger of falling. (47) The back part of the ship fell to the earth first. (48) The men waited until they were fifteen feet from the ground. (49) Then they started to jump. (50) Some men hurt themselves, but everyone survived. (51) They saw the front part of the ship in the air. (52) The wind was tossing it around at 5,000 feet. (53) There were six men inside the front part of the ship. (54) The men in the ship began to release the rest of the gas. (55) The crippled ship came downward rapidly. (56) The men tried to slow down the ship. (57) They lowered 200-foot ropes. (58) But the ropes failed to get caught in the trees. (59) Two miners on the ground did their best to help. (60) They grabbed the ropes firmly. (61) But the crippled ship dragged them along the ground. (62) A farmer saw the ship coming straight toward his house. (63) His wife and children in the house were in great danger. (64) He grabbed the rope and tied it around a stump. (65) This didn't stop the ship. (66) But it did turn the ship away from his house. (67) Then he wrapped the rope around a strong tree. (68) The remains of the ship came down to the ground at last. (69) Fourteen men had died and there were 27 survivors. (70) Ten years later, the German dirigible Hindenburg burned in New Jersey. (71) The verdict became final. (72) The big bags were too slow. (73) They were also too expensive and too fragile. (74) They were less efficient than the airplane in every way. (75) It was the end of a brave chapter in aviation history.

EXERCISE 89. From the column at the left, select the best synonym for the italicized word in each sentence. Rewrite the sentences using the synonyms.

sticky
thrown
queer
terrible
unwilling
paused
yelled
attempted
amazed
shake
avoid
delicate
dropped
catastrophe
tore
securely

1 People heard about the unforgettable *disaster*.
2 It was like a *horrible* dream.
3 The men inside *shouted*, "Grab hold!"
4 They wanted to *prevent* an explosion.
5 The men *tried* to slow down the ship.
6 Dirigibles were too slow and too *fragile*.
7 The miners grabbed the ropes *firmly*.
8 The dirigible was *tossed* about by the storm.
9 The men were *astonished* by the sight.
10 The ship began to *vibrate* before it broke in two.
11 Lansdowne was *reluctant* to release the gas.
12 The giant dirigible *plunged* 4,500 feet.
13 The men *hesitated* before they grabbed girders.
14 The framework was twisted into *peculiar* shapes.
15 The metal cables *ripped* through the sheets.

EXERCISE 90. From the column at the left, select the correct word for each blank space in the sentences at the right. Use each word only once. Do not change the forms of the words.

avoided
yelled
tossed
boiled
drifted
separated
twisted
contained
grabbed
expanded
lowered
frightened
wrapped
prevented
crashed
dragged

1 The ship _____ $150,000 worth of helium gas.
2 The framework was _____ into peculiar shapes.
3 The gas bags _____ as the ship rose.
4 The men _____ the ropes from the ship.
5 The front part _____ away from the back part.
6 The control car _____ to the earth.
7 The men were _____ by the sudden plunge.
8 The ship was _____ around by violent storms.
9 The men _____ the girders for support.
10 The farmer _____ the rope around a tree.
11 The men inside the ship _____ to the farmer.
12 They were _____ along the ground by the ropes.
13 They were completely _____ from each other.
14 They _____ several storms during the first day.
15 The release of gas _____ the bags from breaking.

Supply the correct preposition for each blank space.

1   The men were trying to keep the huge ship _____ control.
2   The gas bags could easily break _____ the height _____ 3,800 feet.
3   The dirigible contained $150,000 worth _____ helium gas.
4   Helium gas was expensive _____ comparison _____ other types _____ gas.
5   The commander decided to release gas _____ five minutes.
6   The control car broke away _____ the same time.
7   Colonel Hall was an army observer _____ the trip.
8   The ship tossed about violently _____ the storm.
9   They waited until they were fifteen feet _____ the ground.
10 The wind was very strong _____ an altitude _____ 5,000 feet.
11 Lt. Anderson was hanging from two wires _____ both hands.
12 The lieutenant tied the rope _____ his body tightly.
13 The man pulled him back _____ the ship inch _____ inch.
14 He had telephoned the news _____ the disaster _____ the meantime.
15 It was the most outrageous case _____ American history.

From the column at the right, select the correct line to complete each of the numbered lines at the left. Write each sentence in its correct form.

1   Storms over Ohio   (A)   the men along the ground
2   The Shenandoah contained   (B)   getting the ship level
3   Hot air currents push   (C)   expensive helium gas
4   Twelve were killed when   (D)   the control car crashed
5   The back part of the ship   (E)   an urgent telephone call
6   Lt. Anderson disappeared   (F)   fell to earth first
7   They tried to stop the ship   (G)   a ship upward
8   Dirigibles were less   (H)   could break the ship's frame
9   They finally succeeded in   (I)   to slow down the ship
10 Their chances of survival   (J)   through a hole in the ship
11 They were in danger of   (K)   around a strong tree
12 The men tried desperately   (L)   efficient than airplanes
13 The crippled ship dragged   (M)   seemed much better
14 Ernest Nichols was getting   (N)   by lowering long ropes
15 He wrapped the rope   (O)   falling to their deaths

EXERCISE 93. Study the following word form chart carefully. The word forms which occurred in the preceding story are italicized.

	ADJECTIVE	NOUN	VERB	ADVERB
1	stormy	*storm*	x x x x x	stormily
		storminess		
2	*cloudy*	cloud	x x x x x	cloudily
		cloudiness		
3	*windy*	wind	x x x x x	windily
		windiness		
4	avoidable	avoidance	*avoid*	x x x x x
5	x x x x x	*progress*	progress	x x x x x
6	powerful	*power*	power	powerfully
7	*thunderous*	*thunder*	*thunder*	x x x x x
8	expansible	expansion	*expand*	x x x x x
9	*reluctant*	reluctancy	x x x x x	*reluctantly*
10	x x x x x	release	*release*	x x x x x
11	comparable	*comparison*	compare	comparably
12	preventive	prevention	*prevent*	preventively
13	x x x x x	*alarm*	alarm	x x x x x
14	x x x x x	*acceleration*	accelerate	x x x x x
15	sudden	suddenness	x x x x x	*suddenly*
16	*sticky*	*stickiness*	stick (irreg.)	x x x x x
17	*invisible*	invisibility	x x x x x	invisibly
18	*unequal*	inequality	x x x x x	unequally
19	disastrous	*disaster*	x x x x x	disastrously
20	x x x x x	exertion	*exert*	x x x x x
21	x x x x x	vibration	*vibrate*	x x x x x
22	x x x x x	confusion	*confuse*	x x x x x
23	x x x x x	astonishment	*astonish*	x x x x x
24	x x x x x	collision	*collide*	x x x x x
25	x x x x x	fright	*frighten*	x x x x x
26	observant	*observer*	observe	observantly
		observation		
27	x x x x x	disappearance	*disappear*	x x x x x
28	tight	tightness	tighten	*tightly*
29	x x x x x	failure	*fail*	x x x x x
30	*urgent*	urgency	x x x x x	urgently
31	x x x x x	reaction	*react*	x x x x x
32	*efficient*	efficiency	x x x x x	efficiently

EXERCISE 95. Use the correct form of each italicized word in the sentence which follows. Notice the first two examples. Refer to the word form chart and examples whenever necessary.

1	*windy*	The violent *winds* tossed the ship around.
2	*disaster*	What caused the *disastrous* accident?
3	*urgent*	The men of the ship _____ needed help.
4	*fail*	Dirigibles finally proved to be expensive _____.
5	*tightly*	He pulled the rope until it was _____.
6	*efficient*	All of the men did their work _____.
7	*suddenly*	The _____ of the ship's fall surprised everyone.
8	*disappear*	The men watched the _____ of the control car.
9	*cloudy*	They could not see well because of the _____.
10	*power*	The _____ engines could not move the dirigible.
11	*expand*	They were afraid of too much _____ of the bags.
12	*reluctant*	The commander made his decision _____.
13	*vibrate*	They searched for the cause of the _____.
14	*collide*	The _____ of objects caused great damage.
15	*frighten*	The _____ man grabbed the nearest girder.
16	*invisible*	The currents of air exerted an _____ force.
17	*sticky*	They noticed that the air had become _____.
18	*react*	The man's _____ to the danger was immediate.
19	*alarm*	There was an _____ sound throughout the ship.
20	*progress*	The weather over Ohio became _____ worse.
21	*observer*	The army lieutenant was an _____ person.
22	*observer*	The army was interested in his _____.
23	*avoid*	The commander felt the storms were _____.
24	*avoid*	During the first day, he _____ several storms.
25	*astonish*	The dirigible was an _____ sight from the ground.
26	*astonish*	The men looked up at the dirigible with _____.
27	*prevent*	What _____ measures did the commander take?
28	*prevent*	He was responsible for the _____ of accidents.
29	*confuse*	The men became _____ when the ship broke in two.
30	*confuse*	There was great _____ everywhere in the ship.
31	*comparison*	Helium is expensive in _____ with hydrogen.
32	*comparison*	Is the performance of the two gases _____?

EXERCISE 94. Study the following examples for the preceding word form chart. The numbers correspond to those on the word form chart.

1 **stormy, storm, storminess.** The sky was very *stormy*. There were *storms* in many places. He worried about the *storminess*.

2 **cloudy, cloud, cloudiness.** The sky was very *cloudy*. The *clouds* hid the sun. They noticed the *cloudiness* of the day.

3 **windy, wind, windiness.** It was a *windy* day. The *wind* was very strong. They noticed the *windiness*.

4 **avoidable, unavoidable, avoidance, avoid.** The *avoidance* of the storms was important to their safety. He *avoided* some of the thunder and lightning. Some of the storms weren't *avoidable*. Some of the storms were *unavoidable*.

5 **progressive, progress (noun), progression, progress (verb), progressively.** They *made progress* during the first day. Then their *progress* became slower. They *progressed* very little after that. The bad weather was a *progressive* condition. The weather got *progressively* worse. They ran into several storms *in progression*. The *progression* of events became worse and worse.

6 **powerful, power, powerfully.** The engines had great *power*. The engines *powered* the flight of the dirigible. The engines were *powerful*. The engines operated *powerfully*.

7 **thunderous, thunder, thunderously.** There was much *thunder*. It *thundered* loudly. There were *thunderous* sounds. The ship broke in two *thunderously*.

8 **expansible, expansion, expand.** The bags of gas *expanded* quickly. The *expansion* of the bags was dangerous. The bags were *expansible* within certain limits.

9 **reluctant, reluctancy, reluctantly.** He was *reluctant* to release the gas. He had great *reluctancy* to release it. He finally released the gas *reluctantly*.

10 **release.** He *released* the gas. The *release* of the gas helped a little.

11 **comparable, comparison, compare, comparably.** He *compared* the price of one with the price of the other. He *compared* the two carefully. He *made a comparison* of the two. The *comparison* was important. Helium was expensive *in comparison* with hydrogen. The cost of helium *compared* with the cost of hydrogen was enormous. Hydrogen wasn't *comparable* in price. But the two gases performed *comparably*.

12　**preventive, prevention, prevent, preventively.**　He *prevented* the ship from rising. The *prevention* of a disaster was important. His action was *a preventive measure*. It was a *preventive* action. He acted *preventively.*

13　**alarm.**　The sudden movement *alarmed* everyone. It was an *alarming* thing. Their *alarm* was easy to see. They rushed around *in alarm*.

14　**acceleration, accelerate.**　The ship *accelerated* as it fell. The *acceleration* of the ship was dangerous. He tried to slow down the *accelerating* ship.

15　**sudden, suddenness, suddenly.**　The *sudden* movement surprised everyone. The *suddenness* of the movement surprised everyone. The dirigible stopped falling *suddenly. Suddenly,* the ship stopped falling. The ship *suddenly* stopped falling.

16　**sticky, stickiness, stick.**　Their clothes began to *stick* to their bodies. Their wet clothes *stuck* to their bodies. The *stickiness* of their clothes bothered them. The air was *sticky.* The *sticky* air bothered them.

17　**invisible, invisibility, invisibly.**　There were *invisible* currents in the air. The currents moved around *invisibly.* The *invisibility* of the air currents made things difficult.

18　**unequal, inequality, unequally.**　The pressure was *unequal* at different points. The currents pushed against different parts *unequally.* The *inequality* of the pressure caused the trouble.

19　**disastrous, disaster, disastrously.**　It was a terrible *disaster.* The trip *ended in disaster.* The trip ended *disastrously.* The trip ended in a *disastrous* way. The trip was *disastrous.*

20　**exertion, exert.**　The currents of air *exerted* pressure on the ship. The *exertion* of unequal pressure caused trouble.

21　**vibration, vibrate.**　The framework *vibrated* strangely. The *vibration* of the framework was dangerous. The *vibrating* framework made strange sounds.

22　**confusion, confuse.**　The sudden movement *confused* the men. Everyone was *confused* by the movement. Everyone *became confused.* The *confused* men ran in all directions. It was a *confusing* situation. The *confusion* caused more trouble. The men moved around *in confusion.*

23　**astonishment, astonish.**　The sight *astonished* him. He was *astonished* by the sight. It was an *astonishing* sight. The *astonished* man stepped back. His *astonishment* was apparent.

24 **collision, collide.** The men *collided* against the walls. The men *collided* with each other. The *collision* caused damage. The *colliding* objects made much noise.

25 **fright, frighten.** Their *fright* was easy to understand. The sudden fall *frightened* them. They were *frightened* by the fall. They *became frightened*. The *frightened* men rushed around the crippled ship. It was a *frightening* experience.

26 **observant, observer, observation, observe, observantly.** One of the men was an *observer*. He *observed* the operation of the ship. The officers welcomed the *observation*. He was going to report his *observations* to the army. He was an *observant* person. He sat in the control car *observantly*.

27 **disappearance, disappear.** The man *disappeared* through a hole in the ship. The *disappearance* of the man surprised everyone.

28 **tight, tightness, tighten, tightly.** He tied the rope around his body *tightly*. The rope was *tight*. He felt the *tightness* of the rope. He *tightened* the rope around his body.

29 **failure, fail.** The ropes *failed* to stop the ship. The *failure* disappointed the men.

30 **urgent, urgency, urgently.** He made an *urgent* telephone call. He called his friend *urgently*. He realized the *urgency* of the situation.

31 **reaction, react.** He *reacted* quickly in the situation. His *reactions* were very quick.

32 **efficient, efficiency, efficiently.** Airplanes were more *efficient* than dirigibles. Airplanes could be operated more *efficiently* than dirigibles. Airplanes had greater *efficiency* than dirigibles. Airplanes are *efficient*. Airplanes have great *efficiency*. Airplanes operate *efficiently*.

EXERCISE 96. Select the correct way to complete each of the following sentences. Write each sentence in its correct form.

1 Commander Lansdowne's wife was worried because her husband had often told her that (a) the ship's gas bags were distributed throughout the interior. (b) he was in command of the giant navy dirigible. (c) storms could break the frame of the dirigible. (d) the dirigible had roaring power in all of its engines.

2 Above the height of 3,800 feet, the ship's gas bags (a) released expensive helium gas. (b) made the chances of survival better. (c) could not ascend or descend. (d) could easily expand and break.

3 The commander reluctantly decided to release gas because he (a) knew this would prevent the ship from rising. (b) was in the control car under the front part of the ship: (c) saw lightning around the ship. (d) started to step into thousands of feet of space.

4 When a layer of cold air descended on the ship at 7,000 feet, (a) they succeeded in getting the ship level again. (b) the lieutenant disappeared through a hole in the ship. (c) the men jumped from the ship. (d) the ship began to plunge rapidly.

5 The commander could not avoid the approach disaster because (a) the Shenandoah contained $150,000 worth of helium gas. (b) blood rushed to the men's heads as the pressure of the atmosphere increased. (c) the ship was so long that unequal forces were exerted in different directions along its length. (d) everything in the ship had become very confused.

6 The six men in the front part of the ship lowered 200-foot ropes because (a) the framework was twisted into peculiar shapes. (b) the back part of the ship was drifting away. (c) the army observer had climbed down the ladder. (d) they hoped the ropes would get caught in the tops of trees and stop the remains of the ship.

7 The lieutenant who had disappeared through the hole in the ship (a) was killed when the control car crashed to the ground. (b) jumped fifteen feet to the ground and broke his ankles. (c) was swinging beneath the ship. (d) wrapped the rope around a fence post.

8 When two miners, Ode Gorden and Herb Poling, grabbed the crippled ship's ropes, (a) the wind was tossing the ship around at an altitude of 5,000 feet.   (b) the big bag was too fragile and broke in two.   (c) they were dragged along the ground and knocked against trees.   (d) the control car broke away from the front part.

9 When the remains of the Shenandoah finally came down to the ground, (a) the most frightening part of the disaster was just beginning.   (b) Ernest Nichols was getting an urgent telephone call from a friend.   (c) the men tried desperately to slow down the ship. (d) there were twenty-seven survivors.

10 Most people finally decided that dirigibles were not practical because (a) storms over the Ohio Valley in September were dangerous.   (b) the cost of helium was enormous in comparison with the price of hydrogen.   (c) they were less efficient than airplanes in every way.   (d) it was the beginning of the end of a brave chapter in aviation history.

"The End of the Shenandoah" by Thomas Gallagher originally appeared in *Pageant Magazine,* March 1958, page 140ff. Permission for the rewriting of this article was kindly granted by the editors of *Pageant Magazine* as an educational contribution in line with the policies of the publisher. Because of the special considerations involved in preparing readings for students of English as a second language, the story as it appears in the American English Reader was freely rewritten and is not representative of the author's professional writing technique.

Wings Across The

On the morning of May 20, 1927, Charles A. Lindbergh took off from a muddy airfield in New York and headed for Paris. Fourteen hours later he was still flying. During the fourteen hours, he had had some anxious moments. Sleet had gathered on the wings of the plane and the fog was so thick that he could hardly see the tips of the wings. However, he had encountered equally dangerous flying conditions before. Of course, now that he was over the ocean his parachute was useless. He had only one choice; he had to go on.

wing	head for	fog	encounter	parachute
take off	anxious	thick	equally	useless
muddy	sleet	hardly	dangerous	choice
airfield	gather	tip	condition	go on

Atlantic

By James V. Thompson

Although he had waited a long time to make this trip, he did not feel strange or nervous. He was accustomed to flying alone, and he had flown this route in his imagination many times. The idea of flying across the Atlantic had occurred to him one night when he had been carrying the mail between St. Louis and Chicago. That night, he told himself that a non-stop flight between New York and Paris was possible. He knew that airplanes capable of making the long flight over the ocean could be built. A man of skill and endurance could succeed.

although	route	occur	capable	endurance
nervous	imagination	non-stop flight	skill	succeed
accustomed to				

As he was recalling that night, he reduced the altitude of the plane. Close to the surface of the ocean, he found a cushion of warm air. The ice on the wings began to melt; the fog disappeared. For the time being, at least, he was safe. As he flew close to the surface of the water, he could see the waves in the moonlight beneath him. The steady sound of the motor seemed like music in his ears. He had perfect confidence in his plane because he knew that there was not a more dependable plane than his. He thought of it as a partner. The Ryan Aircraft Company had constructed the plane to meet his specifications. He had worked with the chief engineer of the Ryan Aircraft Company, Donald Hall, to produce the airplane as rapidly as possible. Although Hall had worked with the basic design of the Ryan airplane, he had had to make many modifications. The wing span was greater to reduce the wing-loading during take-off and increase the range. The tail surfaces were farther back to maintain satisfactory stability and control. The engine was farther forward. A large gas tank was located directly in front of him so that he was unable to see directly forward. All together it was a very special airplane. He had named it "The Spirit of St. Louis," in honor of the St. Louis businessmen whose financial backing had made the trip possible. Besides their money, he had invested all of his own savings, which came to two thousand dollars, in the venture.

Alone in the plane, Lindbergh knew that it would be fatal to fall asleep. Before the flight, he had trained himself to stay awake for long periods of time. Now he watched the instrument panel intently. He began to imagine what he would do at the end of the trip. He hoped to visit all the countries in Europe. He had always wanted to see them. He especially wanted to go to Sweden because his grandfather, August Lindbergh, had been born there and had talked about the "old country." August Lindbergh had been a farmer. Through his own efforts, he had risen to a seat in Parliament and become a secretary to the king.

recall	beneath	design	directly	fatal
reduce	steady	modification	in front of	fall asleep
altitude	confidence	span	unable	train
surface	dependable	wing-loading	all together	stay awake
cushion	partner	range	spirit	instrument panel
ice	aircraft	maintain	in honor of	intently
melt	construct	satisfactory	financial	imagine
disappear	specifications	stability	backing	effort
for the time being	engineer	control	invest	rise
at least	produce	tank	savings	parliament
wave	rapidly	locate	venture	pioneer
moonlight	basic			

He had been a man of pioneering instincts and liberal sympathies. In 1859, he had come to America to seek new opportunities and greater freedom. He, his wife, and his son had measured the trip across the ocean in terms of days, but their grandson was to measure his trip across the ocean in hours.

After arriving in America, August Lindbergh traveled west to the frontier. He built a log cabin in the territory of Minnesota, thirty miles from the nearest town. His son Charles became a lawyer and settled in Little Falls. He married a school teacher there, and their only son, Charles A. Lindbergh, Jr. was born in 1902.

Charles A. Lindbergh, Sr., made a reputation for himself as an honest, able lawyer. Like his own father before him, he was asked by his neighbors to represent them in the government. He was elected to the United States House of Representatives when his son was five years old. For ten years, the family divided its time between a home in Minnesota and a home in Washington. As a boy, Lindbergh never spent more than one year at a time in the same school. Consequently, he had little chance to form permanent friendships, and he learned to enjoy being alone. He preferred life on the farm in Minnesota to life in the nation's capital. The farm was located on a hill beside the Mississippi River, and he learned to love that part of the country.

At the age of ten, he learned to drive an automobile. When he was fourteen, his family took a trip to California, and he was the driver and mechanic. When he had finished high school two years later, he took over the management of the farm in Little Falls. The family bought its first tractor. When it arrived, he refused to let anyone help him to assemble it. It was clear that he was more interested in machinery than in farming, and in 1918, he enrolled in the University of Wisconsin to study mechanical engineering. He did not finish college because he had decided to become a flier. After that decision, college seemed to be a waste of time. When he took his first airplane ride, he knew for certain that flying would be his career.

---

instinct	frontier	elect	capital	machinery
liberal	log cabin	representative	mechanic	enroll
sympathy	territory	divide	take over	mechanical engineering
seek	lawyer	consequently	management	decision
opportunity	settle	form	tractor	waste
freedom	reputation	permanent	refuse	know for certain
measure	able	prefer	assemble	career
in terms of	represent			

221

CHARLES A. LINDBERGH

After his first course of instruction in flying was over, he obtained some practical experience. He joined a group of other fliers who traveled around the country and gave demonstrations of their skill. In 1923, he entered the United States Army Flying School at Brooks Field, Texas, and he received very thorough training there. Then he took a position as chief pilot for the Robertson Aircraft Company, which carried mail by air between St. Louis and Chicago. He was working for this firm when he made the decision to attempt a solo, non-stop flight to Paris.

At 12:10 in the afternoon of May 21, Lindbergh caught sight of the coast of Ireland. Now that the flight was almost over, he began to relax a little. Once over land, he knew that he had a good chance of landing safely. Finally, after thirty-four hours in the air without sleep, he arrived at Le Bourget Field, in Paris.

More than a hundred thousand people were there to welcome him as a great hero. His name was on everyone's lips. Overnight he had achieved fame; the whole world was ringing with his praises. Wealthy and famous men and women fought for the privilege of paying him their personal tributes. The President of the United States sent a battleship to bring him home.

Though the whole world was praising him, Lindbergh kept his head. He resisted the temptation to profit by his enormous popularity. He could have made millions of dollars very easily by merely signing his name to contracts, but he declined to use his name for selfish ends. However, he was eager to advance the cause of aviation by giving lectures about his flight. He also made a good-will tour of the Caribbean countries in the interests of peace. Today, Lindbergh is admired for both the physical courage which brought him fame and his ability to resist the temptations of success.

---

obtain	welcome	tribute	selfish	admire
practical	hero	battleship	ends	physical
experience	lip	keep one's head	eager	courage
firm	overnight	resist	advance	ability
attempt	achieve	temptation	cause	success
solo	fame	profit	aviation	join
catch sight of	ring	enormous	lecture	demonstration
coast	praise	popularity	good-will	thorough
relax	wealthy	merely	tour	position
safely	privilege	contract	peace	pilot
finally	personal	decline		

(1) When did Lindbergh begin his famous flight? (2) What time of day did he leave? (3) What was the condition of the field? (4) Where was the field? (5) What was his destination? (6) In which direction did he fly? (7) What kind of weather did he encounter? (8) Why did the weather cause him anxious moments? (9) Was he used to bad flying conditions? (10) Why did he have to continue the flight? (11) Why did the flight not seem strange to him? (12) When had he first thought about flying the Atlantic? (13) What conditions in the field of aviation had made the flight seem possible? (14) What was he thinking about when he brought the plane close to the surface of the ocean? (15) What kind of weather conditions did he find there? (16) What could he see in the moonlight below him? (17) What could he hear? (18) What did the motor sound like to him? (19) How did he feel about his plane? (20) Whom had he named his plane after? (21) Where had he gotten the money to finance the trip? (22) Who had constructed the plane? (23) What modifications did the company make in the original design of the plane? (24) Why was he able to keep awake on the long flight? (25) What did he look at in his plane? (26) What did he think about? (27) Where did he want to go after the trip was over? (28) Why did he want to go to Sweden especially? (29) What had his grandfather achieved in his life? (30) Who had helped him rise to a seat in Parliament? (31) What kind of a man had he been? (32) Why had he come to America? (33) Where did he live in America? (34) Whom did his son marry? (35) Where had his son settled? (36) When was Charles A. Lindbergh, Jr. born? (37) What was his father's profession? (38) What kind of a professional reputation did Charles A. Lindbergh, Sr. have? (39) In what way did he follow the example of his own father? (40) How old was Lindbergh when his father became a Representative in Congress? (41) How did his father's election affect the family's life? (42) Was there anything unusual about young Charles' schooling? (43) Why did he learn to enjoy being alone? (44) Of his two homes, in Minnesota and in Washington, which did he prefer? (45) Where was the farm located? (46) What did he learn to do when he was ten? (47) When did he learn to drive an automobile? (48) Where did his family go when he was fourteen? (49) How did he help them on the trip? (50) What did he do when he finished high school? (51) What piece of equipment did the family buy? (52) What did he

do when it arrived? (53) Why did he enroll in the University of Wisconsin? (54) What kind of practical flying experience did he get? (55) What did he do in 1923? (56) Where is Brooks Field? (57) What kind of flying school was there at Brooks Field? (58) What kind of training did he receive? (59) After leaving Brooks Field, what kind of a position did he take? (60) What kind of work did he do after leaving Brooks Field? (61) What firm did he work for? (62) What two cities did he fly between? (63) What did he carry as cargo? (64) When did he catch sight of the coast of Ireland? (65) Why did he breathe easier then? (66) How long had he been in the air? (67) How much had he slept? (68) How many people were at the airport in Paris to welcome him? (69) Why had they come? (70) When had he become famous? (71) How did the President of the United States show his regard for Lindbergh? (72) Why did the President send a battleship to France? (73) How did Lindbergh return to the United States? (74) What temptation did he encounter? (75) How had his parents prepared him to meet the challenge of fame? (76) How did he advance the cause of aviation? (77) For what two reasons is Lindbergh admired today?

SUMMARY SENTENCES FOR LABORATORY PRACTICE

(1) It was the morning of May 20, 1927. (2) Lindbergh took off from an airfield in New York. (3) He headed for Paris. (4) He had some anxious moments. (5) Sleet gathered on the wings of the plane. (6) The fog was very thick. (7) He could hardly see the tips of the wings. (8) But he had flown in dangerous conditions before. (9) He had waited a long time to make the trip. (10) He didn't feel strange or nervous. (11) He was accustomed to flying alone. (12) He reduced the altitude of the plane. (13) The ice on the wings began to melt. (14) He could see the waves beneath him. (15) He had perfect confidence in his plane. (16) He thought of it as a partner. (17) He had named it "The Spirit of St. Louis." (18) St. Louis businessmen had made the trip possible. (19) He had invested all of his own savings also. (20) He knew that it would be fatal to fall asleep. (21) He had

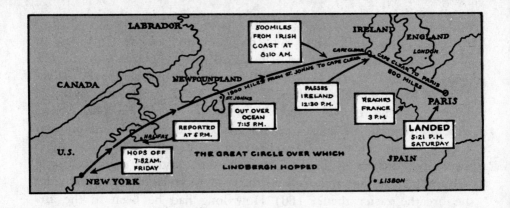

trained himself to stay awake.　(22) He watched the instrument panel intently.　(23) He thought about the end of the trip.　(24) He hoped to visit all the countries of Europe.　(25) He had always wanted to see them.　(26) He especially wanted to go to Sweden.　(27) His grandfather had been born there.　(28) His grandfather had been a pioneer.　(29) He had traveled west to the frontier.　(30) He built a log cabin in the territory of Minnesota.　(31) His son became a lawyer.　(32) He married a school teacher.　(33) Their son Charles was born in 1902.　(34) Lindbergh's father was elected to a government position.　(35) The family divided its time between two homes.　(36) Lindbergh had little chance to make friends.　(37) He learned to enjoy being alone.　(38) He preferred life on the farm.　(39) He took over the management of the farm.　(40) He was more interested in machinery than in farming.　(41) But he didn't finish college.　(42) He had decided to become a flier.　(43) He took a course of instruction in flying. (44) He obtained practical experience too.　(45) He joined a group of fliers.　(46) They traveled around the country.　(47) They gave demonstrations of their skill.　(48) He entered the United States Army Flying School.　(49) He worked for a company which carried mail by air.　(50) He carried mail between St. Louis and Chicago.　(51) He made the decision to fly to Paris.　(52) He wanted to make the non-stop flight alone.　(53) He arrived in Paris after thirty-four hours in the air.　(54) A hundred thousand people were there to welcome him. (55) He had achieved fame overnight.　(56) The whole world was praising him.　(57) The President sent a battleship to bring him home. (58) He was eager to advance the cause of aviation.　(59) He made a tour of the Carribbean countries.　(60) But he was able to resist the temptations of success.

EXERCISE 97.   From the column at the left, select the best synonym for the italicized word in each sentence. Rewrite the sentences using the synonyms.

support
anxious
lasting
dense
relied
promote
proficiency
collected
kept
company
venture
withstood
profession
changed
refused
disastrous

1 The fog at the airfield was very *thick*.
2 He knew that great *skill* would be required.
3 He was not *nervous* as he flew toward Paris.
4 The engineer had *modified* the basic design.
5 He needed financial *backing* for the trip.
6 He *depended* on his plane to go all the way.
7 As a boy he had made no *permanent* friends.
8 He knew it would be *fatal* to fall asleep.
9 He worked for an aviation *firm*.
10 He *maintained* the same altitude for two hours.
11 Ice had *gathered* on the wings very rapidly.
12 He knew that flying would be his *career*.
13 He *declined* to use his name selfishly.
14 He was eager to *advance* the cause of aviation.
15 He *resisted* the temptations of success.

EXERCISE 98.   From the column at the left, select the correct word for each blank space in the sentences at the right. Use each word only once. Do not change the forms of the words.

partner
attempt
capable
thorough
recall
waste
endurance
contracts
range
assemble
prefer
temptation
relax
selfish
steady
enormous

1 He wanted to _____ the tractor himself.
2 Why did he _____ to live on the farm?
3 He received _____ training in a flying school.
4 The trip required a pilot with good _____.
5 He wanted to increase the _____ of the plane.
6 His plane was _____ of making the long flight.
7 He thought of his plane as a _____.
8 He wanted to _____ the non-stop flight alone.
9 What did he _____ as he flew along?
10 He listened to the _____ sound of the motor.
11 He began to _____ when he saw the coast.
12 The _____ to profit from his success was great.
13 He did not use his name for _____ reasons.
14 He refused to sign his name to any _____.
15 His _____ popularity did not bring him millions.

EXERCISE 99. Supply the correct preposition for each blank space.

1 He represented his neighbors _____ the government.
2 He preferred life _____ the farm _____ life _____ Washington.
3 The farm was located _____ a hill _____ the Mississippi.
4 He enrolled _____ a university _____ Wisconsin _____ 1918.
5 He obtained experience _____ joining a group _____ fliers.
6 He worked _____ a company which carried mail _____ air.
7 He knew a flight _____ New York and Paris was possible.
8 Lindbergh took off _____ the morning _____ May 20, 1927.
9 He named the plane _____ honor _____ his financial backers.
10 _____ the ocean, there was no chance _____ using a parachute.
11 He was able to stay awake _____ long periods _____ time.
12 _____ the time being _____ least, he knew he was safe.
13 He arrived _____ Le Bourget Field _____ 34 hours _____ sleep.
14 He gave lectures _____ his flight to help aviation.
15 He made a good-will tour _____ the interests _____ peace.

EXERCISE 100. From the column at the right, select the correct line to complete each of the numbered lines at the left. Write each sentence in its correct form.

1 His family divided its time	(A)	for selfish ends
2 In 1918, he went to college	(B)	to fall asleep
3 After his first airplane ride	(C)	between two homes
4 His grandfather had talked	(D)	about the "old country"
5 The plane was constructed	(E)	from a muddy airfield
6 His airplane was capable	(F)	to study engineering
7 He thought of his plane	(G)	began to melt
8 On May 20, he took off	(H)	in his imagination
9 He had flown the route	(I)	to meet his specifications
10 Close to the ocean, he found	(J)	as a partner
11 The ice on the wings	(K)	of making the flight
12 The sound of the motor was	(L)	he decided on his career
13 He knew it would be fatal	(M)	the cause of aviation
14 He didn't use his name	(N)	like music in his ears
15 He wanted to advance	(O)	a cushion of warm air

EXERCISE 101. Study the following word form chart carefully. The word forms which occurred in the preceding story are italicized.

	ADJECTIVE	NOUN	VERB	ADVERB
1	*muddy*	mud / muddiness	x x x x x	x x x x x
2	*thick*	thickness	thicken	thickly
3	*useless*	uselessness	x x x x x	uselessly
4	*strange*	strangeness	x x x x x	strangely
5	*nervous*	nervousness	x x x x x	nervously
6	x x x x x	occurrence	*occur*	x x x x x
7	*possible*	possibility	x x x x x	possibly
8	*capable*	capability	x x x x x	capably
9	endurable	*endurance*	endure	x x x x x
10	x x x x x	reduction	*reduce*	x x x x x
11	icy	ice / iciness	x x x x x	x x x x x
12	close	closeness	x x x x x	*close* / closely
13	*dependable*	dependability	depend on	dependably
14	specific	*specifications*	specify	specifically
15	x x x x x	*modification*	modify	x x x x x
16	x x x x x	maintaining / maintenance	*maintain*	x x x x x
17	stable	*stability*	stabilize	x x x x x
18	*unable*	inability	x x x x x	x x x x x
19	sympathetic	*sympathy*	sympathize	sympathetically
20	*honest*	honesty	x x x x x	honestly
21	representative	*representative* / representation	represent	representatively
22	x x x x x	division	*divide*	x x x x x
23	*permanent*	permanence	x x x x x	permanently
24	preferable	preference	*prefer*	preferably
25	x x x x x	manager / *management*	manage	x x x x x
26	x x x x x	assembly	*assemble*	x x x x x
27	x x x x x	demonstrator / *demonstration*	demonstrate	x x x x x
28	x x x x x	relaxation	*relax*	x x x x x

229

ADJECTIVE	NOUN	VERB	ADVERB
29 x x x x x	*praise*	praise	x x x x x
30 x x x x x	*temptation*	tempt	x x x x x
31 popular	*popularity*	popularize	popularly
32 x x x x x	advance *advancement*	*advance*	x x x x x

EXERCISE 102. Study the following examples for the preceding word form chart. The numbers correspond to those on the word form chart.

1 **muddy, mud, muddiness.** There was *mud* on the airfield. The airfield was *muddy*. The *muddiness* of the airfield caused trouble.

2 **thick, thickness, thicken, thickly.** The fog was very *thick*. He noticed the *thick* fog. The fog covered the field *thickly*. He noticed the *thickness* of the fog. The fog *thickened* rapidly.

3 **useless, uselessness, uselessly.** The *uselessness* of his parachute worried him. His parachute was *useless*. His parachute hung on his back *uselessly*.

4 **strange, strangeness, strangely.** The feeling wasn't *strange* to him. He didn't *feel strange*. It wasn't a *strange* feeling. He didn't do things *strangely*. There was no *strangeness* in the situation.

5 **nervous, nervousness, nervously.** He wasn't *nervous*. He didn't *feel nervous*. He didn't fly the plane *nervously*. He didn't show any *nervousness*.

6 **occurrence, occur.** The idea *occurred* to him while he was flying. He remembered the first *occurrence* of the idea.

7 **possible, possibility, possibly.** He knew that the flight was *possible*. Very few people realized the *possibility* of the flight. *Possibly* he was wrong, but he didn't think so.

8 **capable, capability, capably.** He had great *capability* as a flier. He was a *capable* pilot. He was *capable* of making the flight. He flew airplanes *capably*.

9 **endurable, endurance, endure.** He had to *endure* difficult conditions. He had great *endurance*. The conditions were bad, but they were *endurable*. His equipment was made of *endurable* material.

10 **reduction, reduce.** He *reduced* the altitude and the speed. The *reduction* in altitude made things better. The plane used less gasoline at *reduced* speeds.

11 **icy, ice, iciness.** *Ice* was forming on the wings of the plane. He could see the *iciness* of the surface. The surface of the wings was *icy*.

12 **close, closeness, closely.** He flew *close* to the surface of the ocean. The *close* waves almost hit his wings. The *closeness* of the water didn't frighten him. He *closely* missed the tops of the waves.

13 **dependable, dependability, depend, dependably.** The *dependability* of his plane was important to him. He knew he could *depend* on his plane. His plane was *dependable*. His plane performed *dependably*.

14 **specific, specification, specifications, specify, specifically.** He *specified* his needs to the company. *Specification* of details was important. He gave the company exact *specifications* for the plane. He gave them *specific* instructions. He told them his requirements *specifically*.

15 **modification, modify.** The engineer *modified* the original plans. The *modification* of the plans required a great deal of time. They made many *modifications*. The *modified* plane flew well.

16 **maintaining, maintenance, maintain.** He *maintained* control of the plane. *Maintaining* control was essential. His mechanic had *maintained* the plane carefully. Good *maintenance* was important too.

17 **stable, stability, stabilize.** The plane was *stable*. It was a *stable* plane. *Stability* was maintained by the tail. The tail *stabilized* the plane.

18 **unable, inability.** He was *unable* to see directly ahead. His *inability* to see ahead caused certain problems.

19 **sympathetic, sympathy, sympathize, sympathetically.** His father had been a man of liberal *sympathies*. He had *sympathy* for liberal ideas. He *sympathized* with liberal ideas. He was *sympathetic* to liberal ideas.

20 **honest, honesty, honestly.** He was an *honest* person. He spoke *honestly*. *Honesty* was important to him.

21 **representative, representation, represent, representatively.** His father *represented* the people in Congress. His father was a *representative*. His opinions were *representative* of the people's opinions. He spoke *representatively*. *Representation* is important in government.

22 **division, divide.** He *divided* his time between two homes. He disliked the *division* of time. He disliked having a *divided* home.

23 **permanent, permanence, permanently.**   He had very few *permanent* friends. He never stayed in one place *permanently*. There was very little *permanence* in his life.

24 **preferable, preference, prefer, preferably.**   He had a *preference* for farm life. His *preference* was easy to understand. He *preferred* farm life to city life. In his opinion, farm life was *preferable* to city life.

25 **manager, management, manage.**   He *managed* the farm. The *management* of the farm wasn't easy. He took over *management* at the age of sixteen. He became the *manager* of the farm.

26 **assembly, assemble.**   He *assembled* the tractor. The *assembly* of the tractor was complicated.

27 **demonstrator, demonstration, demonstrate.**   The pilots *demonstrated* their skill. Their *demonstrations* were exciting. They gave *demonstrations* of their skill. The *demonstrators* were skillful pilots.

28 **relaxation, relax.**   He *relaxed* a little when he saw land. He had no time for *relaxation* during the flight. It wasn't a *relaxing* flight.

29 **praise.**   Everyone *praised* him for his courage. He *received praise* from everyone. He enjoyed the *praise,* but he kept his head.

30 **temptation, tempt.**   He was *tempted* to accept many offers. Some of the offers *tempted* him. There were many *tempting* offers. This way of making money seemed *temptingly* easy. The *temptation* was great. He *resisted the temptation* to make millions.

31 **popular, popularity, popularize, popularly.**   He was a *popular* person all over the world. He was *popularly* welcomed in Paris. His *popularity* was world wide. He *enjoyed great popularity* after his flight. He *popularized* commercial aviation.

32 **advancement, advance.**   Commercial aviation was *advanced* by his flight. He *advanced* the cause of aviation. He assisted the *advance* of aviation. He assisted the *advancement* of aviation.

EXERCISE 103. Use the correct form of each italicized word in the sentence which follows. Notice the first two examples. Refer to the word form chart and examples whenever necessary.

1	*useless*	He worried about the *uselessness* of his parachute.
2	*honest*	People knew about his great *honesty*.
3	*muddy*	The _____ of the airfield caused great problems.
4	*capable*	A pilot would need great _____ for the flight.
5	*reduce*	He knew that a _____ in altitude would help.
6	*unable*	He worried about his _____ to use his parachute.
7	*nervous*	He was too busy to feel any _____.
8	*possible*	No one saw any _____ of crossing the Atlantic by air.
9	*endurance*	He had _____ difficult conditions before.
10	*modification*	The engineer _____ the original design.
11	*divide*	He didn't enjoy the _____ of his time.
12	*close*	He didn't worry about the _____ of the waves below.
13	*occur*	The idea had first _____ to him during a flight.
14	*maintain*	It was important to _____ control over the airplane.
15	*demonstration*	He _____ that light airplanes could cross the ocean.
16	*praise*	He was _____ by people all over the world.
17	*strange*	He didn't feel _____ over the ocean alone.
18	*relax*	There was no time for _____ during the flight.
19	*temptation*	Some of the offers of money _____ him.
20	*popularity*	He became a _____ figure all over the world.
21	*represent*	His father was a _____ in Congress.
22	*sympathy*	He was _____ to the pioneering spirit of America.
23	*permanent*	There was no _____ to any of his friendships.
24	*permanent*	His family never lived in one place _____.
25	*thick*	The fog _____ around the wings of the plane.
26	*thick*	The _____ of the fog made his flight difficult.
27	*prefer*	As a boy, he had a _____ for farm life.
28	*prefer*	He thought farm life was _____ to city life.
29	*management*	As a boy of sixteen, he _____ his parents' farm.
30	*management*	He became the _____ of his parents' farm.
31	*dependable*	He was confident because his plane was _____.
32	*dependable*	The _____ of the plane gave him confidence.

EXERCISE 104. Select the correct way to complete each of the following sentences. Write each sentence in its correct form.

1 Lindbergh's parachute became useless because (*a*) he could hardly see the tips of the wings. (*b*) he had taken off from a muddy airfield. (*c*) he was flying over the ocean. (*d*) sleet had gathered on the wings.

2 The idea of flying across the Atlantic Ocean had occurred to him (*a*) on the morning of May 20, 1927. (*b*) one night when he had been flying between St. Louis and Chicago. (*c*) when he met the chief engineer of the Ryan Aircraft Company. (*d*) when he assembled the family's first tractor.

3 He had perfect confidence in his plane because he knew that (*a*) a non-stop flight between New York and Paris was possible. (*b*) a large gas tank was located directly in front of him. (*c*) the Robertson Aircraft Company had carried mail between St. Louis and Chicago in its planes. (*d*) there was not a more dependable plane than his.

4 The wing span of Lindbergh's plane was greater than the normal Ryan plane (*a*) to give the pilot skill and endurance. (*b*) to fly close to the surface of the ocean. (*c*) to reduce the wing-loading and increase the range. (*d*) to help the pilot stay awake for long periods of time.

5 Lindbergh had named the airplane "The Spirit of St. Louis" in honor of (*a*) the St. Louis businessmen whose backing had made the trip possible. (*b*) his grandparents who had come to America to seek new opportunities. (*c*) a group of fliers who traveled around the country. (*d*) the cause of aviation.

6 At the end of the non-stop flight, he wanted to go to Sweden because (*a*) he was asked by his neighbors to represent them. (*b*) he had had little chance to form permanent friendships. (*c*) he wanted to study mechanical engineering. (*d*) his grandfather August had been born there and had talked about the "old country."

7 Lindbergh's father Charles had made a reputation for himself as (*a*) a secretary to the King. (*b*) an engineer for an aircraft company. (*c*) the president of the Robertson Aircraft Company. (*d*) an honest, able lawyer.

8 After his father had been elected to the House of Representatives, the family (*a*) lived in Washington all the time. (*b*) bought a

farm in Minnesota. (c) divided its time between two homes. (d) moved to California in search of freedom.

9 Lindbergh had little chance to form permanent friendships because (a) he was more interested in machinery than in flying. (b) he never spent more than one year at a time in the same school. (c) he refused to let anyone help him. (d) he lived on a farm in Minnesota.

10 Lindbergh knew for certain that flying would be his career when (a) he learned to drive an automobile. (b) he took his first airplane ride. (c) he enrolled in the University of Wisconsin. (d) he entered the United States Army Flying School.

11 He decided that going to college was a waste of time because (a) he knew how to assemble tractors. (b) he had decided to become a farmer. (c) he had decided to enter aviation as a career. (d) he had invested all of his savings in an airplane.

12 At the time he made the decision to attempt a solo, non-stop flight to Paris, Lindbergh was (a) catching sight of the coast of Ireland. (b) receiving thorough training at Brooks Field, Texas. (c) studying mechanical engineering. (d) carrying mail for the Robertson Aircraft Company.

13 Lindbergh began to relax a little when he caught sight of the coast of Ireland because (a) wealthy and famous people were waiting for him. (b) he had a good chance of landing safely over land. (c) he could have made millions very easily. (d) he had encountered equally dangerous conditions before.

14 When he landed in Paris, he discovered that (a) he had become wealthy. (b) he had achieved fame overnight. (c) he had signed a good contract. (d) the flight was almost over.

15 Lindbergh is admired today not only because he was the first man to fly across the Atlantic alone but also because (a) the President of the United States sent a battleship for him. (b) people fought for the privilege of paying him personal tribute. (c) a hundred thousand people welcomed him to Paris. (d) he resisted the temptation to profit by his enormous popularity.

The story "Wings Across the Atlantic" was adapted from "Charles A. Lindbergh" by James V. Thompson as it appeared in *Vocations and Professions*, edited by Phillip Henry Lotz, published by the Association Press, New York, 1940. Permission for the rewriting of this section of the book was kindly granted by the Director of the Association Press.